DESIGNING SUSTAINABLE CITIES IN THE DEVELOPING WORLD

Designing Sustainable Cities in the Developing World

Edited by

ROGER ZETTER
and
GEORGIA BUTINA WATSON
Department of Planning,
Oxford Brookes University, UK

ASHGATE

Published by
Ashgate Publishing Limited
Gower House
Croft Road
Aldershot
Hampshire GU11 3HR
England

Ashgate Publishing Company
Suite 420
101 Cherry Street
Burlington, VT 05401-4405
USA

Ashgate website: http://www.ashgate.com

British Library Cataloguing in Publication Data
Designing sustainable cities in the developing world. -
   (Design and the built environment series)
   1.City planning - Developing countries 2.Sustainable
   development - Developing countries 3.Urban ecology -
   Developing countries
   I.Zetter, Roger II.Watson, Georgia Butina
   307.1'416'091724

Library of Congress Cataloging-in-Publication Data
Designing sustainable cities in the developing world / edited by Roger Zetter and Georgia Butina Watson.
        p. cm. -- (Design and the built environment series)
    Includes index.
    ISBN 0-7546-4355-7
    1. City planning--Developing countries. 2. Cities and towns--Developing countries--Growth. 3. Sustainable development--Developing countries. I. Zetter, Roger. II. Watson, Georgia Butina. III. Series.

    HT169.5.D47 2006
    307.1'216091724--dc22

                                                                    2005037640

ISBN-10: 0 7546 4355 7

Printed and bound in Great Britain by Antony Rowe Ltd, Chippenham, Wiltshire.

Contents

Part II: Designing People-based Environments

List of Figures

Acknowledgements

The authors would like to express their gratitude to Dr Regina Mapua Lim for her editorial assistance in preparing this book.

The authors and publisher thank the following publishers and organisations for permission to reproduce illustrations. While we have made every effort to contact and acknowledge copyright holders and sources, the many changes of publishers and the merger of publishing companies have sometimes made it difficult to contact the actual copyright holder. If there are errors or omissions please contact the authors and we will gladly correct this in subsequent printing.

Figure 2.12: credit J. Dumarçay for the photograph of Royal Palace in Mandalay, destroyed in World War II. Print by Frank Vincent, 1874 from Dumarçay, J. and Smithies, M. (1995*) Cultural Sites of Burma, Thailand and Cambodia*, Oxford, Oxford University Press, p. 30.

Figure 7.1: credit Karina Landman for her photograph which was originally published in her paper 'Gated Communities and Urban Sustainability: Taking A Closer Look', *2nd Southern African Conference on Sustainable Development in the Built Environment*, Strategies for a Sustainable Built Environment 23–25 August 2000, Pretoria, South Africa.

Figure 9.1: credit The Hajj Research Institute, Umm Al-Qura University Makkah, Saudi Arabia.

Kiscadale Publications for illustrations as follows:

Figure 2.13: A Group of Worshippers in the 'Tuesday' Corner of Shwe Dagon Pagoda c. 1890, photo from Singer, N. (1995), *Old Rangoon*, Gartmore, Kiscadale, p. 42.

Figure 2.14: Building Materials Commonly Used for Vernacular Dwellings c. 1890, photo uncredited from Singer, N. (1995), *Old Rangoon*, Gartmore, Kiscadale, p. 115.

Figure 2.15: Monastery Taken Over by the British Army in 1885, photo by Beato from Singer, N. (1995), *Old Rangoon*, Gartmore, Kiscadale, p. 181.

Figure 2.16: The Chief Commissioner's House in Mandalay c. 1890, photo by Beato from Singer, N. (1993), *Burmah: A Photographic Journey 1855–1925*, Gartmore, Kiscadale.

Figure 2.17: Dak Bungalow c. 1890, photo from Singer, N. (1993), *Burmah: A Photographic Journey 1855–1925*, Gartmore, Kiscadale.

Figure 2.29: Sule Pagoda Road as the Main Commercial District of Rangoon in the 1930s, photo from Singer, N. (1995) *Old Rangoon*, Gartmore, Kiscadale, p. 181.

We have been unable to trace the publisher of the following illustrations:

Figure 2.28: Punakha Dzong, Watercolour by Samuel Davis from: Aris, M. (1982), *Views of Medieval Bhutan: The Diary and Drawings of Samuel Davis 1783*, London: Serindia Publications, p. 115.

Figure 2.28: Paro Dzong, photo by Dr. Banjamin Simpson, 1864 from: Aris, M. (1994), *The Raven Crown: The Origins of Buddhist Monarchy in Bhutan*, London: Serindia Publications, p. 63.

List of Acronyms

AMZ	Artistic Monuments Zone (*Zona de Monumentos Artísticos*)
ASI	Archaeological Survey of India
BID	Business Improvement Districts
BNH	National Housing Bank (*Banco Nacional da Habitação*)
B-2000	Bethlehem 2000
CBH	Cultural built heritage
CBO	Community Based Organisation
CFC	ChloroFluroCarbons
CFD	Computational Fluid Dynamics
CID	Central Improvement Districts
CNCA	National Council of Culture and Arts (*Consejo Nacional para la Cultura y las Artes*)
	CODEM Metropolitan Belém Planning and Adminsitration Authority (*Companhia de Desenvolvimento e Administração da Área Metropolitana de Belém*)
DDF	Federal District Department *(Departamento del Distrito Federal)*
FAR	Floor Area Ratios
FLAAHMZ	Federal Law on Archaeological, Artistic and Historical Monuments and Zones (*Ley Federal sobre Monumentos y Zonas Arqueológios, Artísticos e Históricos*)
FPFV	Popular Front Francisco Villa (*Frente Popular Francisco Villa*)
GC	Gated Community
GEAR	Growth, Employment and Redistribution
HMZ	Historical Monuments Zone (*Zona de Monumentos Históricos*)
IDP	Integrated Development Plans
IMDUM	Municipal Institute of Urban Development and Historic Centre of Morelia (*Instituto Municipal de Desarrollo Urbano de Morelia*)
INAH	National Institute of Anthropology and History (*Instituto Nacional de Antropología e Historia*)
INBA	National Institute of Fine Arts and Literature (*Instituto Nacional de Bellas Artes*)
INEGI	National Institute of Statistics, Geography and Information Technology (*Instituto Nacional de Estadistica, Geografia e Informatica*)
INVI	Housing Institute (*Instituto de la Vivienda*)
IPCC	Intergovernmental Panel on Climate Change
ISS	Institute for Security Studies
LT	Lighting and Thermal
NGO	Non-governmental Organisation

PAN	National Action Party (*Partido Acción Nacional*)
PDGB	Development Plan for the Greater Belém (*Plano de Desenvolvimento da Grande Belém*)
PDU	Belém Urban Masterplan (*Plano Diretor Urbano de Belém*)
PEM	Metropolitan Structural Plan (*Plano de Estruturação Metropolitana*)
REAP	Rapid Ethnographic Appraisal Procedures
SCINCE	Census Information Inquiry System (*Sistema para la consulta de información censal*)
SEDESOL	Ministry of Social Development (*Secretariá de Desarrollo Social*)
SEDUVI	Ministry of Urban Development and Housing Secretary, Government of the Federal District (*Secretaría de Desarrollo Urbano y Vivienda del Gobierno del Distrito Federal*)
SEP	Ministry of Public Education (*Secretaría de Educaión Publicá*)
SERFHAU	Federal Service of Housing and Urbanism (*Serviço Federal de Habitação e Urbanismo*)
UNESCO	United Nations Education, Scientific and Cultural Organisation
WCED	World Commission on Environment Development
WSSD	World Summit on Sustainable Development
ZEDEC	Controlled Development zone (*Zona Especial de Desarrollo Controlado*)
ZEIS	Zones of Special Social Need (*Zonas Espoecias de Interesse Social*)

List of Contributors

Roger Zetter

Roger Zetter is Professor and Deputy Head of the Department of Planning in the School of Built Environment at Oxford Brookes University. His research, teaching, consultancy and publishing interests are in urban-sector aid policies, housing and environmental policies for low-income urban dwellers, with a particular interest in informal land markets, land tenure and urban land policies, mainly in the context of sub-Saharan Africa. He also has extensive research and consultancy experience on refugees, asylum seeking and forced migration. He has conducted research and consultancy for UNDP, Oxfam, ESRC, EU, Joseph Rowntree Foundation, Home Office (UK). His books include *Planning in Cities: Sustainability and Growth in the Developing World* (Zetter and White, IT Publications 2002) and *Market Economy and Urban Change: Impacts in the Developing World* (Zetter and Hamza, Earthscan 2004). His forthcoming book, *The Reception and Integration of Asylum Seekers and Refugees in Europe:Convergence or Divergence?* (Zetter, Griffiths and Sigona) will be published by Macmillan/Palgrave.

Georgia Butina Watson

Georgia Butina Watson is Professor of Urban Design and Head of Department of Planning at Oxford Brookes University. She has co-authored several books and exhibitions on theory and practice of urban design and has been a keynote speaker at many conferences in the UK and abroad. Her professional expertise includes the study of urban morphology, community development and place identity and she is a co-author, with Ian Bentley, of *Identity by Design* (Architectural Press 2006). She has directed many UK and overseas government projects, for example in Mexico and Thailand, and her recent work on sustainable community development in the UK has contributed to the improvement of many settlements and local areas. She makes regular visiting lecturing contributions to UK and overseas universities and her latest project for A-level Geography students on Making Better Places won several commendations and a Silver Medal Award from the British Geographical Association. She is also a founder member of the urban design consultancy Place-ID.

****

Ian Bentley

Ian Bentley is Emeritus Professor of Urban Design at the Joint Centre for Urban Design, Oxford Brookes University. He was lead author of *Responsive Environments* (Architectural Press 1985), author of *Urban Transformations* (Routledge 1999) and co-author, with Georgia Butina Watson, of *Identity by Design* (Architectural Press 2006). He has acted as external examiner across a range of postgraduate courses in urban design, urban regeneration, cultural studies and public art, and has been a keynote speaker at numerous urban design conferences in the UK and internationally. He is a founder member of the urban design consultancy Place-ID, and currently leads the JCUD's outreach programme, delivering the Centre's urban design courses in the workplace to a range of local authority clients.

Mohammed Abdullah Edrees

Mohammed Abdullah Edrees is an Assistant Professor of Urban Design at Umm Al-Qura University Makkah Al-Mukarramah city, Saudi Arabia. He has a BA in architecture, MLA (Masters in Landscape Architecture) and a PhD in Urban Design from Cardiff University in Wales. His main research interests are urban development, land subdivision with particular concern for residential open space and low cost housing. He developed a land subdivision model to improve residential environmental quality. He works for the Hajj Research Institute at Umm Al-Qura University which focuses on crowd control and management at the Hajj and the development of the Hajj site for pilgrims uses. He has several publications in the academic journals concerning residential environments and low cost housing, crowd management and the Hajj site development.

Jane Handal

Jane Handal is an architect and an urban designer with a BSc in architecture from Birzeit University (Palestine) and an MA and PhD in Urban Design from Oxford Brookes University. Her PhD explored the relationship between Urban Design and Development, placing special emphasis on reconstructing identity in post conflict settings. She has worked as an architect in Palestine and as an urban designer/planner for the Ministry of Planning and International Cooperation (under Norwegian and Palestinian Management), between 1995 and 1999 – an era in which the rebuilding of Palestine presented tremendous opportunities and challenges. She has work experience with the World Bank where she worked for six months on urban and social development in North Africa. Dr Handal is currently employed by the Aga Khan Trust for Culture, UK as a manager for their socio-economic projects in Cairo-Egypt.

Luis Gabriel Juárez-Galeana

After finishing his doctorate at Oxford Brookes University, UK, Luis Gabriel Juárez-Galeana returned to private practice, where he has been combining urban design theories and best practice with the commercial realities of urban development. Recently he has submitted a 6,000 dwellings masterplan in East London which includes the application of vertical and horizontal mixed use and conceptualising transport nodes as places for community interaction instead of origin-destination elements only. Other activities include developing in-house research and methods dealing with consultation and participatory design as well applying and testing Space Syntax theories in the urban development market.

Yanet Lezama-López

Yanet Lezama-López has been a conservation officer at the National Anthropology and History Institute of Mexico (INAH) since 1987. She is an architect and holds a Master's degree in architecture from the National Autonomous University of Mexico (UNAM). She worked at architectural studios for several years, where she became a qualified designer. She joined the PhD Programme at the Joint Centre for Urban Design at Oxford Brookes University. Her main research interests are in urban design, conservation of the built heritage and management, as well as community involvement and dealing with conflicts. She is currently carrying out research on urban conservation, place-identity and local communities in World Heritage historic cities for INAH (*Instituto Nacional de Antropología e Historia*) (National Institute of Anthropology and History) in Mexico, where she is also an advisor on urban conservation and planning.

Regina Mapua Lim

Regina Mapua Lim is a designer by profession with degrees from the Rhode Island School of Design (RISD) in architecture, product design and fine arts. Her interest in vernacular architecture and the processes for understanding it in its cultural context stems from design projects involving traditional communities and their building techniques for contemporary architecture. She holds postgraduate degrees in International Studies in Vernacular Architecture and has taught courses, given lectures and design studios at RISD, University Colleges of London, and Oxford Brookes University on: design in a cultural context; socially responsible design; natural hazards and traditional building; and oral and visual research methods.

Jose Julio Lima

Jose Julio Lima is Professor of Urban Design and Planning at Universidade Federal do Pará, Brazil. He completed his PhD in the School of Architecture at Oxford Brookes University. After working in local planning government agencies in Brazil, he has been involved in research on urban regulatory instruments and is interested in socio-spatial segregation and democratisation of urban reform instruments for Brazilian cities. He is currently working with *planos diretores* (masterplans) for medium and small cities in the Amazon basin. He has published in Brazil and abroad including chapters in books such as *Planning in Cities: Sustainability and Growth in the Developing World*, (2002 edited by Zetter et al.), *Brasil Urbano*, and periodicals.

Ana Maria Maldonaldo-Fuse

Ana Maria Maldonaldo-Fuse received her first degree in Landscape Architecture at the National University in Mexico City. Her interests, since then, have been closely related with the use and management of urban landscape, with particular emphasis in social, environmental and economic sustainability. She combined activities as a landscape consultant, university lecturer and collaborations with NGOs and community groups to put her ideas into practice. Her PhD at Oxford Brookes University was focused on developing methods of applying the concepts of diverse aspects of sustainability to urban green open spaces. Currently she contributes as a guest speaker to Mexican universities, she is involved with research projects on urban sustainability with different government institutions and NGOs, and works in private practice.

Koyi Mchunu

Koyi Mchunu has recently completed his PhD at the Department of Planning, Oxford-Brookes University. Prior to joining Oxford-Brookes, he was a lecturer in the Department of City Planning, Cape Peninsula University of Technology, Cape Town. His main research interests include planning theory, with particular interest in cross-cultural planning; environmental justice; low-cost housing strategies; and the application of human rights in the context of the built environment. His research publications include: *Report on Informal Land in Informal Sector Housing* (South African Land Management for Informal Sector 1997); *Race and Technology, the Role Models as Teaching Method* (Centre for Research in Engineering Education, University of Cape Town 1998); 'From Apartheid City to Sustainable City: Compact City Approach as a Regulative Ideal' (in Zetter et al. (eds), *Planning in Cities: Sustainability and Growth in the Developing World* 2002).

Anwar Punekar

Anwar Punekar is Assistant Professor of Urban Design in Malik Sandal Institute of Art and Architecture, Visvesvaraya Technological University, India. Since 2000, he has been researching in the Joint Centre for Urban Design at Oxford Brookes University. His interest in urban revitalisation in culturally diverse contexts comes from his involvement with the revitalisation of historic centres of Bijapur, Badami, Aihole and Pattadkal in India. He is also involved in research for the Commission for Architecture and Building Environment (CABE, UK); Historic Environments and Local Management (HELM, UK) besides teaching on various programmes in the School of Built Environment, Oxford Brookes University.

Norma E. Rodrigo-Cervantes

Norma E. Rodrigo-Cervantes has worked since 1992 as a conservation officer at INAH (*Instituto Nacional de Antropología e Historia*) (National Institute of Anthropology and History) in Mexico City. She has extensive experience in the topics of historic zones designation and their urban issues. Her background is in architecture and restoration of historical monuments. During her PhD studies at the Joint Centre for Urban Design at Oxford Brookes University her research focused on urban strategies for conservation and management of Mexican historic centres designated as World Heritage Cities. Her main professional interests are in the design of management plans addressing the cultural and economic values of these particular places.

Silvia de Schiller

Professor of Architecture and Environment at the University of Buenos Aires, since 1984, and senior researcher in urban sustainability, Silvia de Schiller directs the Research Centre Habitat and Energy, the Laboratory of Environmental Studies and the

Technical Assistance Programme on Environmental Architecture. She graduated from Buenos Aires University, followed by postgraduate studies on housing and planning in The Netherlands and a PhD in Urban Design at Oxford Brookes University. She is the National Representative of iiSBE (International Initiative for a Sustainable Built Environment) and invited lecturer at universities in Latin America, Europe and Japan. She has received awards for innovative research in architecture and prizes in international competitions; she publishes extensively and participates actively in international conferences.

Introduction

Chapter 1

Designing Sustainable Cities

Roger Zetter and Georgia Butina Watson

Overview

The globalisation of architectural styles, building technologies and urban space has dramatically impacted city design in the developing world. These inexorable pressures produce many negative outcomes but two in particular constitute the main concern of this book. On the one hand the destruction of the patrimony of indigenously designed and developed urban places and spaces is accelerating: built environments which are culturally rooted, locally produced, and technologically adapted in time and space are being rapidly eroded. Their potential responsiveness to the needs of a changing social and functional world is largely ignored. Instead, unique built environments are being removed from their context and replaced by global forms and designs which are often poorly adapted to local needs and conditions (King 2004). Segregation of land uses removes the vitality created by mixed activity patterns. On the other hand, these pressures are commodifying the place-identity of historic urban spaces and places, at once detaching them from their continuity with locality, space and time, whilst at the same time re-presenting them as uniquely preserved 'authentic' artefacts for global cultural consumption. These outcomes question the sustainability of new patterns and processes of urban design and the production of local space. They question how place identity is created, recreated and sustained (Hague and Jenkins 2005).

The vast literature on cities and urbanisation in the developing world has framed the sustainability discourse largely in terms of an environmental agenda preoccupied with 'green and brown' issues such as pollution, urban waste, energy consumption, transport and the urban footprint (e.g. White 1994; Satterthwaite 1999). Curiously, and with the recent exception of the compact city debates (Jenks and Burgess 2000), this literature has largely neglected the challenge of *designing* cities as sustainable and liveable places which can adapt their unique cultural identities and specific historic heritage to contemporary needs. This book seeks to redress this deficit by exploring the discourse and practice of urban design in the developing world. Conservation and sustainability in relation to the patrimony and cultural heritage of the built environment are core themes.

Designing Sustainable Cities in the Developing World introduces a new perspective on cities which is innovative in scale, content and objectives.

In terms of *scale*, the mainstream urban literature and research on cities in the developing world is, of course, vast. Dominated by a number of recurring themes, these provide both a valuable context and potent insights to support our own perspective.

Briefly these include: theories of urbanisation; the political economy of cities and the form and consumption of space; demographic, social and spatial reconfiguration under conditions of globalisation and structural adjustment; the dynamics of urban economies and the livelihoods of the mass of low income dwellers; urban poverty and environmental degradation; the scope of policy and intervention to manage rapid informal urbanisation (see for example Romaya and Rakodi 2002; Zetter and Hamza 2004; Zetter and White 2002).

Sustainability features strongly in the urbanisation literature, but is preoccupied with macro scale processes, issues of governance and institutional capacity and the political economy of urban environmental sustainability (e.g. Burgess et al. 1997; Pugh 1996, 2000; Stren et al. 1992).

Our perspective both complements these themes yet is more localised. Focused as they are on the macro scale, these prevailing discourses on urbanisation in the developing world tend to neglect an understanding of the intricate processes by which people design their own places and spaces, how they sustain yet adapt local technologies and traditions, and how they deploy innate capacities to adapt cultural precepts to a modern idiom. To the extent that urban morphology and the internal spatial structure of cities are examined, this usually turns on two rather than three dimensional investigation (e.g. Drakakis-Smith 2000; Gugler 1996; Potter and Lloyd-Evans 1998), or it is concerned with housing and shelter, where of course a massive literature on informal self-build processes exists (e.g. Fernandes and Varley 1998). Our focus is predominantly with three-dimensional urban morphology. Our scale is larger than the house but smaller than the city: it is concerned with the ordinary spaces, places, and the form, design, use and activity patterns of localities and neighbourhoods where city dwellers enact their everyday lives.

Turning to *innovation of content* there are, of course, many micro-level studies of particular cities and particular traditions of city building in the developing world. In this context, a growing body of literature documents the vitality of vernacular architecture and the diversity of building technologies and design, mainly at the intimate scale of the house (Oliver 1997, 2002). Whilst the resilience of vernacular architecture as a tool of sustainable development constitutes an important element of this book, our perspective is generic rather than particular, it stresses adaptability rather than the intrinsic qualities of specific styles and technologies, and its scale, as noted above, is larger than the individual building – typically the scale of vernacular interest. By contrast, another dominant theme in the literature provides historical insights into city design and the impact of earlier globalisation processes – in this case European imperialism (Home 1997; King 1976, 1990; Wright 1991). An understanding of colonial urban history and the adaptation of exogenous city design are important to our book's context.

In their different ways these sources provide generic perspectives on the phenomenon of city building and the design of places and spaces – part of our ambition. But these perspectives tend to be rooted in the specifics of place and historical time. Much of the literature on the colonial city is preoccupied with the monumental legacy and with the colonial planning of 'new' towns and settlements. This provides valuable historical insights but lacks an understanding and exploration of urban design as a dynamic process of adaptation and sustainability. This is our theme. In what ways can and do local technologies, cultural traditions and the indigenous vernacular respond to the dynamics of change – whether local or global? In what ways can these urban development processes provide sustainable approaches to designing cities, localities, places and spaces?

Third, in terms of our *objectives*, our central concern is to advance the role of urban design as a mediator between rapid and unregulated urbanisation on the one hand and sustainable city building on the other. Our approach offers particular insights into sustainable city design under conditions of globalisation and development. Dominated as it is by the environmental agenda, and the market enablement paradigm (Burgess et al. 1997; Zetter and White 2002; Zetter and Hamza 2004), to date the sustainability discourse has ignored the design and development of cities defined in terms of the cultural identity and indigenous built resources of cities, the assembly of buildings and their constituents of places, spaces and neighbourhoods. We explore the concept of sustainability in this context, not only because we contend it sheds a new perspective on the concept itself, but also because it offers practical solutions to the challenge of making cities in the developing world more liveable, adaptable and environmentally secure.

We argue that a viable response to the relentless pressures of urban growth, the deteriorating quality of urban life and the homogenisation of urban form and design in the developing world, is to explore the resilience and adaptability of local urban traditions, technologies, place identities and cultural precepts in city design and development. Our scale is smaller than the city, but larger than the individual house. We focus on assemblies of buildings and the spaces and places they create, typically found at the neighbourhood scale – localities where city dwellers experience and participate in the day-to-day rhythms and realities of urban life.

However, crucially, our approach to sustainable urban design is not only framed in terms of 3-D physical characteristics, urban morphologies and technical challenges. The pattern and built form of the city, as Brand (2000) points out in his investigation of sustainability and urban form in Medellin, Colombia, is a socio-spatial construct reflecting the conflicting values and competing interests that dictate urban change and the consumption of urban space. Contrasting community, professional, political and user interests create a nexus, located in time and space, in which sustainable urban design cannot be a pre-defined goal or objective physical end state. Rather, it is an open-ended process of reconciling competing values and priorities in the building, re-building and adaptation of liveable cities. In this respect, proactive civil society and structures of governance which enable polarities to be debated and articulated, become highly instrumental elements for establishing the constructive co-existence of competing 'urban designs'. Our stance, in this book, gives primacy to local communities and their capacity to articulate their socio-spatial needs in sustainable ways (Carley et al. 2001; Devas et al. 2004). In this sense, urban design can become an important tool for achieving environmental justice.

Thus, in summary, the parameters defining the scope of this book are:

- the primacy of urban design, complementing other disciplinary and substantive perspectives, in mediating the development of the urban sphere;
- a concern with the design of locality, spaces and places, rather than strategic or macro urban scales;
- an investigation of how place identity is authenticated;
- an exploration of generic urban design characteristics derived from particular case studies;
- recognition that designing sustainable cities is 'contested territory', involving socially constructed processes and the conflicting values and interests that accompany processes of urban change;
- a profound concern to examine new ways of promoting sustainability under conditions of rapid urban change.

Themes and Contents

The book is divided into two main sections, although the themes in the two sections overlap.

Part I: Urban Form and Transformation comprises seven chapters around the generic themes of conservation and development, renewal and design, cultural representation and continuity, values and politics of identity. It addresses the issue of urban form and design in the context of rapid urbanisation and development and the particular susceptibility of historic and traditional areas of cities to the pressures of social and economic changes. These chapters show how these pressures may be understood and resolved by principles, policies and practices of sustainable urban planning and design, together with appropriate institutional and statutory frameworks.

In 'Cultural Sustainability and Development: Drukpa and Burman Vernacular Architecture', Regina Mapua Lim examines the relationship between culture and vernacular architecture by exploring the trends of continuity and change in two contrasting Buddhist communities – the Drukpa of Bhutan and the Burman of Myanmar/Burma. She shows how the contrasting affinities between religious and secular styles in these two culturally related traditions have conditioned both their vulnerability and the differential responses to exogenous forces for development and internal expressions of 'national identity'. Evidence of both change and resilience in the form and technology of indigenous architecture is presented, in which the vernacular traditions reveal a precise physical record of cultural adaptation. In contrast to the relatively secluded environment of Bhutan, the invasive colonial history and the ethnic plurality of Burma/Myanmar have had a significant bearing on the more aggressive transformation of vernacular architecture. The particular importance of Lim's chapter is to draw attention to the importance of spiritual continuity in mediating the way pressures for material change impact the form and use of vernacular buildings and the design of urban spaces.

The extent to which religious continuity mediates or accedes to the material pressures of a secular world is further developed in Jane Handal's chapter, 'Rebuilding City Identity through History: The Case of Bethlehem-Palestine'. Here, of course, we are dealing with a much more politically charged arena where contemporary conflict between Palestine and Israel overlies millennia of competing religious claims for historically created urban spaces. Handal conceptualises this tension in terms of countervailing forces of 'emotion' and 'rationality' involved in building and rebuilding the cultural landscape of place identity in a space-time continuum. She uses the B2000 project to exemplify her theme. This was an internationally conceived and funded millennium project to revive Old Bethlehem which was suffering from acute physical and economic deprivation compounded by three decades of Israeli occupation. She shows how the project commodified and distilled a complex history, reconstituting the sacred spiritual and cultural character of the area in a disturbingly lifeless thematic museum piece – a contemporary rationalisation of emotive (in other words historically and culturally derived) forces.

Her argument is that the forces of 'emotion' and 'rationality' simultaneously encode identity and enable it to evolve and innovate. It is crucial that we understand this encoding process before intervening to remedy the imbalances and discontinuities introduced by exogenous agency – in the case of Bethlehem by global tourism and regional conflict. Her study shows how failure to reveal the encoded identity produces a violent erosion of that identity in which intervention further destabilises the disharmonious balance between 'emotive' and 'rational forces'. In other words, rebuilding place identity is more about discovering the distinctive *processes* encoded in that identity, rather than the distinctive, and often idealised *character* of the built heritage itself.

Of the four chapters in the book on Mexico, Norma E. Rodrigo-Cervantes' study of 'Urban Conservation in Mexican Colonial Cities: The Historic Centre of Morelia', reflects on the contemporary significance of the historic core of the city and processes of city centre transformation which are destroying a unique heritage of buildings and urban design.

Taking up one of the core themes of the book, Rodrigo-Cervantes investigates the interplay between sustainability and conservation. In the case of Morelia, founded early in the Spanish settlement era in 1541, the familiar pressures of accelerating rural-urban migration, decentralisation of commercial uses, the flight of middle class inhabitants to the urban periphery, rising city centre land values, are together producing a conventional picture in which physical decay and dilapidation paradoxically co-exist with unsympathetically designed new commercial developments. These forces are destroying the historic core of the city.

She argues that a strongly preservationist tradition of conservation in Mexico is embodied in the laws and institutions for the protection of the cultural patrimony. Defined in monumental and static terms, this tradition has failed to concede a more fluid interpretation based on the concept of sustainability which would be more responsive to contemporary pressures. Rigidity combined with the commodification of the built heritage neglect the importance of finding solutions rooted in more sustainable policies for conserving the historic core of the city.

She also emphasises how another key component of the sustainability discourse – the localisation of initiatives in Agenda 21 – provides a vital entry point to developing and embedding conservation policies and programmes which are more sensitive to local needs and aspirations. Thus she demonstrates the negative impacts of a highly centralised institutional framework of government agencies for conservation which both overlap yet fail to coordinate.

This problematic backcloth is reinforced further by the severe discontinuity between planning and conservation policies and instruments, and also the agencies responsible for these activities. Without their effective coordination, the scope for reformulating the physical preservation of isolated buildings into a holistic model for managing change in the historic urban landscape is likely to be frustrated.

In her chapter, 'Involving Local Communities in the Conservation and Rehabilitation of Historic Areas in Mexico City: The Case of Coyaocán', Yanet Lezama-López, like Rodrigo-Cervantes, also deals with the destruction of the historic heritage of Mexico created from a colonial Hispanic tradition which was transported, adapted and modified to become a now vital part of indigenous patrimony.

Her chapter introduces another theme of the book – the challenge of involving local communities in the creation of sustainable living environments through the conservation and adaptation of their built heritage. She demonstrates how unregulated and competing interests produce first the deterioration and ultimately the destruction of historically significant urban spaces. Localities which represent the evolution of a cultural identity as well as possessing economic vitality are gradually eroded. Cocoayán is just such a locality. Founded in 1521 and located in the south eastern part of Mexico City, it typifies a traditional vernacular and folkloric style, interspersed with churches and public buildings which came under increasing pressure for change.

Lezama-López argues two key and interlinked points. First, she reinforces Rodrigo-Cervantes' contention that conservation law and practice in Mexico is flawed by the dominant concern only for buildings and monuments, rather than a spatially and socially embedded discourse. Her second and related contention, therefore, is that any viably sustainable approach to conservation of the public realm must be constructed around concepts and practices which are shaped by participatory processes and understanding. At present, conservation in Mexico is detached from local communities and located in an essentially sterile and abstract history represented by the preservation of monuments and buildings simply as physical structures.

She shows how different local groups – residents, shopkeepers, street traders and artists, as well as tourists – have different conceptions of the quality, value and heritage of their locality and what it represents. But they can be constructively engaged in developing a shared vision. Only by involving all the stakeholders can a commonly held view emerge of what conservation is, what should be conserved, and how. In other words, conservation strategies must include local communities of interest without which inequitable and fragmented interventions will occur. The failure to empower local people will produce neither a sustainable environment nor the conservation of culturally valuable urban localities.

Two chapters address the themes of the cultural politics of heritage and the politics of identity. Anwar Punekar's study of 'Value-led Heritage and Sustainable Development: The Case of Bijapur, India' reveals the familiar context of conflicts – conflicts between conservation and rapid urbanisation, between an indigenously diverse built heritage and an essentially western dominated, and now globalised, ideology of conservation, and between national level heritage protection at the expense of local level conservation integrated into wider planning strategies. In Bijapur, as in much of India, religious, ethnic and cultural diversity, not to mention the colonial overlay, resonate in the built environmental heritage. The current picture of a deteriorating historic urban fabric is not just a matter of concern in terms of the depletion of a significant built heritage. The deterioration process itself has produced cultural alienation and segregation among the local communities because the policies designed to arrest this decay are not underpinned by an understanding of the needs of the different communities they are designed to serve.

Punekar's study reinforces two of the key themes of the book. In the first place, in Bijapur as much of the developing world, the built cultural heritage is identified solely in terms of its historical and 'monumentalist' importance to communities. The 'archaic vision', as he terms it, is attributable to a number of causes. The need to tackle widespread urban poverty is a much more pressing socio-economic priority than urban conservation. Lack of institutional capacity and appropriate instruments are other factors. The relevance of western-dominated 'international' conventions, principles and praxis for conserving and managing the cultural heritage resources is increasingly doubted. These are powerful barriers to developing more culturally sensitive and locally aware practices. However, their removal is contingent on his second point.

Here, in his second theme, he argues for an unequivocally 'values-led' approach to conservation to overcome the fractured cultural politics of conservation. The archaic vision is problematic precisely because it ignores the conflicting and diverse values embodied in conserving the built heritage and, as a result, alienates contemporary communities from links with their own heritage. He proposes exploring a much 'wider bandwidth' of values across different community interests, professionals from other fields, special interest groups and conservation professionals. This, he contends, will ensure the necessary democratisation of conservation which is better able to bridge the widening gap between local communities and their patrimony, a gap which many other chapters have also pointed to. The concept of cultural landscape – a dialectic between the natural setting, human intervention and human interpretation – supports an analytical methodology of Rapid Ethnographic Appraisal Procedures which, as his case study shows, can reveal a more nuanced understanding of the different values attributed to 'cultural heritage'.

Koyi Mchunu's theme is also heritage and urban design as social and political constructs. In 'Urban Planning and Sustainability in South Africa', he addresses the concept of urban sustainability in terms of globalisation processes, the commodification of urban design and the neglect of community engagement. However, using the examples of gated communities and the claim for space to practice traditional initiation rites in the African townships of Cape Town, he seeks an explanation of the contradictory patterns and processes of sustainable urban design in terms of the political discourse of contemporary planning theory and its impact on planning practice. Investigating sustainability in the context of post-apartheid South Africa, he argues that the persistence of modern rational planning contributes towards urban fragmentation whilst, at the same time, the sustainable development discourse masks the real conflict of interests that accompany processes of urban change.

On the face of it, sustainable development resonates well within the South African urban context of sprawling suburbia, mono-functional zoning, low-density development, and the social inequities of the separated and fragmented urban landscape. Indeed the sustainability principles are encapsulated in the country's planning processes and policies, namely the municipal level Integrated Development Plans (IDP).

Yet the outcomes betray these principles since the design of contemporary urban space in South Africa is producing new forms of fragmentation and conflict along class and ethnic lines, not sustainable urban environments. On the exponential growth of gated communities, valid though security and safety concerns may be, Mchunu argues that they may equally be interpreted as masking a new form of exclusion, unsustainable spatial fragmentation and segregation along class as opposed to racial lines.

Turning from privileged to marginalised communities, Mchunu shows again how the designation of space by urban planners, in this case for practicing traditional initiation rites, has sacrificed sustainability principles to the exigencies of modernist planning machinery and a 'rationalist' solution to the competing demands for urban space. The initiation process becomes unsustainable because, and this is the key point, concepts of environmental sustainability, particularly where disadvantaged urban dwellers are concerned, were too narrowly defined.

These outcomes resonate with wider experience and challenges. Whilst planners and urban designers are increasingly sensitised to issues of difference, diversity and marginalised groups, at the same time, Mchunu's evidence highlights the irony of the role of state institutions in mediating the design of sustainable urban space at a time when their capacity to act is increasing being undercut by forces beyond their control. Equally, the 'will to plan' for sustainable spatial and social integration in post-apartheid South Africa has fallen prey to the standardized concepts and formulae of rational modernist planning, and to new dogma enshrined in legislation, manuals and government regulation.

Part II: Designing People-based Environments explores key planning and design instruments and processes which are needed to achieve sustainable urban design and to conserve valuable and still viable built heritage. This part examines how people-based urban environments must be attuned to cultural precepts, encode the history and collective identity of residents, build on community-empowered models of design, as well as being physically adapted to environmental conditions. These parameters constitute the praxis for contemporary urban design in the developing world which can adapt tradition to modernity in environmentally sustainable ways.

Contributions by Lima and Edrees consider the significance of planning policies, the former at the strategic scale the latter at the neighbourhood design level, for achieving equitable, liveable and sustainable cities. De Schiller et al. introduce a technocratic perspective on these issues with their examination of urban energy consumption and its impacts on city and building design. Contributions by Juárez-Galeana and Maldonaldo-Fuse focus on community level needs and action: how communities can organise and participate in the design and conservation of the environments they live in and use. Again the thematic concern is with developing sustainable policies, practices and interventions, but from the perspective of community-based needs and locally organised processes.

The scope offered by sustainability precepts for achieving social equity in urban design is the theme of Jose Julio Lima in 'Urban Reform and Development Regulation: The Case of Belém, Brazil'. Lima argues that active debate in the developed world, on how sustainable urban form and, in particular, the degree of compactness can deliver some advantages such as social equity, has not been mirrored in the developing world. Specifically, he examines the social function of different urban planning instruments which have been developed in three contrasting periods in the political-economy of Brazil since 1975, and their capacity to achieve equitable urban forms in Belém. He demonstrates that the manipulation of urban form in the different spatial strategies, as a means of satisfying social justice objectives, has certainly increased over this period. However the implementation of policy has not, in practice, produced equity-oriented, redistributive outcomes. Rather, what has occurred in Belém is largely the development-led production of spatial structure and the consolidation of development patterns in locations already served by urban infrastructure.

Although the outcomes are both disappointing but probably unsurprising, Lima's chapter at least demonstrates how sustainability principles can be incorporated in urban plans for cities in the developing world, just as much as in the contrasting conditions and processes of urban change in the developed world.

The prospect of achieving more equitable outcomes, as Lima suggests, lies in two directions. On the one hand it requires improvements to the regulation and the instruments for guiding the implementation of plans at the metropolitan and local levels. On the other hand, we have to recognise the conditioning environment of the political-economy of the county at the macro-level. Whilst the former is susceptible to change in response to local political, social and economic forces, the latter raises more fundamental questions about the role of post-modernist planning processes in a globalising world.

'The Impact of Land Subdivision Processes on Residential Layouts in Makkah City, Saudi Arabia' by Mohammed Abdullah Edrees shifts the geographical and substantive focus. His concern is with residential development, rather than mixed use areas and city centres, and with planning and design standards to regulate the implementation of new development, rather than the policy and institutional framework for conserving the existing built heritage. His exemplar is the residential *barha* – public open space which is both an extension of small groups of houses but also located between the residential neighbourhoods in Arabic cities. The *barha* serves important functional, social, recreational, culturally-adapted, symbolic and micro-environmental purposes in Islamic society, notably in Saudi Arabia. He shows the disjunctive effects which occur when new residential environments neglect to accommodate and sustain the well-developed design principles found in the more traditional residential layouts. Urban expansion is inevitable; but new residential development and layouts in Makkah have not conformed to Shariah precepts despite their formalisation in the planning codes of the country. Instead the new developments reflect western-style, car-based, grid layouts, and density levels which satisfy developers and technocratic planning interests. But from residents' perspectives they lack the intimacy and spatial 'coherence' of traditional areas, the environmental adaptation to microclimatic imperatives, and especially they fail to provide the vital *barha*.

Edrees demonstrates how this disjuncture can be reconciled by effective design guidance for both the *barha* and the residential layouts as a whole. Based on an examination of the design and use of the *barha* in traditional residential areas, he develops this guidance in terms of criteria such as size, security considerations, privacy, facilities, landscaping. Whilst the details are obviously conditioned by the specifics of Saudi Arabia, the principles and methodology are the key points here – how to adapt and update to modern requirements, the cultural norms and precepts, as well as environmentally sensitive urban forms embodied in traditionally designed neighbourhoods. His call for careful evaluation, respect for the cultural values encoded in traditionally designed neighbourhoods, detailed awareness of residents' preferences, and appropriate planning and design instruments, provide a secure way forward.

De Schiller et al. in 'Sustainable Urban Form: Environment and Climate Responsive Design', introduce a different perspective on the question of sustainability – product rather than process. Focused, like the other authors on the way the urban tissue adapts and is modified through time, their concern, however, is not with the social, economic or cultural parameters of change. Instead, the chapter deals with the way physical environmental changes and current architectural and urban design practices – specifically the thermal effects of climate change and the urban energy demand of modern buildings – impact the shape and use of urban space in the developing world. They review this arena at four scales: global, urban, micro-urban, and building scales, arguing that the search for sustainable urban form must reduce the unfavourable environmental impacts at each of these scales if the 'urban heat' island is to be ameliorated. They review associated phenomena such as air movement, radiation and humidity before considering the environmental impacts in Buenos Aires. Using quantitative data from field surveys and environmental modelling, the authors demonstrate both the importance of using a range of methodologies to establish the relationship between environmental factors and urban design at various spatial scales, as well as making a compelling case for modification to urban and architectural design principles. Without this adaptation, environmental and climate change as well as rising urban energy consumption are likely to produce irreversible impacts on the form and use of cities.

These three chapters have concentrated on top-down processes and actions. The chapters by Juárez-Galeana and Maldonaldo-Fuse switch the focus to bottom-up initiatives. They document and explore the way the sustainable development discourse has incorporated community-level needs and action as another crucial dimension for achieving sustainable urban form. They show how effectively mobilised collaborative planning, at the micro-level, can produce creative initiatives for social innovation which underpin environmentally sustainable urban localities.

Luis Gabriel Juárez-Galeana, in his chapter entitled 'Collaborative Public Open Space Design in Self-help Housing: Minas-Polvorilla, Mexico City', discusses how the demonstrable capacity of people to survive in the most unpropitious conditions of low-income informal urban settlements in the developing world, constitutes a vital resource in designing sustainable cities. Reviewing the background of self-help settlements in Mexico City, he first supports the conventional view that the rapid and spontaneous processes of growth – Mexico City doubled in size from 7.3 million in 1970 to over 15.7 million in 1990 for example – and the marginality of a majority of the urban population have indeed produced high levels of environmental degradation. Minas-Polvorilla, for example, is a former quarry and mining area now built over by an informal settlement accommodating over 600 families housed in shacks. But, a different lens reveals that self-build processes constitute both a vital reservoir for community engagement and a crucial opportunity for achieving environmentally sustainable cities. The challenge is to use participatory processes in order to harness the human resources to achieve these objectives.

The case study explores how local residents, especially women, assisted by professionals, generated a comprehensive design solution for their community's concerns. A methodology for community design is described based on workshop interactions. Although developed and adapted to the Mexican social/cultural milieu, this provides a template which could be adapted to other communities and contexts. A series of five structured workshops was held in Minas-Polvorilla. These progressed from initial workshops on problem definition and design principles to workshops on increasingly detailed design and layout proposals.

The overall results of Juárez-Galeana's collaborative planning exercise are promising. With the support of professional advice and training, groups of residents demonstrated the capacity to engage in the design of sustainable improvements to their neighbourhood. Not only was the provision of urban space enhanced: other attributes of sustainable design were also accomplished. Locally accessible shopping areas minimise travel needs. A 'legible' network of streets and public spaces and the locations chosen for main facilities suggest an innate capacity, by low income urban residents, to design sustainable urban forms. Similarly at the house level, designs for incremental expansion and the inclusion of workshops for small scale economic activity again suggest a nuanced understanding of sustainability principles.

Ana Maria Maldonaldo-Fuse in 'Community Involvement in Planning and Managing Sustainable Open Space in Mexico', like both Lezama-López and Juárez-Galeana earlier, also offers a perspective on community enablement in developing sustainable approaches to urban design. Her chapter also complements contributions by Juárez-Galeana and Edrees in dealing with open space provision, an often neglected aspect of the urban fabric in the context of sustainable urban form. She shows how open space is a vital feature of the urban realm of Mexican cities, but how competing demands for urban land, community neglect, and poor planning policies and weak instruments combine to fragment, or threaten to destroy completely, the provision of open space. She presents a methodology for evaluating the specific design qualities and the social sustainability of open space provision in her case study areas – middle sized urban settlements in Mexico. She shows how different forms of ownership and management of urban open space affect the quality of the spaces and thus the levels of use and user satisfaction. Her main conclusion is that the lack of resources, both human and financial, are the principal reasons for the declining value accorded to open space and thus the diminishing role it plays in supporting sustainable urban design.

Conclusions: Key Principles and Towards a Coherent Praxis

The generic benchmark for many chapters in the book is the commonly accepted Brundtland definition of sustainability 'to meet the needs of the present without compromising the ability of future generations to meet their own needs' (WCED 1987: 8). Its relevance to shaping the urban design of indigenously built urban places and spaces, and the conservation of the cultural heritage of local environments is the theme of the book.

However, our intention is not to provide a reductionist vision of sustainability in a revised definition which accommodates the context of urban design. Nor do we promote sustainable urban design as an objective set of principles and practices. Instead, the aim is to explore the interplay between the concepts of sustainability, urban design and conservation in order to show how the patrimony of buildings and urban forms can be shaped and adapted to contemporary urban development pressures in ways which meet this classic definition of sustainability. This interplay provides the dynamic for all the authors. Each chapter extends and elaborates an understanding of this conjuncture of concepts by locating them in specific contexts, histories and cultural traditions of indigenously designed and built environments.

Drawn from the variety of detailed case studies in the book, we can identify a number of concepts and key principles which form the basis for developing a coherent praxis. These constitute a framework for designing and developing urban localities in ways which are not only more sustainable, but also more in sympathy with conserving and adapting the rich cultural heritage of buildings and indigenous urban design. These generic principles, developed in the cities of countries as diverse as Palestine and Mexico, Brazil, Saudi Arabia and Burma, India and South Africa, add a new dimension to, and reinforce our understanding of, sustainability and conservation whilst simultaneously seeking to reconcile these aspirations with the imperatives of development.

*   *Recognise that urban design, urban conservation and sustainability are social constructions located in time and space, which represent the contested territory of different values, aspirations and power.* Preoccupation with urban morphology, conservation of the built heritage and the design of cities as sustainable physical entities masks the real conflicts of interest that underpin the production and consumption of urban space. As many contributions in Part I make clear, the

objective reality of built urban form as a *product* implies a social consensus and rationality which rapidly evaporates when we view the production of urban form as a socio-spatial *process* and construct, increasingly dominated by global market forces. Although post-modernist planners and urban designers, as mediators of urban space, are increasingly sensitised to issues of social diversity, marginalised groups and asymmetrical power structures, the model of rational institutional and professional activity is remarkably persistent. Cities are environments of both harmony and social conflict, as Brand (2000) succinctly notes. Whilst we have the conceptual tools to understand the contradictions of praxis, the practice of sustainable urban design itself, rarely brings environmental justice to communities who need it most.

- *Develop tools and processes which enhance civil society and participatory forms of decision making by local communities in the design and development of their localities.* The wider urban reform agenda of decentralisation, new forms of governance and democratisation (Zetter 2004; Devas 2004) provides the backcloth of citizen empowerment. Building local capacity and enabling local communities to determine their own needs and development aspirations are key elements of the sustainability concept. Sustainable urban design and conservation must be as much bottom up as top down processes. The relevance of these principles to the process of designing local urban neighbourhoods is amply elaborated by Mchunu and in the case studies by Lezama-López, Juárez-Galeana and Maldonaldo-Fuse, for example. There is much evidence that local communities are adept at reconciling traditional design principles and technologies to contemporary demands and capacities. But this capacity must be better harnessed by new ways of thinking about community decision-making structures to ensure that local people can access the necessary tools, support and resources together with appropriate levels of autonomy. The democratisation of conservation must embrace local community groups, equally as much as professional and specialist interest groups, if the urban patrimony is to be sustained in ways which are relevant to the contemporary needs of the communities who live and work in these localities.

- *Create appropriate policy frameworks and implementation capacities better able to mediate external developmental pressures and local urban design needs and characteristics.* As many of the case studies show, international development demands, donor or multinational corporate funding, and 'western' but essentially globalised urban design solutions, create an almost irresistible combination of pressures for change which damage or destroy locality and heritage. Yet, the chapters (notably Edrees, Rodrigo-Cervantes, Lima and Punekar) also indicate the positive ways in which these pressures can be mediated. One aspect is to ensure that locally appropriate urban design traditions are better researched and embedded in planning and design principles, guidance and practice. Enhancing conservation policies, tools and resources is another element in developing coherent strategies which are sensitive to local needs and priorities. These instruments can promote ways in which localities can be adapted to new activity patterns and built forms whilst conserving indigenously designed environments and heritage.

- *Strengthen urban planning institutions and agencies in order to enhance integrated approaches to sustainable urban design.* Institutional fragmentation between agencies responsible for urban planning and design, particularly the conservation and protection of the built environment, is endemic in the developing world. Often central government is vested with the main responsibility for conservation because it is perceived as a specialist function. But this separates it from the mainstream planning activities of local authorities, overburdened with financial debt and the need to provide basic services for their rapidly increasing populations. This institutional isolation of the patrimony inhibits the integration of conservation strategies within the wider framework of sustainable planning strategies. Narrowing the institutional gap between local communities and the management of their built environment is an essential pre-requisite of more effective conservation policies and practices which are fully integrated into local level agencies. At the same time, strengthening the capacity of local government institutions – professional resources, proactive regulatory instruments, development management and coordination – also emerges as a key point in many chapters, in order to underpin improvements to the policy tools and frameworks.

- *Replace the 'monumentalist' and 'iconic' traditions of protecting the built heritage as an object, with approaches which link conservation and sustainable urban design to the contemporary needs of local communities.* In much of the developing world, the cultural heritage of buildings and sites is frequently identified solely in terms of its historical and monumental significance. This outcome reflects countervailing processes. Within the countries themselves, limited institutional capacity and resources on the one hand, as well as a narrowly conceived understanding of the role of conservation on the other, underpin essentially static, preservationist intervention. At the same time, the global market place of tourism needs to sell distinctive localities in order to sustain itself: the historic built environment is a particularly powerful way of presenting this essential imagery of the 'indigenous'. But, of course, this iconography of the built environment reinforces a preservationist ideology since reality must replicate the preconceived image of the 'authentic'. Not surprisingly, this archaic vision of the built environment, as it might be termed – whether induced by national circumstances or international demands – often alienates contemporary communities from links with their patrimony and traditions, as Handal, Mchunu and Punekar point out in different contexts. A much wider professional and institutional vision and set of practices are needed in which the built heritage can be conserved and valued, yet at the same time revitalised, adapted and managed in ways which link to the contemporary needs of local communities.

- *Expand the methods and criteria to document, record and analyse local technologies, cultural precepts of urban design and how spaces, places and neighbourhoods are used, in order to better replicate and adapt them to contemporary needs.* Too often the value of locality to a community or the significance of the built heritage is devalued, or simply ignored in the face of pressures for new development, because appropriate tools to assess and 'validate' its importance are lacking.

Yet, as the case studies by Lim, Handal, Edrees, Lezama-López, Juárez-Galeana Maldonaldo-Fuse, and de Schiller et al. show in a variety of contexts, 'globalised' urban forms are both environmentally unsatisfactory and often locally unpopular. Conversely, detailed analysis of indigenous urban forms can provide viable ways of reconciling tradition and modernity to produce urban places and spaces adapted to contemporary needs.

• *Enhance appropriate education, training and professional skills.* Challenging though it is to resist a western developed pedagogy and professional training for planners, architects and urban designers, there is positive evidence from all the contributors in this book. Developing culturally sensitive techniques for analysing the design and the built form in its local/indigenous context is one strategy. Action planning techniques and participatory methods which draw on and build upon the knowledge and needs of local communities provide a powerful antidote to western dominated principles of urban planning, design of urban space and activity patterns (Hamza and Zetter 2000). The themes of appropriate education, training and professional skills are not, of course, explicitly dealt with by the authors. Yet each chapter provides insights into what these needs are, amongst which multidisciplinary and multi-professional approaches are a consistent theme. All the authors indicate how professional education and training can build in greater relevance and responsiveness to the demands of practice and innovative modes of intervention, and how the skills and knowledge of professionals can adapt to the dynamics of urban change and the social and economic impacts of globalisation on unique urban localities.

In conclusion, this book aims to enrich our understanding of city design as a process rather than a product. Moreover, it provides methodologies rather than tool kits, and guidelines rather than prescriptions, not only to promote this wider understanding but also to support the praxis of designing sustainable cities in the developing world.

References

Brand, P. (2000), 'The Sustainable City as Metaphor, Urban Environmentalism in Medellín', in Jenks, M. and Burgess, R. (eds), *Compact Cities: Sustainability and Urban Form in Developing Countries*, London, E. and F.N. Spon, pp. 91–103.

Burgess, R., Carmona, M. and Kolstee, T. (eds) (1997), *The Challenge of Sustainable Development: Neo-liberalism and Urban Strategies in the Developing World*, London, Zed.

Carley, M., Jenkins, P. and Smith, H. (2001), *Urban Development and Civil Society: The Role of Communities in Sustainable Cities*, London, Earthscan.

Devas, N. (ed), (2004), *Urban Governance, Voice and Poverty in the Developing World*, London, Earthcan.

Drakakis-Smith, D. (2000), *Third World Cities*, London, Taylor and Francis (2nd edition).

Fernandes, E. and Varley, A. (eds) (1998), *Illegal Cities: Law and Urban Change in Developing Countries*, London, Zed Books.

Gugler, J. (1996) *The Urban Transformation in the Developing World*, Oxford, Oxford University Press.

Hague, C. and Jenkins, P. (2005), *Place Identity, Participation and Planning*, Oxford, Routledge.

Hamza, M. and Zetter, R. (2001), 'Reconceiving the Knowledge-base of Planning Education in the Developing World', *Third World Planning Review*, 22:4, pp. 1–23.

Home, R. (1997), *Of Planting and Planning: The Making of British Colonial Cities*, London, E. and F.N. Spon.

Jenks, M. and Burgess, R. (eds) (2000), *Compact Cities: Sustainability and Urban Form in Developing Countries*, London, E. and F.N. Spon.

King, A.D. (1976), *Colonial Urban Development*, London, Routledge and Kegan Paul.

King, A.D. (1990), *Urbanism, Colonialism and the World Economy*, London, Routledge.

King, A.D. (2004), *Spaces of Global Cultures: Architecture Urbanism Identity*, London, Routledge.

Oliver, P. (ed.) (1997), *Encyclopedia of Vernacular Architecture of the World*, 3 vols, Cambridge, Cambridge University Press.

Oliver, P. (2002), *Dwellings: The Vernacular House World Wide*, London, Phaidon (originally published in 1987).

Potter, R.B. and Lloyd-Evans, S. (1998), *The City in the Developing World*, Harlow, UK, Longman.

Pugh, C. (ed.) (1996), *Sustainability, the Environment and Urbanisation*, London, Earthscan.

Pugh, C. (ed.) (2000), *Sustainable Cities in Developing Countries*, London, Earthscan.

Romaya, S. and Rakodi, C. (2002), *Building Sustainable Urban Settlements: Approaches and Case Studies in the Developing World*, London, ITDG.

Satterthwaite, D. (ed.) (1999), *Earthscan Reader in Sustainable Cities*, London, Earthscan.

Stren, R., White, R. and Whitey, J. (eds) (1992), *Sustainable Cities: Urbanization and the Environment in International Perspective*, Boulder CO, Westview Press.

White, R. (1994), *Urban Environmental Management: Environmental Change and Urbanisation*, Chichester, John Wiley.

World Commission on Environment Development (WCED) (1987), *Our Common Future*, G.H. Brundtland, Oxford, Oxford University Press.

Wright, G. (1991), *The Politics of Design in French Colonial Urbanism*, Chicago, University of Chicago Press.

Zetter, R. (2004), 'Market Enablement and the Urban Sector', in Zetter, R. and Hamza, M. (eds), *Market Economy and Urban Change: Impacts in the Developing World*, London, Earthscan, ch. 1, pp. 1–44.

Zetter, R. and Hamza, M. (eds) (2004), *Market Economy and Urban Change: Impacts in the Developing World*, London, Earthscan.

Zetter, R. and White, R. (eds) (2003), *Planning in Cities: Sustainability and Growth in the Developing World*, London, IT Publications.

PART I
Urban Form and Transformation

Chapter 2

Cultural Sustainability and Development: Drukpa and Burman Vernacular Architecture

Regina Mapua Lim

Introduction

This chapter examines the relationship between a culture and its vernacular architecture by exploring the trends of continuity and change in two contrasting Buddhist communities – the Drukpa of Bhutan and the Burman of Burma/Myanmar. It considers in particular the contrasting affinities between secular and religious styles in these two traditions and shows how their vulnerability and differential response to exogenous forces of 'development' and 'national' identity generate both change and resilience.

The common thread in the two case studies is the heritage of Buddhism which paradoxically has been the major proponent for change. It originated in India and came to Bhutan in the form of Mahayana Buddhism from Tibet during the eighth century. The links of Bhutan with Tibet would not be severed for another 12 centuries until Communist China's invasion of Tibet. The influence of Tibetan culture extended from the religious, political, economical, and social spheres of Drukpa life. Similarly Theravada Buddhism reached Burma via Sri Lanka and defined the moral basis for its political framework and expansionist activities.

The British Colonial regime in India, the culture of colonisation and imperialism affected the economic, political, and social institutions of the Drukpas and the Burmans and had implications for cultural heritage and vernacular architecture. Both cultures reacted differently to western cultural influences.

Cultural Heritage, Development and Vernacular Architecture

The cultural environment (Figure 2.1) comprises a variety of elements, each one affecting the evolution of the culture in varying degrees. Analysing the cultural environment is a method of understanding the complexity of a culture, its fragility, its resilience, and its reaction to change. If development as the proponent of change for a better life is truly concerned with the material and spiritual well being of people, this deeper understanding is essential. In this sense it would only be appropriate to define material and spiritual well being within the context of the culture.

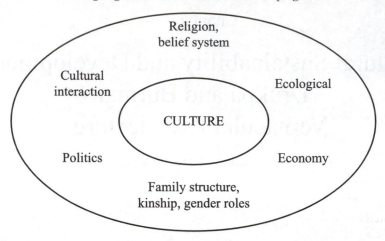

Figure 2.1   The cultural environment

Cultural differences occur because cultural environments are unique and particular to a culture. Nation states often blur these differences amongst ethnic communities within territorially, politically and, at times, religiously defined limits. Perhaps it is with redefining the notion of nation as a community of diverse cultures, each one remaining autonomous for culture specific issues and united for national issues, that 'global' development policies can move towards. Development should be deferential to the culture.

Vernacular architecture is clearly a manifestation, a physical representation of the culture of a people. 'Vernacular architecture' comprises the dwellings and all other buildings of the people. Related to their environmental contexts and available resources, they are customarily owner or community-built, utilising traditional technologies. All forms of vernacular architecture are built to meet specific needs, accommodating values, economies and ways of living of the cultures that produce them (Oliver 1997). If vernacular architecture accommodates cultural needs we begin to realise the complexity involved in its evolution having to serve these needs and within the magnitude of social conditions to which it applies.

In Drukpa and Burman culture, religion, politics, economy, ecology and the social aspects (cultural interaction, family, kinship, and gender roles) have been the most relevant cultural components which give depth to the understanding of the cultural heritage and vernacular architecture. These cultural components have collectively been called the 'cultural environment', one which nurtured and formed the culture.

Evolution of Culture

Religion and Belief Systems

Buddhism was a unifying element that defined the states of Bhutan and Burma. Religion was the bond that held the Drukpas and the Burmans in unity. Their concepts of leadership and kingship evolved from religious doctrines. Society behaved and reacted towards this authority and moral order because of the common beliefs they held. They believed in the teachings of the Buddha as the way to freedom.

Theravada Buddhism adheres to the goal of being an *arhant*, to attain nirvana in the present life, never to be reborn again. Only ordained monks can achieve this status. Mahayana Buddhism deems the notion of the *arhant* as self-serving and instead encourages the adept to follow the Buddha's own example in becoming a *boddhisatva* (enlightened being). *Boddhisatvas* delay the final entry into nirvana returning for several lifetimes to help others on the path to nirvana.

Contrasting religious influences are reflected in Drukpa and Burman vernacular architecture. The closer affinity between ecclesiastic and secular architecture of the Drukpas than that of the Burmans is a reflection of these differences in religious interpretation. The Drukpas of the Mahayana Buddhist school encourage the sharing of the doctrine so all sentient beings may attain nirvana. This sharing of monastic building traditions with vernacular dwellings is also practiced in the close relationship between the monastic and secular community. The marked distinction between Burman ecclesiastic architecture and the vernacular dwellings reflects the elevated status that members of the monastic community have for their special access to the doctrines leading to enlightenment.

Economy

In defining economy one considers the wealth and resources of the society in terms of the production and consumption of goods and services. Economy is the way of life beginning from immediate needs for sustenance, food and shelter, to the regional market exchange of goods, to global trade and its effect on the culture. The community's way of life, whether it be agriculture, pastoralism or trade has bearing on the house form, orientation, location, decoration, building materials and building process.

Drukpa and Burman society evolved from being predominantly agricultural through periods of regional trade, isolation, and global recognition. The economy brought changes in social stratification. Whereas the Burmans controlled this distinction with sumptuary laws, the Drukpas reacted differently. A rural peasant community, the Drukpas never had a powerful aristocracy and the transfer of building technology, art, and culture between the religious and the secular was less restricted.

Burman sumptuary laws produced a marked distinction between the architecture of the religious and the ruling elite and that of the commoners. This sumptuary distinction is not as defined with the Drukpa architecture because of the absence of strong social stratification.

Positive trends in the economy resulted in a surplus of wealth. This excess wealth went into the support of the *sangha*, the Buddhist religious order of ordained members. For Buddhists, status is defined by generosity and how much one can contribute to the cause of religion. It was through royal patronage, community donations, and corvée labour (taxation in the form of labour) that vernacular architecture in the form of stupas, *zedis*, monasteries, *dzongs* (Bhutan's fortress-monastery) were built.

Politics

The Drukpas and the Burmans were first a socio-cultural-ethnic unity before they were a political organisation described as kingdoms. As their territory expanded, their influence and authority extended to other ethnic groups who accepted their hegemony and their cultural values. Both cultures emerged as the dominant ethnic group, which defined cultural identity when it became necessary to have a national culture. This in itself has caused problems in the form of ethnic division within each nation as cultural differences arose within various ethnic groups. The acceptance of Drukpa cultural heritage was less resisted within the predominantly Buddhist kingdom. The harmonious architectural landscape lends itself to this Drukpa cultural dominance. It is not without problems for the non-Buddhist Hindu communities of southern Bhutan, which still seek to find a solution for integrating into this culture.

Political institutions were formed, selected and supported by the society. For the Drukpas and the Burmans, the monarchy and Buddhism were key elements, which defined the political institutions prior to 1900. Changing fortunes in politics had a bearing on architectural form for both cultures, evident in the form of the *dzongs* of the Drukpas, the sumptuous monasteries of the Burmans which were royally endowed, the gold leafed *zedis* or *stupas*, and the *lakhangs* or temples of Bhutan which undergo cyclical construction and deconstruction.

Political institutions were instruments for social control: order symbolising social solidarity. For Bhutan political institutions became venues for the spread of the Drukpa Kagyupa line of Buddhism and consequently Buddhist inspired architecture subservient to maintaining political dominance. The Burman monarchy royally endowed the *sangha*, which became a powerful instrument for maintaining social order. Consequently the Buddhist concept of kingship and public welfare defined the code of conduct and duties of the monarch. The emerging cultural dominance of the Drukpas and the Burmans was not always a peaceful process despite the aversion of Buddhism for violence.

Family, Kinship and Gender Roles

The relationship of the lineage principle which takes into account marriage patterns, inheritance, land ownership, political organisation and social status is clearly illustrated when the Drukpa dwelling is passed on from mother to daughter. The cyclical rebuilding of the family dwelling every 20–25 years, when the eldest daughter marries and assumes the position as head of household, is a community tradition.

The mutual help system keeps the community tightly bound. Men have access to a monastic life and the intellectual study of Buddhist doctrines. Because of matrilocal traditions in Bhutan, men move to villages beyond their place of birth to live in their wives' household. Systems of family, kinship and gender roles are different for each community and are therefore reflected in their dwellings and other forms of vernacular architecture.

Cultural Interaction

As the introduction has noted, the heritage of Buddhism and the British Colonial regime have been the major proponent for change. Over more than 12 centuries Buddhism has exerted a profound influence on religious, political, economical, and social spheres. More recently, British colonisation and imperialism has similarly impacted the economic, political, and social institutions. This has had significant implications for the cultural heritage and vernacular architecture, although with different outcomes for the Drupka and Burman societies.

Ecological Environment

Geographic location, natural resources, and climatic conditions have a direct bearing on the manner in which homes are built, and the construction materials made available by the environment. The ecological environment dictates the source of livelihood and consequently the house forms are defined by these elements.

The Drukpas of Bhutan

To the Bhutanese, their country is known as *Drukyul*, land of the Drukpa sect. The dominance of the Drukpa Kagyupa sect of Tantric Buddhism has given it this name. In 1907, the weakening Buddhist theocracy transferred its political powers to a hereditary monarch. Ugyen Wangchuk's skills of diplomacy permitted the flourishing of local Bhutanese multi-cultures in a relatively peaceful albeit more isolated environment, which was not subservient to a colonial power.

Bhutan is a landlocked country whose geographic location set limits for its contact with much of the outside world (Figure 2.2).

The Drukpas occupied the central zone with a temperate monsoon climate (Figure 2.3). Their settlements along the western and central valleys clearly reflect their Buddhist background. They maintain multi-crop farms and keep animals. The difficult terrain has kept the different valleys largely economically independent particularly in food production. Other valleys are inhabited by other ethnic groups but it is Drukpa culture that dominates when defining the national language, dress, religion, and architecture.

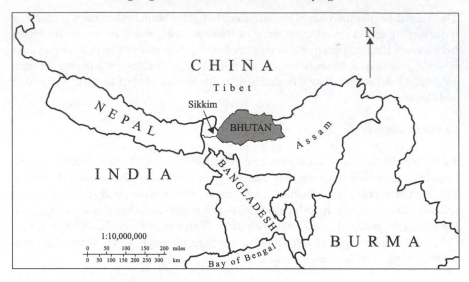

Figure 2.2   Location map of Bhutan

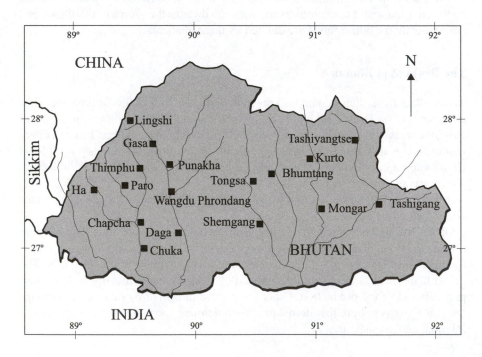

Figure 2.3   Settlements along the central zone of Bhutan

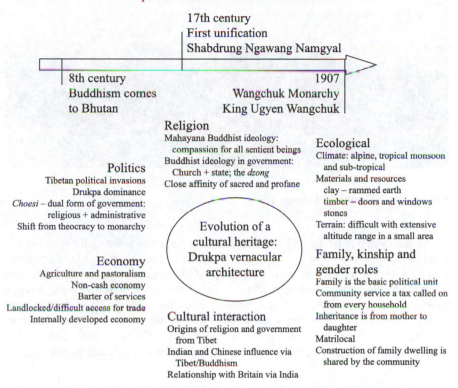

Figure 2.4   Evolution of the cultural heritage and its influence on Drukpa vernacular architecture

Dzongs *as Centres of Culture*

The *dzongs* in each valley symbolised the might of the Drukpa School with each one containing a monastery and an administrative centre (see Figure 2.5). There were 16 historical *dzongs* built in Bhutan during and shortly after the reign of the Shabdrung Ngawang Namgyal (1594–1691). The Shabdrung was the first religious-political leader that unified Bhutan. As a governmental institution, the *dzong* can be considered the socio-political heart of a *dzongkhag* (valley community). Personal and public affairs centred on the *dzong*, familiarity with the architecture influenced building traditions of the farmhouses. *Dzong* architecture with its embodiment of Buddhist values acted as a cultural magnet and a source of inspiration; it became the trendsetter for Bhutanese architecture. As Dujardin observes, 'In Bhutan, religion is the mediating factor that unites and integrates all aspects of culture into a distinct whole, crystallised in material culture' (Dujardin 1994: 152). Other monastic buildings which dot the countryside and remain in harmony with Buddhist inspired architecture include *lakhangs* (temples) (see Figures 2.6 and 2.7), *gompas* (monasteries), *chörtens* (stupas), *mani* (prayer walls), and the *lukhang* and *tsenkhang* (spirit houses).

Figure 2.5   Punakha Dzong, 1999[1]

Visual evidence from 1783 and recent photographs show the resilience of *dzong* architectural tradition (see Figure 2.8). However, none of the *dzongs* have remained exactly as they were built, because the concept of historic restoration in the Bhutanese sense is not one of maintaining buildings as they were but of buildings going through a continuous process of renovation depending on current needs. This process remains deeply rooted in Buddhist ideals, particularly that of impermanence. To a Buddhist, nothing is considered permanent in the unending cycle of life and death. The intrinsic form of each *dzong* may remain the same, as they were strategically planned for the

Figure 2.6   Kurjey Lakhang with the special roof lantern allowed only for palaces, temples and monasteries, 1999

---

[1]   All photos by the author unless otherwise credited.

Figure 2.7   Annual masked dances performed by monks in Ura Lakhang

Punakha Dzong, 1999

Watercolour of Punakha Dzong by
Samuel Davis, 1783

Paro Dzong, 1999

Paro Dzong, 1864 photo by Dr Benjamin
Simpson

Interior courtyard of Paro Dzong with the central
tower housing the most important temples, 1999

Figure 2.8   Comparative images of *dzongs* over time

specific terrain, but detailed changes and improvements are implemented with each renovation. The same process of construction and deconstruction apply to other monastic buildings and vernacular dwellings.

Building technology and belief systems were transmitted to the village level through the *zopöns,* and the system of *gungda ula* directly influencing vernacular dwellings. *Zopöns,* as master carpenters recruited from the villages to build the *dzongs* were also experts in Buddhist ideological values and iconography. *Gungda ula* was taxation in the form of labour, one person per family participating for a period of two weeks in works of national importance. The tradition of one son becoming a monk maintains a strong communication bond. Social life evolves around annual rituals performed by monks in the homes and villages. Buddhist iconography is used in the detailing, ornamentation, and protection of the rural farmhouses (Figure 2.9). *Dzong* building traditions were adapted for the rural farmhouse. Certain iconography was used only by ecclesiastical and official buildings as an indication of status.

The common use of traditional building techniques and a rather strictly defined architectural language have not prevented the individual from creating a unique dwelling specific to his needs. Infinite variations using the same architectural vocabulary may create a uniform settlement portraying cultural harmony even if there are no two dwellings that are exactly the same (Figures 2.9 and 2.10).

'In the rural areas, every village house has been described as the cultural achievement of the entire village community' (Dujardin 1994: 148). Households are bound together in a village by the sharing of services, religious rites and obligations. The construction of a house is a task shared by the community. The sense of identity of the house owner is materialised in the construction of her house as endorsed by the entire community.

Figure 2.9   Constructing vernacular dwellings in Bhutan

Jakar valley, 1999

Paro valley, 1999

Figure 2.10   Vernacular dwellings from different areas of Bhutan

The Burmans

The country of Burma, currently named Myanmar (Burmese) is a union of peoples from different ethnic backgrounds. The Burmans are the dominant ethnic group occupying much of the central plains and parts of the Irrawaddy delta, they are principally agriculturists and predominantly Buddhist.

Buddhism provided the Burmans with a clearly defined programme for moral action and placed great emphasis upon means of demonstrating merit to indicate one's

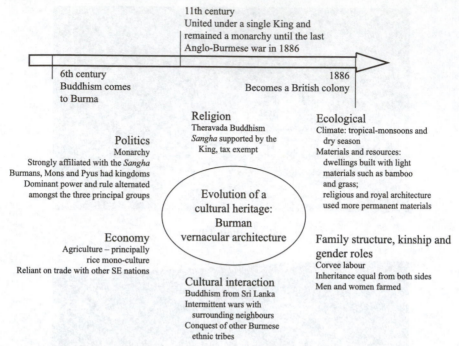

11th century
United under a single King and
remained a monarchy until the last
Anglo-Burmese war in 1886

6th century
Buddhism comes
to Burma

1886
Becomes a British colony

Religion
Theravada Buddhism
Sangha supported by the
King, tax exempt

Ecological
Climate: tropical-monsoons and
dry season
Materials and resources:
dwellings built with light
materials such as bamboo
and grass;
religious and royal architecture
used more permanent materials

Politics
Monarchy
Strongly affiliated with the *Sangha*
Burmans, Mons and Pyus had kingdoms
Dominant power and rule alternated
amongst the three principal groups

Evolution of a
cultural heritage:
Burman
vernacular architecture

Economy
Agriculture – principally
rice mono-culture
Reliant on trade with other SE nations

**Family structure, kinship and
gender roles**
Corvee labour
Inheritance equal from both sides
Men and women farmed

Cultural interaction
Buddhism from Sri Lanka
Intermittent wars with
surrounding neighbours
Conquest of other Burmese
ethnic tribes

**Figure 2.11   Evolution of the cultural heritage and its influence on Burman
vernacular architecture**

status in society. Religious ideals created Pagan as the centre uniting ethno-cultural
and socio-economic differences among the three groups: Mon, Pyu, and Burman.
Bellwood (1992–1994: 61) informs us that the Burman rulers of Pagan synthesised
competing languages, economies (trading for the monsoon coasts and rice agriculture
for the central plains), and thwarted common enemies (invasions from the mountains
and seas). By the eleventh century, Theravada Buddhism which came via Ceylon was
flourishing under royal patronage in Pagan.

The strict concept of *Yazadaing* (sumptuary laws), which is still traditionally
observed, was enforced to emphasise the distinction between ecclesiastical
architecture and vernacular dwellings. *Yazadaing* rules dictated the shape of a man's
house according to his status. Heights of buildings, use of material, and manner of
construction were symbolic of a person's status. For the common citizen, tall buildings
were not permitted and the use of brick and masonry was restricted to ecclesiastical
buildings.

Yazadaing laws were followed by the subjects of the Burmese kings. In the sphere
of architecture, everyone except for the king, the monks, and the highest officials had
to obey the following:

•   to use only light material – wood, bamboo, grasses or leaves;
•   to construct buildings of one storey only;

- not to build a 'standing' house but a 'kneeling' house, the front slope of the roof being required to be longer than the rear slope;
- not to build a false storey, a porch above the entrance, or a staircase perpendicular to the façade;
- not to build a secondary building with a pitched roof;
- not to insert a secondary door in the main door;
- not to adorn the outside or the inside of the house with paint, lacquer, gold or sculptures (Lubeight 1997).

Sturdier and more permanent materials such as masonry and hardwood timber were reserved for higher status buildings. For the rural community, the quality of permanence imbued in religious buildings represents the permanence of Buddhist ideals, the social structures of that community, and its close relationship with its spiritual leader (Lubeight 1997). On the other hand, the quality of impermanence for vernacular dwellings may well reflect the Buddhist concept of the impermanence of this lifetime and the belief in the cycle of rebirth.

Royal patronage and public endowment of religious institutions enhanced the religious centres of Pagan, Pegu, Rangoon, and Mandalay with monuments for perpetuity. Art, talent, expense and labour were never restrained for the building of these institutions (Figures 2.12–2.14). *Corvée* labour was used for public works such as the building of roads, irrigation projects, and religious architecture. That these building traditions never filtered down to the humbler vernacular dwellings is because of *yazadaing*.

Cultural Interaction

With the expansion of agriculture and the surplus of rice production, trade brought the Pagan kingdom into contact with other Southeast Asian nations. Between 1500–1600,

Figure 2.12   Royal palace in Mandalay, 1874, destroyed in World War II

Source: Print by Frank Vincent, 1874, from Dumarçay and Smithies 1995: 30.

**Figure 2.13   A group of worshippers in the 'Tuesday' corner of Shwe Dagon
              Pagoda c. 1890**

**Figure 2.14   Building materials commonly used for vernacular dwellings
              c. 1890**

all over Southeast Asia we see the rise of recognised religious centres with largely urban populations with the mechanism for organised trade. It is the entrepôts that become political and social centres of trade.

However, prosperous trade was affected by a mini ice-age in the seventeenth century. Up until the eighteenth century economic development amongst the Burmans, and most of Southeast Asia, lagged behind that of Europe. It was at this point that European prosperity, wealth, and stature began its upward course. European interest in colonisation and imperialism brought Burman and European cultures into contact with one another initially through trade. By 1826, Arrakan, Assam and Tenasserim were ceded to the British. Rangoon had become the centre of colonial Burma. The colonial period brought about changes in the urban architecture. Some religious buildings and royal palaces were converted to government offices. Many monks were turned out of their monasteries and the buildings temporarily taken over by the British Army (Figure 2.15).

Figure 2.15   Monastery taken over by the British Army in 1885

Source: Photo Beato.

New building types such as prisons, schoolhouses, commercial buildings, urban residences, (Figure 2.16), and the more rural Dak houses took elements from the vernacular dwellings for the practical solutions they offered.

Verandahs, piles, floor level ventilation windows, use of local materials were reinterpreted and applied to these new building forms. The residences of the more affluent were built of teak and they no longer followed the strict code of *yazadaing* and liberally borrowed influences from monastic architecture and the practical

Figure 2.16   The Chief Commissioner's house in Mandalay c. 1890

Source: Photo Beato.

elements of the vernacular dwelling such as the main living areas being located above
the ground floor, steep roofs, verandahs, and generous window sizes (Figure 2.17).
Multiple roofs, once reserved for high status and religious buildings, were commonly
used for domestic dwellings of the new commercial elite. Urban density increased
fire risks, the more affluent dwellings both of the British and wealthy local merchants
used less flammable materials such as tile and iron roofs, brick, cement, and timber.

Figure 2.17   Dak Bungalow c. 1890

The traditional farmhouse dwellings remained simple. Status was defined by how much one gave to the Buddhist Church rather than the wealth one accumulated. Merits were gained in return for generosity. The common people dedicated this life for gaining merits for a positive rebirth in the next life. This may well explain the qualities of impermanence in the vernacular dwelling as opposed to the qualities of longevity and grandiosity of religious architecture.

Cultural Heritage and Development in Bhutan

In 1907 Ugyen Wangchuk became the first hereditary monarch. His diplomatic relations with the British paved the way for a less isolated future for Bhutan. Contact with other nations beyond its immediate boundaries would later be used as an asset in protecting its sovereignty (Figure 2.18). His rule established the concept of nationhood. Ugyen was supported by the British for his ability to control ethnic strife, which eased border relations with British India. Buddhism was a positive influence for unifying Bhutan's ethnically diverse communities.

Relations with the British were cultivated on the side of the Bhutanese for the resources it would offer for development. Advances in the sciences, medicine, and agriculture were assets to which these relations gave the Bhutanese access.

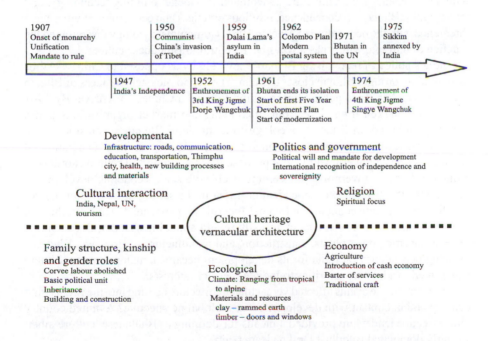

Figure 2.18   Evolution of the cultural heritage and its influence on Bhutan vernacular architecture

The reign of the third King Jigme Dorji Wangchuk (1952–1972) marked the gradual opening of the country to the outside world and the economic and social development Bhutan would undergo. India would provide the capital, education, professionals and even the labour force that development undertaking would require. The resources flowed into the country further strengthening the monarchy and uniting the country under Drukpa leadership. Inspired by Indian democracy, the King revised the structure of government to include elected officials at the district level and decision-making policies to include the family in the villages as the primary unit. He incorporated traditional decision-making structures, that of the *dzong* or district level, the village and family with the concept of democracy. The importance of spiritual development and the partnership between the religious and the secular were recognised by the kings of Bhutan. The Wangchuk kings were of Drukpa heritage, tracing their lineage to the Shabdrung. Religion validated Drukpa dominance, which in turn became the essence of national culture. The present King Jigme Singye Wangchuk continues to work on national unity and the role of the monarchy as the principal agent of development.

Communism in China and Indian Intervention in Bhutan

Before China's intervention in Tibet, Bhutan had active trade and diplomatic relations and a shared history of common cultural heritage of religion, politics, and society with Tibet. Bhutanese architecture owes much to Tibetan building technology, and iconography. Bhutan's independence, religious practices and economic activities were threatened with the occupation of Tibet in 1951. Communist ideology discouraged the practice of religion, which has always been central to Bhutanese culture.

India's policy of recognising Bhutan's sovereignty as opposed to China's claims of suzerainty brought Bhutan closer to India. The economic backwardness of Bhutan was the main barrier to getting her prepared to repel a Chinese offensive. By 1961 we see the marked transition: from 'medieval' non-market organisations and a government based on Buddhist ideology to a 'modern' Bhutan, a transition from a self-subsistence economy to a planned trading economy; from a theocratic and absolutist form of government whose purpose was the support of religious orders to a modern form of government concerning itself with socio-economic development (Ura 1994: 25). Bhutan was dependent on India in the setting up of institutions for building up a modern economy and state. Modernisation extended to the introduction of light industry, improvements in agriculture and animal husbandry, development of hydroelectric power plants, construction, and manufacturing. However, Bhutan's growing dependency on India for its development became a major concern. Bhutan was forced to adjust its priorities to India's security interests.

How have these events affected vernacular architecture coming into the twenty-first century and in contact with development on a global perspective? A united country with effective leadership provided a means for defining a 'Bhutanese' culture albeit strongly dominated Buddhist Drukpa leadership.

In the twenty-first century, effective administration through the *dzong* system continues, maintaining the tight bond between church and state. Use of the *dzongs* requires constant renovation from functional changes and improvements brought about by damage. These cultivate innovative building techniques based on tradition but not totally bound by historic precedents. Buddhist culture is central to these renovations. The transfer of knowledge for improvements is dispersed on the village level through the *zopöns* and applied to domestic architecture. Economic benefits brought about by development opportunities such as trade, education, and employment are reflected in the vernacular architecture in the form of new building components such as iron roofing, plumbing, electricity, and timber-framed detailing once affordable only by state institutions. New *lakhangs* have been constructed in the reign of the present King which lacks neither traditional craftsmanship nor contemporary innovation (Figures 2.19 and 2.20).

The consciousness to retain a 'Bhutanese' style has led to the opening of a state school teaching traditional crafts, which include painting, sculpture, and woodworking. With economic prosperity and the continuing interest in traditional culture these trained craftsmen are in great demand. A significant amount of the farm income goes into the dwelling, for the temple room's sacred objects – brass sculptures, wall paintings, and *thangkas*, which are Buddhist religious paintings.

Motor roads built to improve communications for the primary purpose of defence has stimulated socio-economic development. It has fostered the transfer of goods, the movement of people, and cultural interaction from one valley to another. 'Regional aspects of traditional house construction are now being introduced in other regions; these will lead to new traditional configurations in the near future' (Dujardin 1994: 140). Specific archetypes once isolated within the valley have been seen in other valleys. Domestic architecture, after the trend of *dzong* improvements, now uses

Figure 2.19   Kurjey Lakhang in Jakar valley, 1999. The temple on the left was constructed in 1993, the one on the right c. 1907

Figure 2.20 Tongsa Dzong with its iron roof, 1999

building materials transported from India. Some construction methods may not engage the community's tradition of mutual help giving one's dwelling a sense of community identity.

Development has introduced an urban tradition into what has always been a rural society. There are no historical precedents for a Bhutanese urban culture. New building types have emerged. Projects such as an airport (Figure 2.21), schools, hospitals, hotels, shophouses, a library (Figures 2.22–2.24), look towards the vernacular dwelling as a basis for formulating its Bhutanese image. *Drukpai lusö*, 'the cultural traditions of the Bhutanese' invoke a set of norms governing ritual behaviour and appearance prescribed by the state and enforceable by law. Formal acts of deference and national styles of building and dress all come under this heading. 'Culture' in official eyes has produced architectural hybrids for new building types. These hybrids use *dzong* and domestic archetypes and apply it to new buildings. Termed the 'Bhutanisation' of architectural buildings, it is a process of applying superficial building décor with historical precedents in order to fall within the official 'culture' code. None of the new urban building types have been as inspired as the internally generated architecture of the *dzongs* wherein the variety of building forms each suited to specific sites has managed to present a harmonious and distinctive archetype (Figures 2.22–2.27).

The organisation of urban space has been another struggle. On the village level, the careful placing of each house with the consensus of the community is strategically located to define common space, for protection from weather conditions, and other community concerns. Thimphu, the main city, is struggling to find an urban tradition for defining open space.

Development must cope with urban migration from rural settlements. Improvement of the quality of life must rise as fast in the rural areas so as not to intensify rural to urban migration. Today, the dwelling culture remains vibrant in its rural setting.

Figure 2.21   Bhutan International Airport in Paro, 1999

Figure 2.22   School building in Jakar valley, 1999

Figure 2.23   Hospital in Jakar valley, 1999

Figure 2.24   Hotel conforming to 'Bhutanese' style Jakar valley, 1999

Figure 2.25   Shophouses in Thimphu based on a variation of the farmhouse, 1999

Figure 2.26   Shops, restaurants, offices and hotels taken in Wongzin Lam, the heart of the commercial district of Thimphu, 1999

Figure 2.27   Shops, restaurants, offices and hotels taken in Wongzin Lam, the heart of the commercial district of Thimphu, 1999

Improved social services, health and education, have brought about an increase in population. Population growth has in turn brought about primary concerns for the fragile ecosystem that must support it. Traditional building techniques rely on the availability of natural resources. Nail-less architecture of Drukpa dwellings use much timber from the forest reserves left unexploited in the earlier years. The present ruling administration is concerned about the adverse impact of increased economic activity and population on the fragile mountain ecosystem and has made environmental preservation a priority.

The set-up of television and telecommunications networks linking the *dzongs* with faxes and telephones and providing Thimphu with global information access via the internet is certain to bring in external influences affecting vernacular architecture. The ability of the Bhutanese to absorb what is needed and to maintain what has been valued from the past will be tested as development continues to introduce change.

Cultural Heritage and Development in Burma

The last Burman King Thibaw (reign 1878–1885) was exiled after the Third Anglo-Burmese war in 1886. This period is marked by changing development concerns with goals that vary to suit the objectives of the specific government's ideology: from colonial Burma through her emergence as an independent nation, and through the struggle to synthesise the ethnic diversity of Burma. Although the colonial state had great military strength, its great weakness was its inability to sustain support from the indigenous population.

The interests of the colonial rulers took precedence over Burmese cultural concerns. The economic, political, social, religious agenda of the new rulers were completely different from the regime they had displaced (Figure 2.28). The Burmans had come into contact and became subservient to a culture quite alien from their own.

Whilst the primary political interest was to protect the territory of India, the economic interests of British Burma were to exploit local resources, to open Burma to international trade, and to create markets for the industrialised products of Europe.

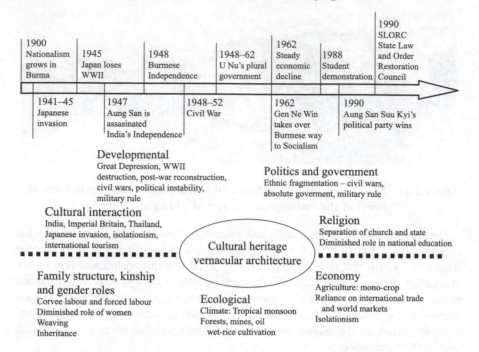

Figure 2.28   Evolution of the cultural heritage and its influence on Burmese vernacular architecture

In 1852, much of Rangoon, as the entrepôt, was razed to the ground to make way for the planned urban site with substantial brick and wooden buildings. The concept of a colonial urban town was transplanted into Burma. Rangoon attracted European, Chinese, Indian, and Muslim traders. The Burmese became minorities in this trading town.

For the colonial regime, the nation was an advantageous way of defining the territory and establishing rule over the entire dominion of different ethno-linguistic groups. From a historical perspective many of these tribes being bound as one nation had been sworn enemies or had formed alliances against one another. To acknowledge cultural differences and to work as one 'independent' nation would be a task for the future independent Burmese.

Vernacular architecture was affected with the changes in social order, the abolition of the monarchy, the establishment of colonial rule, and the migration of non-Burmese traders: the sumptuary laws became irrelevant and were no longer imposed in urban centres like Rangoon. The functions of an entrepôt and the requirements of a large urban population called for planning that discouraged construction method according to some of the rules of *yazadaing*. The use of light construction materials such as bamboo and grass increased the risk of fire in the dense urban situation. Permanent materials such as timber, brick and masonry once reserved for religious and royal architecture became the materials of choice.

Urban density required new forms of architecture. Single storey dwellings with pitched roofs built of bamboo walls and grass roofs as dictated by *yazadaing* were replaced with three-level flats. Administrative offices were built in the fashion of colonial architecture (Figure 2.29).

The vernacular dwelling so suitable to the ecological conditions influenced the language of urban architecture after the turn of the century. Colonial period buildings took vernacular design elements for their practical solutions. Door height and windows with floor level openings for ventilation were implemented even in government buildings. The more prosperous merchants built larger teak houses reminiscent of monastic architecture in the suburbs of Rangoon.

Figure 2.29   Sule Pagoda Road as the main commercial district of Rangoon in the 1930s

Not subjected to sumptuary laws of the monarchy, they built larger, using more permanent materials and adopting architectural forms once reserved for religious, royal and high status buildings. In the rural areas, the humbler dwellings remained unchanged. As a sign of status, the more commercially successful peasants built with timber instead of the more common bamboo and grass.

After independence, and during the period of civil wars, the economic change brought about by isolation and withdrawal from international commerce affected the urban metropolis to a greater extent than the rural areas. The metropolis, as commercial centres without the funding for social services and the maintenance of physical infrastructure that taxation provided from trade, went into decline. But the veneration and construction of prestigious shrines around Shwedagon continued. In the countryside, the vernacular dwellings built of light materials, and in accordance to the rules of *yazadaing* proved resilient to economic hardship. After all, it was the architecture of the common people. Locally grown materials and traditional building skills remained available. People continued to live in ancestral villages and reaffirmed ancestral ways, 'exhibiting not blind traditionalism but prudent conservatism. They were aware that new opportunities and arrangements did not benefit everyone equally. Scepticism as to the wisdom and benevolence of public officials was all too frequently justified; and the perception of modern education as a potential threat to customary values was largely correct' (Owen 1992–1994: 517–18).

In the 1960s, it was not the monarchy or a foreign colonial power, but an indigenously grown military regime that ruled. The regime, as in all others, professed altruistic development goals: economic prosperity, peace and order, synthesis of diverse ethnic communities. Despite the noble platform, the regimes did not overcome the tragic flaw common to military regimes and dictatorships in Southeast Asia, the refusal to pass the mandate to a democratically elected party.

One asks, how well represented are the different ethnic groups in the planning of development policies in a non-democratically elected government? Is the policy suppressing of ethnic diversity for the sake of national unity? Does isolation strengthen cultural heritage? Whose cultural heritage? Without representation on the national level, do those geographically remote cultures become marginalised? With the modern government's powerful channels to integrate, dominate and reform, will the 'Burman' culture synthesise or smother the ethnic minorities?

Conclusion

Historical events and circumstances will always vary but what remains constant is how people as a defined group draw on their culture when reacting to change. The opportunity Bhutan had of cultural unity made possible by its size and population, the peace and isolation that geography and political circumstance provided, permitted its culture to evolve to a greater extent more indigenously. Its definition of development in terms of material and spiritual well being has been defined to a great extent from within the culture. In the Bhutanese cultural context, it had to do with the acquisition of education with respect to morality, intellect, and knowledge, so as to rise above inborn prejudices and ignorance of the world. Those who possessed such wisdom and intellect were considered developed (Thurman 1995). It went beyond basic material prosperity even if the Buddhist concept of development as described in the role of the Shabdrung's first unified government was to remove human suffering and to take practical measures to eliminate immediate material causes of suffering and actively encourage the conditions necessary for prosperity.

Bhutan's history excludes western colonisation where the colony becomes subservient to another culture. Bhutan remained less developed at the turn of the century because of Britain's decision to limit the finances necessary for development. This may have turned out advantageous in the preservation of its natural resources, cultural traditions and its independence. The investment in development had made other nations economically subservient to the economic goals of the investor-coloniser. The concept of colonisation as bringing in Western culture to improve the lives of the natives of the colony had less altruistic results for many of the colonials. The concept of taking one lifestyle as superior and not taking into account that traditions evolved to suit the complex cultural environment was a common oversight during this period of Western imperialism. The vernacular architecture it presents remains strongly rooted to Buddhist values, the ecological environment, and the economy (also in terms of sustaining the community of builders, artists and craftsmen); it is supported by the religious and political leadership, and has remained attuned to the needs and capabilities of the community. In many ways its evolution was internally generated. Bhutan has at this point managed development in a more controlled and culturally integrated manner. Its clarity in maintaining a balance between cultural tradition and Western concepts of development has been largely beneficent for its rural communities and has dictated its own pace for change.

On another perspective is Burman culture, which through the course of history had its turn as the dominant ethnic group among the now nationally defined Burmese State. Colonisation brought changes in the ruling authority transferring it from the traditional rulers to a foreign authority. Economic goals of the colonisers were different and their understanding of the Buddhist religion and local belief systems were studied and not necessarily believed or practiced. These attitudes had significant bearing on Burman vernacular architecture. New archetypes were introduced; the concept of *yazadaing* or sumptuary laws went with the abolition of the monarchy; an urban culture subservient to economic trade emerged. Likewise, traditional ways of building and the language of vernacular architecture had its influence on the new archetypes of the colonial period, even if mostly for climatic and practical purposes. This cultural interaction between colonial power and colony also diffused the internally generated cultural elements of traditional Burman life. The size of Burma, the number of diverse ethnic groups, the dominance of Burman culture as a method of defining national identity, have painted a more complex picture of development for this country and in particular Burman culture. What is worth noting is the resilience of the vernacular archetype through these drastic changes. As a nation, Burma (Myanmar) has had difficulty defining national culture because of ethnic diversity and the different perceptions of development. It has yet to strike a balance between recognising the individuality of cultures, providing for it, and working together as a nation state.

Bringing vernacular architecture into the focus of this investigation on cultural heritage and development has given clarity to what may have become hypothetical observations and conclusions.

This study has presented the symbiotic relationship between the cultural environment and vernacular architecture, and of vernacular architecture being a physical manifestation of how a culture adapts to change.

Development should look to cultural heritage for the wisdom inherent in the values and belief systems that provide moral guidance, the economy and way of life, which sustains the community in keeping with their moral beliefs and social structures.

References

Amundsen, I. (1994), 'Bhutan: Living Culture and Cultural Preservation', in *Rehabilitation, Revitalization, and Preservation of Traditional Settlements*, vol. 67/IASTE, pp. 67–94, Berkeley, CEDR, University of California.

Aris, M. (1982), *Views of Medieval Bhutan: The Diary and Drawings of Samuel Davis 1783*, London, Serindia Publications.

Aris, M. (1994), *The Raven Crown: The Origins of Buddhist Monarchy in Bhutan*, London, Serindia Publications.

Aris, M. and Hutt, M. (eds) (1994), *Bhutan: Aspects of Culture and Development*, Gartmore, Scotland, Paul Strachan – Kiscadale Ltd.

Aung San, S.K. (1991), *Freedom From Fear*, London, Penguin.

Bellwood, P. (1992–1994), 'Southeast Asia Before History', in Tarling, N. (ed.), *The Cambridge History of Southeast Asia*, vol. 1, Cambridge, Cambridge University Press, p. 61.

Boisselier, J. (ed.) (1994), *The Wisdom of the Buddha*, London, Thames and Hudson.

Dujardin, M. (1994), 'Bhutan's Human Settlements: The Dynamics of Tradition and Modernity', in Aris, M. and Hutt, M. (eds), *Bhutan: Aspects of Culture and Development*, Gartmore, Scotland, Paul Strachan – Kiscadale Ltd.

Dujardin, M. (1997), 'From Fortress to Farmhouse: A Living Architecture', in Schicklgruber, C. and Pommaret, F. (eds), *Bhutan: Mountain Fortress of the Gods*, New Delhi, India, Bookwise Ltd.

Dumarçay, J. and Smithies, M. (1995), *Cultural Sites of Burma, Thailand and Cambodia*, Oxford, Oxford University Press.

Gravers, M. (1999), *Nationalism as Political Paranoia in Burma: An Essay on the Political Practice of Power*, Richmond, Surrey, Curzon Press.

Khosla, R. (1975), 'Architecture and Symbolism in Tibetan Monasteries', in Oliver, P. (ed.), *Shelter, Sign, and Symbol*, London, Barrie and Jenkins, pp. 71–83.

Lim, R. (1999), *Cultural Sustainability and Development: Drukpa and Burman Vernacular Architecture*, Oxford, Oxford Brookes University, unpublished MA dissertation.

Lubeight, G. (1997), 'Uses and Functions: "Yazadaing (Burma)", Buddhist Burma, and Monastery Burma', in Oliver, P. (ed.), *Encyclopedia of Vernacular Architecture*, vol. 1, Cambridge, Cambridge University Press.

Maseland, J. (1997), 'Bhzop Bhutan and Drukpa Bhutan', in Oliver, P. (ed.), *Encyclopedia of Vernacular Architecture*, vol. 2, Cambridge, Cambridge University Press.

Oliver, P. (ed) (1997), *Encyclopedia of Vernacular Architecture*, 3 vols, Cambridge, Cambridge University Press.

Parry, H. (undated), 'Burma', in Hammerton, J.A. (ed.), *People of All Nations: Their Life Today and the Story of Their Past*, vol. 2, London, The Fleetway House, p. 1056.

Schicklgruber, C.and Pommaret, F. (eds) (1997), *Bhutan: Mountain Fortress of the Gods*, New Delhi, India, Bookwise Ltd.

Singer, N. (1993), *Burmah: A Photographic Journey 1855–1925*, Gartmore, Scotland, Kiscadale.

Singer, N. (1995), *Old Rangoon*, Gartmore, Scotland, Kiscadale.

Strydonck, Guy van, Pommaret, F. and Yoshiro, I. (1989), *Bhutan: A Kingdom of the Eastern Himalayas*, Boston, Shambala.

Tarling, N. (ed.) (1992–1994), *The Cambridge History of Southeast Asia*, 2 vols, Cambridge, Cambridge University Press.

Tenzing, D. (1993), *An Introduction to Traditional Architecture of Bhutan, Thimphu*, Royal Government of Bhutan.

Thurman, R. (1995), *Essential Tibetan Buddhism*, London, HarperCollins.

Ura, K. (1994), 'Decentralization and Development in Medieval and Modern Bhutan', in Aris, M. and Hutt, M. (eds) *Bhutan: Aspects of Culture and Development*, Gartmore, Scotland, Paul Strachan – Kiscadale Ltd.

Ura, K. (1997), 'Tradition and Development', in Schicklgruber, C. and Pommaret, F. (eds), *Bhutan: Mountain Fortress of the Gods*, New Delhi, India, Bookwise Ltd.

White, J. (1909), *Sikhim and Bhutan: Twenty-One Years on the North-east Frontier 1887–1908*, London, Edward Arnold, repr. New Delhi, Asian Educational Services.

Chapter 3

Rebuilding City Identity through History: The Case of Bethlehem-Palestine

Jane Handal

Introduction

Place identity is the process of building and rebuilding meaning, in a space-time continuum, on the basis of emotive forces – the 'heart' – as formed and reformed by the flow of rational forces, the 'head'. The need to adapt to era-specific realities and, in the age of globalisation, to assimilate extensive flows of meaning and to compete economically in the world market, demand engagement with the rational forces of the 'head'. On the other hand, cultural projects, political identifications, religious revelations and collective reminiscences of an imagined community demand that we engage emotive forces of the heart. These two forces shape the cultural landscape of place. They find expression in the physical environment, its set of activities and in the control, production and management systems. These attributes show great capacity in structuring place identity by encoding identity and enabling it to evolve and innovate under varied emotive and rational challenges. It is also through those attributes that identity is eroded if a mismatch between the emotive and rational forces arises.

These forces are not, to borrow Marx's term (as cited in Marx 1970: 210) 'abstract concepts'. What is somehow masked in this term is a sense of how the values of emotive and rational forces imbue the meaning, perception, and reproduction of identity in the cultural landscape throughout history. To turn against these abstractions, it is essential to emphasise that these forces are made and remade by the human agency of a place. 'People make abstractions that then take on a life of their own, seeming to make history for us. But perhaps by recognising these abstractions for what they are, maybe then we can remake history' (Olwig 2002: 220).

In the age of globalisation, the mismatch between emotive and rational forces of place, is leading to the erosion of place identity and the resurgence of defensive identities constructed upon national, ethnic or religious foundations.

Within this context, the question which this chapter explores is in what way can these countervailing emotive and rational forces be integrated in urban planning and design interventions to accommodate change whilst sustaining place identity? The chapter argues that rebuilding place identity is more about discovering the distinctive processes rather than the distinctive character of place. The analysis is set in the politically inflamed and culturally and religiously diverse context of Bethlehem-Palestine. This is an historic tourist city, of universal significance, and subject to particularly intense movement of international capital in the millennial era, largely channelled through tourism.

Background

In the current era, the importance of place identity is widely perceived, although rather more in principle than practice. Informed by an understanding of identity determined either by an idealised past or by the phenomenon of globalisation and urban change, the rebuilding process runs the risk of either mummifying identity and transforming cities into museums, or replacing the heritage with the monotony of global high capitalism. In either case, the sense of a sustainable and living place identity is at stake.

As far as the latter scenario is concerned, the processes of capital and power transfer through globalisation displace the specific emotive forces which are vital for the survival of the distinctiveness of places: loss of identity is ever-increasing. The forms of production and transformation associated with global capitalism are underpinned by urban design and planning guidelines which are based on the principle of a supposed universal rationality. Their currency is valued, because they support the continued profitable working of the capital accumulation process. This process contributes to the homogenisation of place and the loss of distinctive identities.

In developing countries, the planning and design systems, fuelled as they are by the external development assistance, technology and know-how, further damage place identity. The dominant or orthodox model of development aid, as Hamdi and Goethert (1997) call it, which is implicit in aid conditionality is centralist and hierarchical: major decisions are made at national or international levels in centres of power and investment. This model serves the needs of governments and the vested interests of powerful individuals, development experts and large commercial enterprises. Planning and design approaches support these characteristics: they are often mechanistic and exclude the array of local community groups from the decision making process. Consequently, the very processes which are vital to the health and survival of a sense of belonging, ownership and cultural continuity of those communities – the opportunity to negotiate, to co-operate, to build incrementally, and to express cultural/religious beliefs and political associations in urban forms and lifestyles – are displaced. Places are not perceived as living bodies that convey the unfolding human development process.

Similarly, place identity as an idealisation of the past – the first model – also embodies internal contradictions which are particularly evident in historic tourist cities. Against the tide of rapid urban growth and change, to local inhabitants and visitors alike, historic cities represent an environment that is familiar and stable which is linked to an 'idealised' past and, in a globalised market of ever-increasing 'sameness', an 'otherness' and distinctiveness not as yet attained in the new. In this context, Lynch (1972) argued that an individual's sense of well-being and effective action depend on stable references from the past which provide a sense of continuity. Historic cities, as the 'collages of time', are the very references that connect past, present, and future (Lynch 1972: 235). For local inhabitants, historic cities are significant for understanding cultural diversity and are rich sources for the sense of place and rootedness as major components in building social solidarity and national identity (Al-Sayyad 2001: 3–4). According to Anderson, membership of an imagined community, of which the nation-state is a reasonably stable and long-lasting example, requires an element of belief in the community's 'reality'. For Butina Watson and Bentley (2006), the meanings read into historic built form are most likely to be drawn on for constructing imagined communities of the most stable, 'deepest' kind; to which the most stable, deepest aspects of our own identities relate.

As well as being sites of cultural consumption, historic sites are economic commodities for various strategies of economic regeneration and place promotion. Globalisation is accompanied by the creation of new competitive nuclei of local production and consumption (Massey 1984, Cooke 1989). Each locality is catapulted into a competition to market those distinctive qualities that will allow it to gain a competitive edge over its rivals (Harvey 1989). Harvey further notes that, for the options open to localities for increasing their stake in the market-place, those strategies which can attract consumer spending and which can be relatively limited to the area in question, are seen as providing the best returns. The 'presentation of self' becomes all important, and aspects of local identity which can help to define this image, as well as generating local spending and revenues are co-opted into an expanding market of local signs and images.

The process of re-presenting place identities to promote tourism can involve many pitfalls. An obvious problem, as Robinson (2001) explains, is that the tourism industry largely conceives of the cultures, beliefs and historic associations (emotive forces) of local communities either as value free, and thus largely an inconsequential aspect of development, or/and as a product to be packaged and consumed. In this process, as decisions for change are taken *outside* the host community in centres of power and investment, places are represented in accordance with the aspirations, tastes, preferences and budgets of first-world tourist developers, donor bodies and government agencies. Robinson (2001) argues that the issue, in such cases, is not that of change, *per se*, but one of *the extent to which a host community feels a sense of ownership of change*. In reproducing the built environment to meet the expectations and preferences of the 'tourist gaze' (Urry 1990), the elements of placeness, continuation, evolution, stability and familiarity are eroded. Gentrification and ownership change are two major adverse impacts of this process of change.

This manipulation of emotive forces (culture and history) by the rational forces of tourism is often compounded by the commodification process whereby traditions, rituals, beliefs and 'ways of life' (emotive forces) are packaged, imaged and transformed, into saleable products for tourists (Cohen 1987). McKean (1996) argues that commodification, in itself, need not generate conflict if it carries the consent of the host culture and the latter can reap the benefits of reasonable levels of commercialisation. This view is also shared by Macdonald and Thomas (1997) who pointed out that the presentation of cultural artefacts and cultural history can be identity-affirming and liberating for cultures seeking to explain their traditions, values and history. The key issue in this process of commodification, as Robinson (2001) argues, relates to enabling local inhabitants to decide for themselves what aspects of their culture should be displayed and how they should be presented.

Inter-cultural conflict may be induced over ownership and representation of identity, either when the commodification process results in a trivialisation of ethnic groups and their cultural practices and traditions, or when it is controlled by agencies with little insight or understanding of the meanings and historicity of such practices. When commodification serves the recreational desires and economic purposes of the developed world, tourists continue to be offered what McCannell has termed 'reconstructed ethnicity' (1984: 361). Morris (1995: 96) pointed out, toured communities are increasingly required to live out their manufactured ethnicity for the gaze of the other, with the result that the destruction of some traditions and their replacement by others is required by the state and then negotiated by various ways by those whose bodies and practices are thus required (but do not necessarily directly consent) to incarnate policy.

For the change induced by tourism to be viable and sustainable, both cultural (emotive forces) and economic (rational forces) dimension of historic places need to be kept in view, and not artificially hived off into separate areas of inquiry.

Within this understanding of place identity, the mismatch between the emotive and rational forces is now elaborated within the context of Bethlehem-Palestine.

The Mismatch between Emotive and Rational Forces in Rebuilding the Identity of Bethlehem

In order to celebrate the dawn of the third millennium of the birth of Jesus Christ, the Bethlehem 2000 – B2000 – project, with an estimated budget of US$200 million, was initiated in response to an urgent call to the international community from the Palestinian Authority for assistance in preparing Bethlehem for the bi-millennial celebrations.

By the end of the 1990s Old Bethlehem-Palestine, the source of so much political and religious history, was clearly suffering from severe deprivation: physical and economic problems were extensive and the institutional base had been weakened by three decades of Israeli occupation. Despite its deprivation, Bethlehem had a distinctive morphological structure, a lively administrative and commercial centre, a multi-religious community (Muslims and Christians from various denominations) which enjoyed a harmonious co-existence, and a strong sense of pride in being Bethlehemites and Palestinians.

The countdown to the Millennium celebrations started and the project was fuelled by the transfer of aid in the form of money, technology and know-how. Areas and sectors were targeted for improvement according to the project authority's priorities as the central decision maker. Project documents were prepared setting out objectives, project inputs and outputs, deadlines and reporting schedules. Project documents also set out, in prescriptive detail, all the activities which each subcontractor would need to undertake as part of the project: investment programmes, pre-investment feasibility studies, and a variety of reports dealing with urban and infrastructure design, promotion plans, private sector development, computerised databases and staff development plans.

A high percentage of the project's budget went to foreign consultants who were brought in to produce tourism and public sector development studies and proposals for solving the urban decay. Building on these studies and proposals, working plans for overseeing infrastructure and urban renewal of major public areas in the town, for developing the tourism sector and for planning a 16-month calendar of events, were prepared and designed either by expatriate consultants or large architectural practices. The planned schemes and designs were subject to a review based on acceptability to donor bodies, subcontractors and the project authority, and based on economic and administrative feasibility. However, the municipality and the local community groups together with their knowledge, cultural values, political reminiscences, interpretations of the town's identity, and their traditional modes of control and management of the urban environment, were considered to be far too fragile to be involved in any decision making process.

At the implementation stage, large entrepreneurs and businessmen drawn from elite groups carried out infrastructure and urban design projects. Publicity boards that carried the names of donor bodies and implementing agencies of different projects were put-up by the B2000 project authority as a form of informative community participation well after the major and minor decisions were taken. Main streets and squares were 'glossed out' to hide the collapsing, badly serviced surrounding quarters from the tourist gaze. The administrative services and villagers who sold their fresh produce in the old market were transferred to the new parts of the town in an attempt to reduce the number of users of the historic core who were seen as diminishing its value as a museum of Christianity. With the aim of meeting the needs of an expected three million tourists, who were the main 'objects' of development, an estimated US$100 million were invested in private tourism development projects. Finally, the remaining funds were spent on sophisticated electronic equipment for the municipality to fulfil the commitment to institutional capacity building.

By December 1999, the success of the project was heralded by its authority and donor agencies!

Only the powers of observation were necessary to see the huge gulf between the reality on the ground and the apparent falsehood of these evaluations. While the unique identity of the town was recognised as an invaluable commodity in the rhetoric of the decision makers of the project (the B2000 project authority, its set of consultants and donor bodies), in practice, however, a lack of understanding of Bethlehem's identity led to a mismatch between this and the globalised outcomes of the planning and design interventions, and thus eventually to the erosion of its distinctive identity.

Bethlehem's identity, as understood through different historical periods, has been established by the association of its inhabitants, and the world at large, with both its sacredness and its political reality. Being a beacon of spirituality, Bethlehem has always possessed a form of sacred reality. It has never been a mere physical conglomerate that was built as an ensemble. Its earthly urban reality was determined, in different eras of history, by its multifaceted spiritual and cultural character. The highly charged political history of the town has also been a major force behind the constitution of the town's distinctiveness. It is the catalyst behind the creation and consolidation of viable collective values and shared experiences which has maintained the social bonds among a mosaic community with different religions, traditions, interests and places of origin. References from the religious and political forces are profoundly embodied in a distinctive way of life characterised by social solidarity, mutual aid and territorial associations, and in meaningful urban forms and representations in the town's living heritage. These references embed local communities' roots and provide them with a sense of ownership, a sense of social, cultural and political continuity, and a sense of pride in being Bethlehemites and Palestinians. This overarching presence of what might be called 'emotive forces' conveys a shared inheritance against which the relentless influence of external developmental pressure – the rational forces – has created and recreated the city as a living reality, unfolding gradually over the centuries.

In general, the deep-rooted emotive forces and the creative, but slow paced impulses of the rational forces, have conditioned, nurtured and balanced each other in the formation and reformation of Bethlehem's identity throughout history until recent times. Despite a volatile political history, and dramatic social, physical and economic change in the past, the inhabitants have collectively enacted the capacity to sustain the 'emotive forces' which they *passed down* from generation to generation and *passed across* to changing modes of production, control and management of the historic urban environment. The pluralistic local community which gave Bethlehem its distinctive meanings was the main guardian of its identity. Due to the political instability of the region, local government, with its weak resources, was never an ultimate decision-maker; but local community groups were partners in shaping development to retain the town's unique character and vitality. Through this partnership, the meanings of the urban fabric, and the multiple socio-cultural values (emotive forces) of the community groups were *passed up* to local governmental bodies and hence interventions and planning and design strategies for change (rational forces) managed to balance the legitimate needs of various actor groups with the protection of the town's identity.

In the Millennium era, however, the overarching presence of emotive forces was curtailed under the influence of overruling rational forces reflected in a stillborn urban, social and economic development project that aimed at making the town a setting for the Millennium celebrations. The crux of the contested integration between the rational and emotive forces was derived from the wide gap between the conceptions of local people as to Bethlehem's identity, and those of the B2000 project authority, the *quango* decision maker of the project.

In contrast with the previously illustrated complex and perpetual past-present identity of Bethlehem distilled throughout history, the project authority, with its set of foreign consultants, perceived the distinctiveness in Bethlehem's identity to emanate merely from its religious status as the birthplace of Jesus Christ. By confining Bethlehem's identity to this era of history, upon which they planned and designed the future of the town, the B2000 project emptied the town's 'present' identity of much of its substance and significance and blocked the natural fluidity between the past and the future.

As a corollary, the once lively historic town, bustling with a variety of users and uses, was developed as a stage-set thematic museum of Christianity (Figure 3.1 over). Also, with its ready made standardised solutions, the B2000 project flattened the distinctiveness of the town's identity and promoted abstract identities that were not underpinned by lived and practiced values and sustained collective experiences.

Depriving urban forms of their emotive meanings eliminated any sense of place which had been the main component in sustaining a sense of belonging and feeling for the roots that kept the town together in times of seismic political upheavals.

Figure 3.1   The streets of the Bethlehem Old Town around midday before (left) and after (right) the millennial interventions[1]

---

[1]   All photos by the author.

As the creative communication between human beings and their cultural matrix was stifled, the long nurtured intercultural integration was unsettled and defensive fundamentalist identities and trends erupted particularly among young people in their twenties and early thirties. An identification with a continuous process of interaction between the rational and the emotive forces in the modes of control, production and management of the urban environment, which had generally been sustained throughout history, was also forsaken by the B2000 project authority. This was in the interest of a decision-making process that was characterised by centrism and paternalism. The local pluralistic community groups who for generations had been guardians of the town's identity, were neither integrated in planning nor in promoting the urban scene. Their views, their needs, their knowledge, their experience and their very spontaneous, incremental, but culturally responsive actions, as the creative forces that sustained the town's identity throughout history, were replaced by a top-down, professionally dominated control and management system. This system merely served the vested interests of experts and powerful individuals, and the motives of the government. Such a model of urban development, based on the motive of economic growth and primarily concerned with meeting the demands of the tourist gaze, was seen by the B2000 project authority as the principal mode for promoting an international recognition of Palestine and Palestinians as a nation. As the outcomes of the project fell far short of their expectations, local people became cynical about the Palestinian National Authority's governance system.

The entrenched warfare between emotive and rational forces, that had haunted the B2000 project since its start and which subsequently led to its failure, eroded the unique identity of Bethlehem. This warfare found expression in rigid and fatal dichotomies which emerged in the course of planning, design, representation and interpretation of the project, and were set up in: 'meaning of Bethlehem as interpreted by the decision makers of the B2000 project' versus 'meaning of Bethlehem as interpreted by local people'; 'past identity' versus 'present identity'; 'objectives of decision makers' versus 'needs of local people'; 'experts knowledge' versus 'vernacular knowledge'; 'a stage-set heritage museum' versus 'a living historic locality'; 'the use of place' versus 'the interpretation of space'; 'growth' versus 'quality of life'; 'competitiveness' versus 'progressiveness'; and 'globalisation' versus 'distinctiveness'.

The 'worthy lesson' that stems from an understanding of place identity in the context of Bethlehem-Palestine is that a contested integration between emotive and rational forces in the cultural landscape lead to the erosion of place identity.

Hence, the question that can be posed at this stage is: in what way can the emotive and rational forces of a place be integrated to accommodate change while protecting place identity?

Addressing the Integration between Emotive and Rational Forces: The 'New Realism' of the Study

In developing an understanding of Bethlehem's identity within the perspective of the emotive and rational forces, a different conceptual insight is needed into the complexity of their integration on one hand, and the manner in which different modes of integration can nurture or erode distinctiveness from the cultural landscape, on the other.

In Bethlehem's context of perpetual political instability, uncertainty, indeterminacy, cultural and religious diversity, and accelerating change, an approach to urban planning and design that did not maintain a balanced integration between emotive and rational forces has failed to sustain place identity in the cultural landscape. Hence, it is only through a *balanced integration between the emotive and the rational forces in the cultural landscape* that future change can be accommodated and identity can be protected. It is through this balance that learning how to supplant a fatal and identity-negating urban planning and design approach, of which Bethlehem 2000 was a prototype, by an identity responsive one can take place.

Its unique religious status, its history of long political ideological conflicts, its diverse cultural and religious social structure and its intense transformation with the movement of international capital through tourism, makes Bethlehem-Palestine a very distinctive place. This distinctiveness which has yielded strongly pronounced emotive and rational forces, also contributes to compounding their contested integration and, consequently, to the loss of the town's identity in the millennial era. Despite these context-specific challenges that might impose limitations on how much can be generalised from the empirical context of Bethlehem, however, and as distilled from the previous sections, a dissonant integration between emotive and rational forces is a universal predicament in sustainable development. Hence, a balanced integration between the emotive forces (heart) and the rational forces (head) in the cultural landscape can be heralded as a universal 'new realism' in the field of urban planning and design.

Though a new realism in the fields of urban planning and design, the balanced integration between emotive and rational forces has, in fact, existed for a long time.

The balanced integration of the rational (head) and emotive (heart) was the basic concern of ancient civilisations and religions. The balance between the head as the seat of discursive and divisive intelligence, and the heart, as the seat of feelings and organ of intuitive knowing, was a concern mentioned in the Bible, the Upanishads, the Quran, and other sacred writings of the world (Nasr 2001: 6–7). In Chinese wisdom, it is the *yang* value that needs to be balanced by the *yin* value – expansion by conservation, competition by cooperation, and an object-centred consciousness by spiritual-centred consciousness (Morowitz 1992).

The new realism called for in Bethlehem-Palestine, also finds resonance in various other disciplines, including social science, natural science, and architectural practice. In the 1960s, Habraken's *Support Structures* (1961) offered a new perspective on balancing people's needs with professionals views in the field of architecture and built environment. *Support Structures* made a huge impact in creating new architectural designs in housing production, not as rigid monuments, but as a responsive architecture embracing internal and external places within which people could feel comfortable and at home. To allow this to happen, Habraken suggested an involvement of 'users' in decision making throughout the planning, design and building process of dwelling environments.

Similarly, in the social science domain, achieving a balanced integration between the demands of the individual in his/her private life and the demands of the large institutions of the public life via *mediating structures*, has been a concern of Berger and Neuhaus since the 1970s (Berger and Neuhaus 1979). They argued that mediating structures, which included the neighbourhood, the family, the church, and voluntary associations, are essential for a vital democratic society, and their recognition in public policy allows people to be more 'at home', and political order to be more meaningful.

The balance between emotive and rational forces advocated here also coincides with the balanced integration between freedom and order articulated by Schumacher (1973) in his revisions to the development ideology. Schumacher (1973: 53–54) puts it this way:

> In the affairs of men, there always appears to be a need for at least two things simultaneously, which, on the face of it, seem to be incompatible and to exclude one another. We always need both freedom and order. We need the freedom of lots and lots of small, autonomous units, and, at the same time, the orderliness of large-scale, possibly global, unity and co-ordination...What I wish to emphasise is the duality of the human requirement ... For his different purposes man needs many different structures ... For constructive work, the principle task is always the restoration of some kind of balance.

Also in the fields of both social and natural science, Capra (2002) extends the understanding of living systems, which emerged from biological and cognitive theories, to argue the need for a balanced integration between the emergent structures and designed structures of human organisations in the social domain. Emergent structures are defined by Capra as the creative innovations and adaptations that human communities, through their knowledge, intellect, and learning abilities exchange by social interactions and create in the context of a particular organisation. Designed structures, on the other hand, are the rules and routines established by leaders and managers which are necessary for the effective functioning and stability of the organisation. Capra explained that a balanced integration between the two structures allows human communities to be partners in the change process, in rethinking and restructuring the organisation right from the start and in designing a future that already has them in it.

As this brief resumé makes clear, a balanced integration between emotive and rational forces has engaged a wide academic community for a protracted period. After addressing this balance as the process in which change is achieved and identity protected in the rebuilding of cities through history, and following the recommendation of Jane Jacobs 'once one thinks about city process, it follows that one must think of catalysts of these processes ...' (Jacobs 1961: 12), the questions that need to be addressed now are: what are the catalysts and means for balanced ends? And, how can that balance lead the way ahead towards identity-responsive urban planning and design interventions?

Shaping the Way Ahead: Rebuilding the Identity of the City Through History

In addressing these questions, this section builds upon the resonance between the *balance* in the case of Bethlehem-Palestine and other disciplines to point out universal truisms. By these truisms, founded on the balanced integration between the emotive and rational forces, identity is sustained through managing change rather than halting it. These truisms should not be considered as constituting some absolute, universally applicable 'good practice'. Good practice, after all, is contextual, and real-life settings are never universal – they have to 'take place' and cannot come into being without particular emotive and rational forces. These truisms are positive raw material which can be called on to construct fruitful new visions which, when investigated within the emotive and rational forces of a place, can form working practices that sustain identity.

This section concludes by introducing further questions which, whilst on the face of it familiar, demand answers which are not obvious and which open up avenues for further theoretical and empirical research. Improved answers to these questions will allow a more comprehensive understanding of the role of the balance in informing future urban policies, plans, programmes and projects, which are better attuned to the common ground of values and needs which users, controllers and producers of a place share.

Rebuilding the identity of the city through history, as explained in this chapter, highlights the profound tension of protecting place identity and accommodating change. Symptomatic of the tension is the fact that the process of '*rebuilding*' holds the meaning of protecting the *status quo ante* development while developing new approaches and interventions. A balanced integration between the emotive and rational forces of a place, proved to be the way forward in achieving change (*building*) while protecting place identity (*re*). If the *building* process is not constructed upon a comprehensive understanding of the *re* processes, the challenge of developing identity-responsive change that is locally viable and strategically sustainable, would be forgone.

A comprehensive understanding of the *re* processes, i.e. the distinctiveness of place (or the lack of it), involves an understanding of place identity as evolved from the past to the present and as projected into the future. An understanding of the *re* processes enables an assessment of the problems, opportunities, threats and strengths of a place and hence, enables change to be focused where need is greatest. It explains how distinctiveness in a place's identity is formed, evolved, and contested by the integration of the various constituents of the emotive and rational forces in the cultural landscape. The flow of rational forces, formed of meanings, images, people, capital and goods across the borders of a place, is defined. Also determined via this understanding are the emotive forces of a community, formed of their cultural beliefs, religious affiliations, inter-communal relations, collective associations, sense of territorial belonging and ownership. It offers an insight into how the emotive forces were passed down from one generation to another, the extent to which they have been transformed by rational forces and the way in which they have been passed across to the cultural landscape (control, production and management systems, the physical environment and its set of activities). An assessment of the institutional structures, planning and design regulations and development policies, the capabilities of local and national government organisations, and the extent to which both people and government are willing to change and participate in the change, is also achieved through an investigation of the *re* processes.

This investigation also examines how various actor groups involved in the control, production and consumption of a place, evaluate its identity as established from the emotive and rational forces and their integration in the cultural landscape. The understanding of place identity as evolved from the past to the present is also complemented by an understanding of place identity as projected into the future in the needs and aspirations of various actor groups of a place. This step is crucial, because the multiple investigation of the needs and aspirations of various actors allows a deeper insight into areas of mutual support and conflict. Areas of mutual support are necessary to drive future urban planning and design interventions which are context specific and responsive to the needs of various actors.

To obtain a comprehensive understanding of the *re* processes and restore them into the building of place identity, different strategic methods and context specific tools of inquiry have to be purposely combined and developed.

To restore the *re* processes into the building of place identity as established in the course of this chapter, i.e. protect place identity while accommodating change, a balanced integration of the emotive and rational forces has to be restored in the cultural landscape as formed of the physical environment, its sets of activities, and the control, production and management systems. As distilled from the case of Bethlehem, these are the systems that show great capacity in structuring place identity by encoding identity and enabling it to evolve and innovate under varied emotive and rational challenges, and it is through these attributes that identity can go awry if a balanced integration between the emotive and rational forces is halted.

In other words, the control, production and management systems, the physical environment and its set of activities are the *enabling structures* that allow a balanced integration between emotive and rational forces to take place. Hence, it is only through re-institutionalising this balance in the enabling structures that place identity can be sustained.

It is essential to emphasise that the enactment of a balanced integration between the emotive and the rational forces into the enabling structures cannot be sporadic or occasional. However, it has to be represented in the different levels of the enabling structures – intangibly in the control, production, and management systems and tangibly in the physical environment and its set of activities.

So, what are the catalysts for, and the impacts that are likely to be achieved from, a balanced integration between the emotive and rational forces in the different levels of control, production, and management systems of an urban environment?

As distilled through evaluations of the B2000 project, a top-down, standardised, and professionally dominated control, production and management system that excludes the needs and aspirations of different cultural groups and their cultural values and local knowledge passed down from generation to generation (characteristics all or some of which urban design and planning systems in many parts of the world have), has proved a failure in sustaining place identity. Such an approach can also make local people angry and cynical towards governance strategies adopted by government bodies. Hence, urban planning and design approaches that are the very opposite to this negation of place identity and that turn the tide from domination and control to co-operation and partnership ought to be sought.

The alienation of public institutions from private institutions, of managers from communities, from professionals to people, or from 'the top' to 'the grass roots' in human institutions, has been a shared concern among Capra (2002), Berger and Neuhaus (1979) and Habraken (1972) in disciplines of natural science, social science and architectural practice. Such alienation poses a fatal crisis. It is a crisis because the top comes to be devoid of the meaning and identity existing at the grass roots, and the top is therefore viewed as unreal or even sinister by grass roots.

Partnership is the balancing act between 'place identity as interpreted by government organisations' and 'place identity as interpreted by local people', 'objectives of governments' and 'needs of diverse community groups', 'experts knowledge' and 'vernacular knowledge', and 'local resources' and 'external resources'.

Participation and partnership between the top and the bottom are seen as pivotal by different disciplines. Capra (2002) argued a need for adopting new power relations in human organisations by adopting a balanced integration between the laws and policies of its designed structures and the collective creativity and values of the communities as crystallised through their emergent structures. A partnership between the community and government allows the emergence of solutions for change that are sensitive to the cultural context of a place while enhancing the sense of ownership and belonging of local communities. For Habraken (1972) too, the involvement of users in the decision making process allows the emergence of structures that supports a balanced integration between the needs of users and the professionals' technical practices.

To balance emergent structures (creativity and knowledge of local communities) with designed structures (policies and regulations), reforms in urban policies are needed to allow government to exercise its responsibility, while enabling communities to play a role in the production and management of their urban environment.

Capra (2002) and Berger and Neuhaus (1979), stress that when public policies are abstract and detached from the values and realities of a specific context (as is the case in Bethlehem), they impose one version of a comprehensive order of meaning which ignores the cultural particularities of a society and the distinctiveness of the locality. As a result of this uniformity, the political order gets 'delegitimated' by people. When that happens, officials tend to secure political order by coercion rather than by consent. They emphasise that sound and more meaningful public policies that allow the 'top' to pursue the strategic role of the public organisation without being oppressive to the 'grass roots', can be achieved if the local social and cultural dimension is recognised. Emphasising diversities of a community while getting people organised under communal beliefs and shared experiences is defined by Hamdi (2005) as the essence of good governance.

In this respect, good governance balances capitalising on rational forces (investment returns and government achievements) with capitalising on the emotive forces (local resources and assets). It builds on the resources of local communities and empowers them to be partners in the planning and design process. It also builds the capacity of government organisations to allow them to network with community organisations.

One of the most debilitating results of the B2000 project and its imbalanced governance strategies, is a feeling of powerlessness in the face of a governmental organisation controlled by officials who alienated local people and globalised their cultural values and by experts whose values local people did not share. Such planning and design approaches displace the very emotive constituencies which are vital for the survival of place identity and the integration of its multi-cultural community groups. The emotive forces, as distilled from the case of Bethlehem, allow people to find ways for preserving their diversity while working within collective associations that maintain indispensable social bonds. People can also be creative in sustaining and innovating their emotive forces by passing them down from generation to generation and passing them across to different levels of production, control and management of the urban environment. It is this legacy of tacit communal knowledge embedded in the emotive forces, that empowerment strategies ought to recognise and sustain.

Capra's (2002) views on organisational learning are congruent with these concepts of empowerment. Capra argued that knowledge and learning are social phenomena. In his model of knowledge creation, he explained that knowledge is always created by individuals and it is brought to light and expanded by social interactions. Hence, knowledge cannot be treated as an entity that is independent of people and their social context. Replicating, transferring, quantifying and trading knowledge, as he stressed, will not improve organisational learning. Capra suggested that to enhance the creativity of an organisation that is responsible for the emergence of new context-specific orders, organisationally designed systems have to support and strengthen communities.

Berger and Neuhaus (1979) explained that recognising the social institutions (neighbourhood, family, church, and voluntary associations) in public policy, as mediating structures between the individuals and the public organisations, preserves the individual's identity and reduces the threat of alienation to the public order. The aim of empowering social institutions such as NGOs and CBOs is not dismantling public organisation. Rather, it is pursuing its vision within democratic governance that enhances, rather than undercuts, identity choices available to a pluralistic society with a multitude of particular interests.

Building on this scrutiny of the catalysts for, and the impacts that are likely to be achieved from, restoring a balance in the control, production, and management systems of an urban environment, a number of questions arise which open new doors to explore the potential value of the balance in sustainable development. These are as follows:

- As partnership and participation are tools for achieving balance, how would the balance allow us to break new grounds in participation?
- In what way can much-needed reforms in urban policies be lead by the concept of balance to achieve partnership between the government, CBOs, NGOs and the private sector in and across different control, production and management levels of the urban environment?
- How can the balance define new roles, responsibilities and duties for different stakeholders in a partnership in a way that is responsive to the cultural, political and social context of a place?
- What does the concept of balance imply in terms of strategies for building local assets of communities and capacities of government for improving public/private partnership?
- Can the balance help to direct urban planning and design projects to adopt long term development strategies rather than relying on short term emergency projects?

Now that the balance between the emotive and the rational forces in the control, production, and management systems has been scrutinised, the question to be posed at this stage is: what are the catalysts for a tangible representation of a balanced integration between the emotive and the rational forces in the physical environment and its set of activities?

The chapter has so far proposed changes that a reconceived balance might induce in the control, production and the management systems of an urban environment. This perspective is clearly an important one, but it is critical not to drift into considering the built environment itself in a reductionist way – feeling that the right product will somehow automatically emerge if the process itself is right. In other words, any assumption that a balanced integration between the emotive and the rational forces in the built form and its set of activities ought to be a by-product of an ideal identity-responsive control, production, and management system, would be far from the truth. Even in any process of user involvement, no matter how sensitively used, it is in the forms, functions and rehabilitation techniques which designers and experts put into play in the built environment, that people live and work. If a balanced integration between the emotive and the rational forces is not represented in such forms and functions, then the urban design and planning interventions can only be fundamentally flawed from users' perspectives. If a place is interpreted in this negative way, as was the case in Bethlehem, then local people are far less inclined to adopt an active attitude and a sense of ownership towards it, which correspondingly reduces the sustainability of those interventions over time. Besides, monotonous urban forms and activities which are normally a corollary of an imbalanced integration of the emotive and the rational forces in the built environment, eliminate sense of place, damage the sense of belonging and feeling of roots which are major components in sustaining the cohesion of place-based communities.

It seems clear from all this that to offer the most promising basis for an identity-responsive transformation, there must be a balanced integration between the Head and the Heart in the form and function of a place. Again, capitalising on the economic benefits and investments of rehabilitation/conservation can only be realised if balanced by capitalising on the cues and symbols of the emotive forces that find expression in the physical environment and the internal pattern of life with its set of collective community actions which have generated the historic, identity-responsive environment in the first place. This balance allows an understanding and preservation of the past, tradition, and cultural diversity to combat a sense of transience, of a lack of belonging or lack of community, while maintaining cultural continuity.

Through the balance, change is not halted in the urban environment but rather managed to ensure that the full range of qualities that give a place its distinctiveness – its past, its buildings, its open spaces, its cultures and its social life – are sustained for future generations.

By this balance, future urban upgrading projects, in the different levels of their planning, design and implementation, will reject *a priori*, universal solutions, and will favour identity-responsive approaches rooted in the concrete reality of place. It is only through forming a partnership between the people who own the place and have a vested interest in the planning for development and change that there can be balance in the sustainability of identity with that of urban planning and design projects.

For Habraken (1961: xi), achieving such identity responsive transformation can be pursued through the idea of the 'natural relationship' which is a core message of a balanced integration between the Head and the Heart in the form and function of the built environment. Habraken called for a reinstatement of a balanced integration between people's needs and creativity, and professionals' views and technical knowledge in the design and building process of dwelling environments. Habraken's call for this balance emanated from his concern with standardised architectural forms that offer too few opportunities which people might call on to improve their lives – a concern increased in the capitalist era, when the increase in which corporate ownership of land became a fundamental factor influencing the decision making process, allowing particular agents (governments, powerful individuals, development experts and large commercial enterprises) to exercise power over particular sites, whilst prohibiting users from having such control.

'Typological repertoire' such as those suggested by Bentley (1999), Lynch (1975) and Norberg-Schultz (1971) are also necessary for achieving change while protecting identity. If embedded in the emotive and rational forces of a particular place and put into play within a balanced integration between people's needs and creativity and professionals' knowledge, these repertoires can restore a balance in the form and function of the built environment.

Further questions that require investigation arise from this discussion:

• Can the concept of balance introduce new tools and techniques into the typological repertoires of Bentley, Lynch and Norberg-Schultz to enhance the designed and the emergent structures in an urban environment and further encourage their balance?

• Would embedding the repertoires into the emotive and rational forces of a place require an adjustment in their inquiry methods to be context-specific?

- Is there a specific method to detect and understand the meaning of various cues and symbols that finds expression in the physical environment and its set of activities, both retrospectively and as projected from the present into the future?
- Can there be a structure of incentives to stimulate the balance and encourage its recurrence in and across different levels of control, production and management systems, the physical environment and its set of activities? How can this enabling environment promote the balance in a way that would encourage rather than deter new investments?
- How can an enhanced understanding of the balance lead to the formulation of evaluation criteria to ensure that past 'best practices' for urban development are evaluated objectively and are built on in future interventions?

Our understanding of the concept of balance can only be deepened by undertaking systematic and rigorous research to address the questions outlined above.

Concluding Note

In a time of dramatic and violent change, accelerated by globalisation, sustainable urban futures lie in sustainable urban pasts. Place identity, as understood within the emotive and rational forces, is a process that depends on continuity, a natural fluidity between the past and the future, while also possessing the faculty of adapting, evolving and innovating under the influence of rational forces so long as it remains connected to its emotive sources. If the change process sustains the cultural values, social diversities, political identifications and collective associations of a community and its embodiments in the urban environment, its set of activities, and the control, production and management systems of a place, as passed from the past to the present, then sustainable urban futures are guaranteed. Without a balance between the emotive and the rational forces of a place in urban planning and design interventions the process of rebuilding the identity of the city through history will be aborted – identity will either have no correspondence with reality or be relegated to museums, and so will the built environment.

References

Al Sayyad, N. (2001), 'Global Norms and Urban Forms in The Age of Tourism, Manufacturing Heritage, Consuming Tradition', in Al Sayyad, N. (ed.), *Consuming Tradition Manufacturing Heritage, Global Norms and Urban Forms in The Age of Tourism*, London, Routledge, pp. 1–34.

Bentley, I. (1999), *Urban Transformations: Power, People and Urban Design*, London, Routledge.

Berger, P.L. and Neuhaus, R.J. (1979), *To Empower People: The Role of Mediating Policy Structures in Public Policy*, Washington, DC, American Enterprise Institute for Public Policy Research.

Butina Watson, G., and Bentley, I. (2006), *Identity by Design*, London, Architectural Press.

Capra, F. (2002), *The Hidden Connections*, London, HarperCollins Publishers.

Cohen, E. (1987), 'Authenticity and Commoditization', *Annals of Tourism Research*, 15:3, pp. 371–86.

Cooke, P. (ed.) (1989), *Localities*, London, Unwin Hyman.

Habraken, N.J. (1961), *Supports: An Alternative to Mass Housing*, Dutch edition, Netherlands, Scheltema and Holkema.

Hamdi, N. (2005), *Small Change: The Artistry of Practice and the Limits of Planning in Cities*, London, Earthscan.

Hamdi, N. and Goethert, R. (1997), *Action Planning For Cities: A Guide to Community Practice*, Chichester, John Wiley.

Harvey, D. (1989), *The Urban Experience*, Baltimore, Johns Hopkins University Press.

Jacobs, J. (1961), *The Death and Life of Great American Cities*, New York, Random House.

Lynch, K. (1972), *What Time is This Place?*, Cambridge MA, MIT Press.

Lynch, K. (1975), *The Image of the City*, Cambridge MA, MIT Press.

Marx, K. (1970), *A Contribution to the Critique of Political Economy*, Moscow, Progress.

Massey, D. (1984), *Spatial Divisions of Labour: Social Structures and Geography of Production*, London, Macmillan.

McCannell, D. (1984), *Reconstructed Ethnicity: Tourism and Cultural Identity in Third World Communities*, Annals of Tourism Research, 11, pp. 361–77.

McDonald, R. and Thomas, H. (1997), 'Nationality and Planning', in McDonald, R. and Thomas, H. (eds), *Nationality and Planning in Scotland and Wales*, Cardiff, University of Wales Press, pp. 1–14.

McKean, C. (1993), 'The Scottishness of Scottish Architecture', in Fladmark, J.M. (ed.), *Heritage: Conservation, Interpretation and Enterprise*, London, Donhead, pp. 77–93.

Morowitz, H. (1992), *Beginnings of Cellular Life*, New Haven, Yale University Press.

Morris, M.(1995), 'Life as a Tourist Object in Australia', in Lanfant, M.F., Allcock, J. and Bruner, E. (eds), *International Tourism: Identity and Change*, London, Sage, pp. 177–92.

Nasr, S.H. (2001), 'The Spirit of the Cities', in Serageldin, I., Shluger, E. and Martin-Brown, J. (eds), *Historic Cities and Sacred Sites*, Washington, DC, International Bank for Reconstruction/World Bank, pp. 3–11.

Norberg-Schulz, C. (1980), *Genius Loci: Toward a Phenomenology of Architecture*, New York, Rizzoli.

Olwig, K. (2002), *Landscape, Nature and the Body Politic: From Britain's Renaissance to America's New World*, Madison, University of Wisconsin Press.

On the Issues.org and Speakout.com (2003), Israel Map, http://www.issues2000.org/images/israel_map.gif, visited on 7 September 2003.

Robinson, M. (2001), 'Tourism Encounters: Inter- and Intra-cultural Conflicts and the World's Largest Industry', in Al Sayyad, N. (ed.), *Consuming Tradition, Manufacturing Heritage: Global Norms and Urban Forms in the Age of Tourism*, London, Routledge, pp. 34–68.

Raheb, M. and Stickert, F. (1998), *Bethlehem 2000: Past and Present*, Heidelberg, Palmyra.

Schumacher, E.F. (1973), *Small is Beautiful: A Study of Economics as if People Mattered*, London, Abacus.

Shomali, Q. and Shomali, S. (1997), *Bethlehem 2000: A Guide to Bethlehem and its Surroundings*, Waldbröl, Flamm Druck Wagener GmbH.

Urry, J. (1990), *The Tourist Gaze: Leisure and Travel in Contemporary Societies*, London, Sage.

Chapter 4

Urban Conservation in Mexican Colonial Cities: The Historic Centre of Morelia

Norma E. Rodrigo-Cervantes

Sustainability and Conservation

The now accepted definition of sustainability is 'To meet the needs of the present without compromising the ability of future generations to meet their own needs' (WCED 1987: 8) and that one of the requirements of sustainability is adaptation to particular circumstances and local conditions. The concept of conservation, however, is less agreed. This reflects changing concepts of the purpose and processes of conservation, although it has always been associated with the need for a cultural identity (Chanfon-Olmos 1988). In general terms, it involves the retention of present assets in a way that, if intelligently utilised, can assist their adaptation to new uses (Delafons 1997, Lichfield 1997). Conservation principles resonate with the quest for sustainability in the following sense: conservation also requires adaptation to particular circumstances and local conditions in order to ensure that existing assets are used rationally to meet the present needs in a resource efficient way.

This chapter investigates the interplay between conservation and sustainability, in the context of Mexico. It seeks to show how the two concepts, and the policies which flow from them, can be mutually supportive to the benefit of the built environment. A sustainability perspective reinforces the case for conservation and enriches the scope of policies protecting the built cultural heritage. The chapter develops this argument in the context of a case study of Morelia, a colonial city founded in 1541 and the first Hispanic settlement in the State of Michoacan established for evangelising the western part of the New Spain.

Of the two concepts, arguably conservation, as we have already seen, is the more problematic – at least in the context of this chapter. In practice, conservation embraces certain questions about *what* should be conserved, *how* and *for whom*. From this stem two general approaches to conservation that directly affect the manner of *how* and *for whom* the existing assets should be used or adapted (Ashworth 1997). This has often affected, as a consequence, the cultural built heritage. One conservation approach is preservationist, where pure conservation is sought for the products of the past, but new development or change in the urban fabric is seldom permitted, whether those changes are creative or not. The other approach is conservation as heritage which seeks to conserve the past as a commodity in order to be consumed by certain targeted markets, mainly tourism.

Another important perspective on the conservation-sustainability praxis is that a key initiative for sustainable urban management from Agenda 21 suggests the restoring of the built environment fabric to meet collective needs (Satterthwaite, 1999). This can be understood as the continuous utilisation of the built heritage in a more rational way, adapting present needs but lengthening the life of the asset as well. The challenge of conservation means fitting modern uses without risking the loss of inherited built resources for future generations. Conservation has intrinsically embraced this in principle, and in the particular sense of sustainability, this could bring a re-legitimisation or new validity to conservation practice.

As we shall see these are vital challenges in the Mexican context. Part of the reconciliation of sustainable and conservationist approaches lies in the closer integration conservation practice with city planning processes. This requires much detailed work at the development control stage (Larkham 1996). But it also means that planning authorities should bring conservation and sustainability aims into closer union in their planning strategies to create a robust framework of principles and policies. This suggests that an approach to conservation should be adopted which combines effective preservation of an asset with sustainable development (Delafons 1997, Mason 1997). In this context, the local plan is perceived as a fundamental instrument in the control and management of historical resources.

A final contextual element in this chapter is to emphasise the fact that the way urban spaces are developed and managed in different cities is the product of different forces, traditions and of particular conservation policies. These variables – the localisation mentioned above – have to be taken into account. Thus in Mexico during the twentieth century, a large amount of legislation to protect the cultural heritage was introduced at the three levels of governance: Federal, State and Municipal (Diaz-Berrio, 1990, Olive 1997). Despite this, little motion exists towards a conservation policy which is alert to a sense of the necessity for sustainable economic growth, social importance, sensible environmental planning in historic sites and thinking about the long-term future. At this juncture the question to be addressed is this: could a sustainable approach to conservation be adopted in the Mexican cultural context?

This chapter explores these ideas and the developmental issues affecting the urban form of city centres in Mexico using the colonial city of Morelia as the case study. This historic colonial city is very typical of the pressures and processes occurring in similar historic urban landscapes from the country's colonial period. Morelia was designated as a World Heritage Site by UNESCO in 1991, on the occasion of the 450th anniversary of its foundation. This designation has obviously ensured that it has received particular attention in environmental planning and political agendas.

Consciousness of the Cultural Heritage in Mexico

At this point it is necessary to develop an understanding of the nature and manifestation of a certain consciousness towards the cultural built heritage in the Mexican context. Some of the events, which have denoted this awareness, will be explained in terms of the value of the historic environment.

In Mexico, the national legal framework which protects monuments and historical sites was first established in 1902 (Olive 1997), as in many countries of the developing world (Hardoy and Gutman 1991). Even so, concern about the condition of particular monuments and relics in Mexico dates back to the 1850s; this reflects the interest in the remarkable richness of its archaeological past. During the Revolution, two laws were adopted between 1914 to 1916 in an attempt to stop the destruction occurring in haciendas, churches and related buildings. Later on, in 1930, protective legislation was introduced to control development and give protection to some historic sites (Diaz-Berrio 1990). Two more laws were promulgated with national coverage before the current law which was adopted in 1972: this is the Federal Law for the Conservation and Research on Archaeological, Historic and Artistic Monuments.

Lichfield (1997) suggests that the cultural built heritage (CBH) is the inherited urban fabric with particular cultural, historic and aesthetic values among others. It is considered not only as a resource but also as an asset for the present and future society and consequently it should be conserved and managed in an effective way. Similarly the CBH in Mexico is also considered as national patrimony. It is mainly divided into two elements – Historic and Archaeological Zones. Most town centres founded after the Spanish conquest (1521) and built before 1900 are considered as *Historic Zones* – the subject of this chapter.

Mexican legislation accords equal weight to both historic and archaeological sites in terms of governmental policies. Hence we can appreciate that the Mexican national patrimony is a wide concept. But because of the extraordinary importance of the archaeological past in Mexico, the value given to historic zones differs from the experience of other Latin American countries. This is paradoxical because as of July 1999, from a total of 19 World Heritage Sites recognised by UNESCO, which include some of the nation's greatest archaeological and architectural treasures, eleven of them are historic zones. These are predominantly the centres of the colonial cities, such as Morelia, and the conservation laws embrace two approaches: listed buildings and historic zones themselves. Yet in comparison with the archaeological heritage, the historic zones have not received the same attention and funding by the Federal Government.

Re-use of Listed Buildings and Regeneration of Historic Zones

Listed Buildings

These buildings, also called historic monuments, date mainly from the sixteenth to the end of the nineteenth century, and must qualify on at least one of the following values: aesthetic, cultural, historic, or if a famous person lived in the building. They appear on the schedule prepared by the National Institute of Anthropology and History (INAH), the institution for the protection of the cultural built heritage in Mexico, created in 1939 (Olive, 1997). This agency has federal coverage, although there is a regional agency for every state in Mexico.

Historic monuments are usually added to the schedule in the course of updating surveys conducted by the INAH. For Morelia the last schedule dates from 1986 and a re-survey to update it started in 1999, although this has not yet been published. According to the 1986 survey, 273 monuments were listed as Grade A (there are three categories). Houses typically constructed with one or two stories based around interior courtyards are generally not listed. At the time of the 1986 survey it was considered that 6632 buildings were still to be listed, of which only 157 were protected by the 1972 Federal Conservation Law (INAH 1972, 1986). The preliminary findings of the 1999 survey estimated that one third of the historical fabric is today at risk (Hiriart-Pardo, 1999).

Any intervention or extension to a listed building requires a special licence or consent issued by the INAH. There is an implicit understanding, in sustainable conservation, of the need for good design, the use of modern technology to enable building adaptation, and that regulations should be flexible for sensitive conversion and renewal (Feilden 1994). Nevertheless, in Morelia's regional agency there are only five staff with the required level of expertise working on the issuing of licenses and assessing interventions in historic buildings for the whole state of Michoacan.

Moreover, most of Mexico's conservation legislation has been elaborated by lawyers with little collaboration from historians or architects. As a result, many of the legal provisions and the criteria dealing with historic and aesthetic values are rather subjective and technically imprecise. This creates confusion when the law has to be then interpreted in practice (Diaz-Berrio 1990, Ramirez 1994). Moreover, the common trend within conservation laws of the country has been traditionally preservationist. Given this tendency, it is unlikely that those involved in the conservation system will show the necessary flexibility in interpreting regulations or in assessing the scope for adaptation or creativity needed in rehabilitation and conservation projects.

Historic Zones

Historic zone designation started in Mexico during the 1930s (Diaz-Berrio 1990). This approach relates to groups of historical buildings connected with historic national events, or areas linked to unique or special aspects of the country's life and history. Consequently historic zones are areas of special architectural or historic interest that are valuable to preserve or enhance. Historic areas must be defined in a *Declaration of Zone* prepared by the INAH and approved by the President of the Republic in a *Decree of Zone*.

The purpose behind the designation of a historic zone is to protect the character of an area by controlling the context for alterations and development. The approach reflects similar trends in European countries. In fact, during the twentieth century, Mexican concern about protective legislation for its historic national heritage has closely followed some of the European legal models, mostly those of Britain, France or Italy (Diaz-Berrio 1990, Olive 1997). The model, however, has not been applied with due care for the different cultural context.

In Morelia, the built up area of the city is about 2,600 hectares, and the designated historical zone is 232 hectares. The Committee for Conservation of Traditional and

Colonial Aspects of Morelia officially defined the perimeter of the area in 1956: this was ratified unchanged except that San Pedro Park was added to the perimeter at the time of its formal Declaration as a Historic Monument Zone by the INAH in 1990.

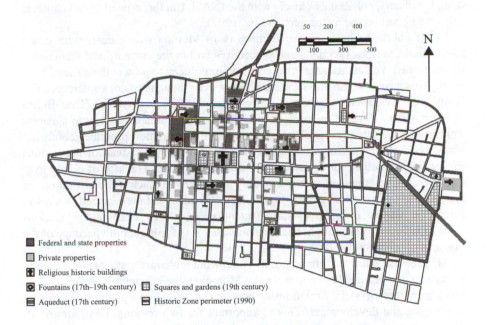

Figure 4.1   **Historic Zone of Morelia and listed buildings of Morelia City**

It is generally the case that areas and buildings of historic value are most likely to be conserved if they are in use, either for the purpose for which they were built, or for new purposes (Mason 1997). In Morelia a set of Urban Regulations of Historic Sites and Transition Zones of Morelia, was issued by the INAH and the Town Council on 27 November 1997 with the purpose of indicating how the adaptation of existing stock could be achieved according to the changing demands of business, commerce, leisure and lifestyle. However, these measures are mainly focused on specifying the adaptation of isolated buildings and not the integrated conservation of the whole historic zone.

Conservative Legislation in Practice

In Mexico, at federal government level, the main agencies related to urban planning and conservation are: the Ministry of Urban and Social Development (SEDESOL), the Ministry of Public Education (SEP) and the National Council of Culture and Arts (CNCA). Except for the last agency, each is sustained by a separate federal law, and they are independent of each other. This is also the case for the National Institute of Anthropology and History (INAH), which forms part of the Ministry of Public Education (SEP); it is sustained by the federal law of 1972, and is the lead institution in terms of the conservation and protection of the national patrimony. To assist its functions, the Municipality, state government and the other agencies noted above should, in theory, collaborate closely with the INAH. But this type of coordination is only established on special projects (Olive 1997).

In the political-administrative framework of Morelia which deals with urban conservation, various functions and procedures within the current legal framework are duplicated. Yet, at the same time, each law introduced to protect the cultural built heritage has its own jurisdiction and regulations, even though this does not necessarily delimit the relevant agency only to those aspects within its own discretion (Diaz-Berrio 1990, Ramirez 1994). At the present time, the city has three conservation agencies representing the three levels of government, and the situation produces confusion when the law is being implemented (Hiriart-Pardo, 1999). Instead of regulations reinforcing each other, they provide overlapping functions. The lack of clarity over who exercises what powers would probably not matter so much if the institutions in charge were well coordinated (see Figure 4.2). But this is not the case and as a result the conflict between different legislative intentions and the application of regulations in the historic zone has brought negative impacts for the cultural built heritage of the city, as will be illustrated later.

This confusion is not confined just to Morelia but is characteristic of conservation policy and practice in Mexico as a whole. Moreover, the continuing challenge is to develop an awareness of the relationship between conservation and the wider context of planning and development. This is important for two reasons. First, almost all designated zones are in the heart of the main urban areas and so a comprehensive approach is needed. Second, the main scope for improving the quality of the environment in historic zones is typically the responsibility of the Municipality – for example maintenance of public open space, maintaining public buildings, traffic management, parking, advertisement controls, footpaths, street furniture, and so on. By contrast, the main functions of the conservation agencies are to issue permits, assess the scope for restoration or rehabilitation of properties within the historical zone and supervision. Clearly the two functions need to be coordinated.

On the other hand, Mexico has traditionally retained a centralised government, where the decision making powers of the municipalities have been weak and ambiguous (Massolo 1996, Rodriguez 1997). Nevertheless, in 1983, the Municipal Government acquired a certain level of autonomy with the modification of Article 115, section V, of the National Political Constitution. This gives local authorities autonomous powers for planning and controlling local urban development plans separate from the Federal and State levels of government, as well as the powers to issue permits and licenses for construction and control of land use.

In relation to a sustainable conservation strategy, the conservation system must work jointly with local planning authorities to integrate conservation policies for the historic zone in order to make urban development plans more comprehensive (Delafons, 1997; Mason, 1997). However, in the case of Mexico the practice of a

Levels of government	Administrative entities	Law	Agency functions
Federal REPUBLIC OF MEXICO	**SEDESOL** Social Development Ministry	1982	Protection and conservation of monuments and sites
	CNCA National Council of Culture and Arts	1982	Provision of economic resources Support to state and local governments Listing
	SEP/INAH Public Education Ministry National Institute of Anthropology and History: National Centre	1972	Improvement in the urban environment: tourism and transit
State STATE OF MICHOACAN	**SEDESOL** Agency of Protection and Conservation of Historic Monuments and Sites and Public Works Office	1974	Planning and controlling the urban development projects in towns and cities: funding, conserving, improving, etc. Protection, conservation and supervision of monuments and historic sites
	SEP/INAH **Regional Centre** National Institute of Anthropology and History	1972	Regulation of land uses Permits and licences for construction of new buildings in the historic zone Improvement in the urban environment: tourism, transit Regulation and supervision of urban image: façade modifications, display ads
Municipal MORELIA CITY	**TOWN COUNCIL** Urban Development, Public Works, Historic Centre and Ecology Agency	1983	Formulation and administration of municipal development plans Improvement in the urban environment: tourism, transit, electricity, telephone, and urban supplies, among others
	IMDUM Municipal Institute of Urban Development and Historic Centre of Morelia	1972	Conservation, preservation, maintenance of buildings and urban environment Permits and licences for construction, modification and provision on plots,
	INAH/Regional Centre National Institute of Anthropology and History	1983	buildings and reserves Regulation of land uses Issuing regulations and dispositions according to the needs

Figure 4.2   Planning and conservation administrative and legal framework in Morelia

centralised government has been changing very slowly, and the relationship that should exist between conservation system and local planning is still being developed. Hence, if this relationship is not well established, it is unlikely that proposals for the development, conservation and enhancement of these important areas will be successful.

Urban Growth and Urban Conservation Issues

During the functionalist and rationalist period of architecture and urban design (1940–1960), traditional styles of building were considered obsolete in terms of construction materials, performance, and the adequacy of building form to meet new living requirements such as car-parking (Tapia-Chavez 1999). New construction technology brought the capacity for increasing the number of floors in buildings as well as major changes to the traditional architectural features of Morelia. Accordingly the new buildings have typological differences such as height, door and window proportions, renderings, alignment and aesthetic values among others.

Notwithstanding these changes, there are only a few examples of twentieth century architecture in Morelia city centre. Because of strict regulations since 1956, with the aim of preventing rapid urban change, the regulations have forbidden modifications which could affect the historic character of the zone. As time went by however, these regulations were only applied to the facades (proportions and materials). New designs started to imitate the historic facades so that architects and developers could get a licence for reconstruction more easily. As a consequence, it is sometimes difficult to know from the outside the exact age of certain buildings while their interiors are very modern.

More powerful changes to the urban fabric relate to the impact of the slow process of migration from the rural areas to the state capital cities in Mexico since the 1940. In Morelia's case this process accelerated after the middle 1970s because of several consecutive economic crises in the country. Following the famous earthquake in Mexico City in 1985, the federal government commenced a national level decentralisation programme and many government offices and services were moved from the megalopolis to the medium size cities such as Morelia. Consequently, at the end of the 1980s the population of Morelia reached half a million inhabitants, almost doubling its 1980 population of 297,500 (Aguilar-Mendez 1996, INEGI 1995).

Whilst the functionalist architectural movement had only a limited impact on the city's historic heritage, these recent migration processes have resulted in many urban changes. Morelia manifests today all the pressures and problems of accelerated growth in its historic zone, which also functions as the city centre. Office and commercial services have concentrated in the historic core and have gradually displaced residential uses. During the 1980s, the period of intensive growth, this phenomenon was completely uncontrolled (Lopez-Castro 1991, Ramirez 1994). As a result the population living in the historic zone has declined from over 37,000 in 1898, to little over 20,000 in 1995 (INEGI 1995). Some original landowners still reside in their properties; but since the late 1970s those who could afford to do so have been moving out in search of better living conditions, car-parking and better public amenities. At the present time there is no strong evidence that the middle classes desire to live in or come back to the historic centre.

It appears that landowners who rent out their property are really only just maintaining it rather than conserving it. As a result of inadequate institutional coordination and responsible regulation of development, landowners often subdivide buildings, without supervision in order to raise housing density levels and maximise returns from minimal investment. Apart from high-density tenements and commercial uses resulting from this attitude, other typically intensive uses are sweatshops and warehousing. Nevertheless evidence suggests that some landowners prefer to sell their property in order to capitalise on high land values rather than the rental value of the property itself.

Lack of technical staff in the conservation field has caused long delays in issuing licenses for restoration projects. This has discouraged many landowners from developing projects in a sympathetic way (Hiriart-Pardo 1999). Many developers often carry out modifications on the buildings behind 'closed doors', most likely over weekends again due to a poor coordination of local authorities in supervising the projects. Some landowners allow their properties to deteriorate or completely decay to justify demolition consent. Sometimes, in order to obtain this license they themselves block drain pipes in the old buildings and other deliberately destructive actions in order to accelerate the deterioration process.

With the exception of a few low-income tenant housing quarters, rent and land values in the city centre are higher than in the 1970s (Hiriart-Pardo 1999). Rent levels in the main city core areas are much more expensive than in high- or middle-class residential areas. As a result city centre properties can only be afforded either by the public sector for office functions or rich investors interested in commercial and tourist uses. These kinds of investors are most likely to be national or even foreign commercial chains, such as *Macdonald's* or *Burger King*, a process which is resulting in further displacement of local traditional shopkeepers.

At the same time, buildings in the historic zone have had to be modernised in order to compete with decentralised commercial offices and shops. These larger shopping malls are very similar to North American models, with examples from recent international companies like *Costco* and *Wal-Mart* among others, with car-parking facilities and changed façades. But how can historic buildings be entirely renewed in this way without affecting their characteristic features?

In adapting historic buildings to new uses the facades of colonial houses have sustained certain modifications, for example their windows have become doors. However, as mentioned before, the main problem lies in the interiors of the buildings where landowners try to intensify land use on individual plots. The original plot proportions have been heavily subdivided, in some cases because the land value is higher than the property value. Interiors have been demolished, without authorisation, whilst only façades has been conserved. Attempts have been made to control changes to the physical fabric in the case of listed monuments, although only the regulation of changes to the façades has been accomplished.

Hence, in conclusion, in Morelia a semblance of historic character has been possible by retaining facades, but not regarding the fabric and uses behind – whether this is through property modification to accommodate new uses or through demolition. At the end of the day, this is creating negative impacts on the built cultural heritage. It is wasting built resources, and also falsifying authenticity and history. This is denying the challenge of conservation.

Street Vendors

The economic crisis and the unemployment trends of the country evident during the last two decades have produced many problems for the historic zones of most Mexican cities. One particular problem is associated with street trading. Thousands of unemployed people have taken to the streets in the urban centres, where they have found their main market – tourism and employed people (Harrison 1998, Pena 1999).

In the early 1980s a few groups of street vendors appeared on some streets and squares in Morelia's historic zone usually on special celebration days (of which there are plenty). However at the beginning of the 1990s the vendors started to remain at their places daily even after the celebrations had ended. Since that time their number has rapidly increased and their zone of activity has spread much wider: by 1999 there were over 1500 street vendors. In past years, there were several attempts by the government authorities to move them out by force. But this only created violent clashes between authorities and street vendors. Later, the Municipality offered them several relocation sites, but the attempts to convince the street vendors to move have not been successful. The vendors claim that there are no guarantees of receiving another stall, besides which they saw the whole process as political propaganda since they thought the projects would never be concluded. So they remain in place having taken over the public space in the *Portales* around the Cathedral, several adjacent squares and many streets.

Investment in Morelia Historic Zone

The three main conservation agencies involved in the conservation system of Morelia have been maintained by Federal public investment. On the one hand they have mainly focused their work on isolated buildings, relying on scarce Federal funding to carry out their restoration work, although with preservationist trends, as was outlined above. However, the conservation system in Morelia has not developed the necessary links with the private sector to produce broader enhancement and area schemes of urban conservation for the historic centre. On the other hand municipal conservation activity in the area, during the last decade, has mainly focused on street furniture and maintenance of the main squares, the restoration of the town council building and the change of pavements in some streets.

Private developers have found a range of difficulties when seeking consent for building restoration or rehabilitation in the historic area, as compared with other areas of the city. Another reason that developers have been discouraged is that when designing these types of projects, the current conservation legislation has plenty of restrictions, but does not provide proactive support or guidance on how to develop the projects in a feasible way (Hiriart-Pardo 1999). In practice, the legislation, with its intricate system of regulations, has constrained the private sector. Equally, the preservationist tendency adopted by the conservation institutions has also constrained the flexibility to adapt old buildings to new uses, which is very necessary for projects not sponsored by the public sector. As in other Latin American countries (Bromley and Jones 1999), it appears that the situation of properties and plots being heavily subdivided as well as the complexity of their ownership has also inhibited the private sector from further investment.

As Bromley and Jones (1996) claim, there has been a lack of private investment in most historic centres for most of the last century as upper and middle-income households have migrated to the periphery and private and government functions have moved far away from the city centres. Similar trends can be found in Morelia with the exception that government offices did not start to move out until 1999, as a consequence of the *Master Rescue Plan for the Historic Centre* which, as will be briefly explained below, is part of the conservation policy framework for the historic zone.

Current Conservation Policy

The Municipal Institute of Urban Development and Historic Centre of Morelia (IMDUM) was created in 1994 under a former municipal government drawn from an opposition right wing party (PAN). The institute is a consultative body in charge of developing the Strategic Directive Plan for Morelia, which includes a Local Plan for the historic centre. However, it seems that the Directive Plan is unlikely to be finished because of lack of resources, or because of changes in the political make up of the Municipality.

The pressures on a city such as Morelia as a World Heritage site, are somewhat different from other colonial cities in the country. As a result the city's administration, together with the state government, have tried to take a more direct role than the conventional Directive Plan by promoting 'The Master Plan for the Rescue of Morelia's Historic Centre'. This is a specific version of the Partial Plan developed by the previous Municipal government.

The main aims of the Master Plan for Rescue are as follows: decentralisation of government offices, removal of the bus station and relocation of street trading. The justification for the first two aims is that it will be possible to diminish street vendor sales by means of reducing the movement of people to the city centre – over 50,000 people daily. The administration has stressed the belief that without street trading the urban image problems of the centre will be solved. The publicity campaign associated with the Plan involved press and radio and television spots showing the streets of Morelia with and without street vendors stalls and the slogan 'it's your decision'.

Nevertheless, the removal of this activity does not seem to be easy because of strong opposition from street vendor unions (there are more than 15). But the campaign has started a curious controversy amid the citizens of Morelia. On the one hand most of them contend that the street vendors must be relocated urgently to 'save' or 'rescue' the historic centre. On the other hand people do not stop buying from them, and recognise that, although they produce a poor urban image, cause litter and pedestrian obstruction, they offer much cheaper prices than formal commercial outlets.

Meanwhile, from May 1999, the Municipal authorities started to move out of several city centre offices. However, some of the vacated buildings do not have a future planned use – notable exceptions being two buildings which have been proposed for a city museum, such as the *Clavijero* Palace. In the past some important buildings that have remained empty for long periods of time in Morelia have been occupied by force by political or student groups, for instance the *San Agustin* convent in 1976 (Rodrigo 1994). A similar prospect lies in store now. Hence this Master Rescue Plan presents several disadvantages:

*   Local residents wanting access to governmental offices (over 11,000 people a day), will have to travel further in order to get to those services, especially taking into account the fact that public transport is poor and almost all existing routes terminate and commence in the city centre.
*   Limiting the movement of people to the city centre jeopardises not only the street vendors' economy but also formal commercial sectors.
*   Empty historic listed buildings will be in danger of misuse or occupation.
*   Residential uses are being discouraged but commercialised as a function of tourism.

Morelia is indeed a touristic centre – over 250,000 visitors at Easter time for example. It is undeniable that the tourism market attracts interest from public and private sector investors in the area. The Master Plan for Rescue often suggests that Morelia should appear in the Federal Development Plan of Tourism, given its World Heritage Site. The Plan seeks to promote the role of tourism as one strategy to attract investment to the historic centre. However a 'heritage strategy' (Ashworth, 1997) implies that selling a centre to tourists requires adaptation of buildings mainly for hotels, recreational or shopping uses.

Conclusions

The most important urban pressures and issues which confront Morelia's historic zone have been discussed. These are the key factors which should be taken into account when elaborating conservation policies at the local level. However, before elaborating these policies, there is still the need in Mexico to find appropriate conservation strategies and tools at the local level which will foster the retention and, where possible, the expansion of residential uses and small scale businesses rather than only promoting the role of tourism in these historic zones. In doing this, public conservation agencies and local authorities also have to develop a more coordinated relationship to devise effective conservation policies and to embed them in the local urban development plans. Without this approach, it will be impossible to obtain a sustainable model for the historic centres.

To date, the conservation system in Mexico has not been able to establish the close relationship with local authorities which is needed to produce and include conservation policies in the local urban plan; but then again Municipal autonomy, within a well-established centralised model of government, is weak and powers are vague as well. In addition, the Federal government also provides for the State Governor the same facilities to regulate, plan, fund, conserve and improve towns and cities, as well as the power to issue permits for land uses, change of use and development on plots, building consents, development standards and so forth (Diaz-Berrio 1990, Olive 1997). Furthermore, as Morelia is the capital city of the State, both levels of government co-exist there, thus it is unlikely that the Municipality can take autonomous decisions in the city without the coordinated participation and political will from the Federal and state authorities.

Equally, the process of identifying, listing and protecting the built heritage has been inconsistent in Morelia; the last listing survey of historic buildings was in 1986, and its updating did not start until 1999. This process is a basic requirement because of the need for a constant evaluation and control of modifications and development in historic zones, as well as testing if the strategies have been successfully followed. But after so long a gap from the last 'evaluation', the preliminary findings of the most recent survey (1999) have shown discouraging evidence about the damage which has taken place to the urban built environment, produced by range of processes of change to the urban historic landscape which Morelia has experienced.

In developing countries like Mexico it is very difficult to say definitively 'no' to a heritage approach, in other words to promote the role of the tourism market, when developing conservation strategies for a historic areas. This is because, under conditions of almost perpetual economic recession, the historic fabric is seen as a resource to sustain local economies, even though inflexible preservation approaches of the heritage model have also left negative impacts on the built cultural heritage. Therefore, it is indispensable that a range of possible solutions needs to be established which would identify how demand for change should be managed in order to avoid the total dilapidation of the patrimony, and in order to analyse how the urban form can meet the present and practical needs while its environmental resources are being continuously used.

To do this, however, it is necessary to have clear awareness of the conservation strategy to follow: neither preservation nor heritage. Conservation practice in Mexico will have to move from the basic process of physical preservation of isolated monuments and sites only, towards a holistic management of the historic urban landscape. The experience of Morelia's historic zone in coming to terms with its historicity and its role, during the last three decades, has not been harmonious. There is still the need to balance current conditions with future prospects in the context of its particular urban identity and the resources of its historic patrimony.

References

Aguilar-Mendez, F.A. (1996), *El Crecimiento Territorial de las Ciudades Mexicanas*, Mexico, DF, Universidad Autonoma Metropolitana, Escuela de Ciencias y Artes.

Ashworth, G.J. (1997), 'Conservation as Preservation or as Heritage: Two Paradigms and Two Answers', *Built Environment*, 23:2, pp. 92–102.

Bromley, R.D.F. and Jones, G.A. (1996), 'The Conservation Cycle in Cities of the Developing World: Implications for Authenticity and Policy', *Urban Geography*, 17:7, pp. 650–69.

Bromley, R.D.F. and Jones, G.A. (1999), 'Investing in Conservation: The Historic Centre in Latin America', *Built Environment*, 25:3, pp. 196–210.

Chanfon-Olmos, C. (1988), *Fundamentos Teoricos de la Restauracion*, Mexico, UNAM, Coleccion Posgrado.

Delafons, J. (1997), 'Sustainable Conservation', *Built Environment*, 23:2, pp. 111–20.

Diaz-Berrio, S. (1990), *Conservacion del Patrimonio Cultural*, Mexico, INAH.

Feilden, B. (1994), *Conservation of Historic Buildings*, Oxford, Butterworth-Heinemann.

Hardoy, J.E. and Gutman, M. (1991), 'The Role of Municipal Government in the Protection of Historic Centres in Latin American Cities', *Environment and Urbanisation*, 3:1, pp. 96–108.

Harrison, M. (1998) 'Street Vending in Mexico City', *Third World Planning Review*, 19:4, pp. 313–87.

Hiriart-Pardo, C. (1999), 'El centro Historico de Morelia, un Lugar en Pugna', in Acevedo-Salomao, E. (ed.), *Michoacan: Arquitectura y Urbanismo*, Morelia, Facultad de Arquitectura, Estudios de Posgrado, Universidad Michoacana de San Nicolas de Hidalgo, pp. 115–21.

INAH (1972), *Ley Federal sobre Monumentos y Zonas Arqueologicas, Artisticos e Historicos*, Mexico, INAH.

INAH (1986), *Catalogo de Monumentos Historicos y Artisticos de Morelia, Michocan*, Morelia, Gobierno del Estado de Michoacán, INAH.

INEGI (1995), *Conteo Nacional de Poblacion en el Estado de Michoacán*, Morelia, Instituto Nacional de Estadistica, Geografia e Información, Gobierno del Estado de Michoacan.

Larkham, P.J. (1996), *Conservation and the City*, London, Routledge.

Lichfield, N. (1997), 'Achieving the Benefits of Conservation', *Built Environment*, 23:2, pp. 103–10.

Lopez-Castro, G. (1991), *Urbanizacion y Desarrollo de Michoacán*, Zamora, Colegio de Michoacan, Gobierno del Edo. de Michoacan.

Mason, D.R. (1997), 'Managing Development at Cultural Heritage Sites: Conservation Practice and Sustainability', in Bran, P.S. (ed.), *Evaluation of the Built Environment for Sustainability*, London, E. and F.N. Spon, pp. 300–12.

Massolo, A. (1996), 'México', in McCarney, P.L. (ed.), *The Changing Nature of Local Government in Developing Countries*, University of Toronto, Federation Of Canadian Municipalities, pp. 227–52.

Olive, J. C. (1997), 'Problemas Legales Sobre la Proteccion del Patrimonio', in Barros, C. (ed.), *El Centro Historico*, Mexico, INAH.

Pena, S. (1999) 'Informal Markets: Street Vendors in Mexico City', *Habitat International*, 23:3, pp. 363–72.

Ramirez, R.E. (1994), *Las Zonas Historicas de Morelia y Patzcuaro ante el T.L.C.*, Morelia, UMSNH.

Rodrigo-Cervantes, N.E. (1994), *Hotel Convento de San Agustin; Restauracion y Nuevo Uso para el Monumento y su Contexto Historico Urbano*, unpublished MPhil dissertation, Mexico, Posgrado de Arquitectura, DF, UNAM.

Rodriguez, V.E. (1997), *Decentralisation in Mexico: From Reforma Municipal to Solidaridad to Nuevo Federalismo*, Boulder CO, Westview Press.

Satterthwaite, D. (ed.) (1999), 'The Key Issues', in *The Earthscan Reader in Sustainable Cities*, London, Earthscan Publications Ltd.

Tapia-Chavez, A. (1999), 'Del Porfirismo al Funcionalismo, El Caso de Una Arquitectura Ignorada', in Acevedo-Salomao, E. (ed.), *Michoacán: Arquitectura y Urbanismo*, Morelia, Facultad de Arquitectura, Estudios de Posgrado, Universidad Michoacana de San Nicolas de Hidalgo, pp. 103–8.

World Commission on Environment Development (WCED) (1987), *Our Common Future*, G.H. Brundtland, Oxford, Oxford University Press.

Chapter 5

Involving Local Communities in the Conservation and Rehabilitation of Historic Areas in México City: The Case of Coyoacán

Yanet Lezama-López

Introduction

Much has been said and written in recent years about 'sustainable development'. What makes so important the most commonly accepted definition of this concept (the Brundtland Commission's statement to meet 'the needs of the present without compromising the ability of future generations to meet their own needs') (World Commission on Environment and Development 1987: 8) is that 'important though global environmental issues are, sustainable development … is and should be about the wider issues of ensuring social justice and improving the quality of life' (Trevor 1999: 112). Drawing on Satterthwaite's (1999: 95) sustainable development goals as applied to cities, this chapter addresses the importance of meeting those needs in two respects. Firstly, it considers the need for 'people's choice and control – including homes and neighbourhoods which they value and where their social and cultural priorities are met'. Secondly, it reviews the political needs which include 'freedom to participate … in decisions regarding management and development of one's home and neighbourhood, within a broader framework'. Sustainable development also implies minimising the waste of 'cultural, historical and natural assets within cities that are irreplaceable and thus non-renewable – for instance, historic districts' (ibid.: 96). Conservation of the built environment, as Delafons states 'has obvious relevance to this objective since, by definition, it conserves existing assets and, sensibly applied, can facilitate their adaptation to new uses' (1997: 112).

The principles of equity and public participation in decision making have been recognised as central for achieving greater sustainability in the built environment (Brandon et al. 1997). Further, evidence indicates that community participation can lead to significant improvements in the planning and management of urban settlements (Wates 1998). Hence, urban development programmes involving the conservation of historic areas in México should consider the role of community involvement in protecting and enhancing these areas whilst maintaining their social and cultural diversity. This chapter is concerned with these aims, premised on the assumption that finding the balance between the different local groups' aspirations, interests and concerns for the conservation and rehabilitation of historic areas will lead to more equitable and sustainable solutions to the problems Mexican historic areas are facing.

This chapter addresses two main aspects with regard to conservation in Mexican historic areas. First, it argues that conservation is mainly focused on the protection of physical aspects of the zones without considering their spatial and social dimensions: particularly, it is concerned with the lack of community participation at all stages of the planning process from the definition of conservation programmes to the implementation stages. Second, it discusses how different local groups operating in the historic area of Coyoacán have developed their own views and interests about the current situation and the future of the zone, the fundamental conflicts between them, how this affects the conservation of the historical built landscape, and the inequitable situation this has produced.

Conservation of Historic Areas in México: Legal Framework

México has had a tradition of legislation with respect to the protection of its national heritage since the end of the nineteenth century (see Lombardo 1985). According to the present legislation a Historical Monuments Zone (HMZ *Zona de Monumentos Históricos*) is 'the area which includes several historical monuments related with significant national events or that linked with former relevant facts for the Country' (Art. 41, Federal Law on Archaeological, Artistic and Historical Monuments and Zones FLAAHMZ: INAH 1972). Article 14 of this Federal Law's Appended Regulations (INAH 1975) establishes that the competence of the federal powers within a HMZ will be limited to the 'protection, conservation, restoration and recovery' of the zones. According to Olive this could have been intended on the one hand, to avoid jurisdictional conflicts between the federal institution in charge of applying the law and the local powers – to municipal or state level – and on the other hand to 'allow the latter to exert their government powers' (1997: 199).

Olive (1997) reports that the legislation also provides a legal framework for the conservation of a HMZ in two main respects. First, it ensures that all the peripheral features of the zones or the public amenities e.g. advertisements, external electricity or telephone cables, petrol stations, kiosks, stalls, etc) do not 'harm' the zones. Second the legislation authorises that every new building should be constructed within existing perimeters with the aim that the new buildings do not 'alter the harmony' (Olive 1997: 200) of the zones (see Art. 42 and 43 FLAAHMZ, and 42 of its Attached Regulations). Both articles refer only to physical aspects.

The designation of an HMZ in México involves a long process in which first the study and the boundaries must be drawn by the staff of the National Anthropology and History (INAH) before the final decree is signed by the President of the Republic, and therefore published in the Official Gazette of the federation (Art. 37 FLAAHMZ: INAH, 1972). Between 1972 and 1989, 12 HMZ had been through this process across the whole country (Díaz-Berrio 1990). Several more were added in the last decade to reach a total of 57 in 2004, of which eight localities comprising 12 HMZs in the Federal District are included, including the case study zone of Coyoacán (INAH 2001; INAH/SCZ-CNMH 2004).

Public Participation in Conservation

Although there has been growing awareness in México of the need to link community involvement with programmes for the conservation and rehabilitation of HMZs (Díaz-Berrio 1990, Olive 1997, Rosas-Mantecón 1994, 1996), and this is established in the General Law on Human Settlements (Art. 49: DOF 1994), this has not been common practice. The second article of the Federal Law (INAH 1972) establishes that INAH and INBA, the federal agencies in charge of the historic and the artistic patrimony respectively 'will organise or authorise neighbourhood and civil associations as well as agricultural workers unions as auxiliary entities … to … preserve the cultural patrimony of the Nation'. The first Article of the Appended Regulations to the 1972 Federal Law (INAH, 1975) points out that the consequent aims will be, *inter alia*, 'to assist federal authorities in taking care of, or preserving a zone or monument'. This commitment has been endorsed by federal authorities. Thus in 1991 the head of INAH argued that 'whatever the conservation task, … the law is needed and it must be supported by the majority of the community through its real and formal representations', and also suggested that for the application of the law, social factors in terms of 'those who use the heritage' should be taken into account (García-Moll 1991: 53, 54). Years later Teresa Franco, holding the same position, advocated the need for 'the participation of several actors: the community that lives in the buildings and uses the public spaces, the owners, the developers, the urban planners' in the preservation of the monumental historic and artistic patrimony of the country (Franco 1997). However, public participation for the conservation and rehabilitation of historic areas has not been implemented in a methodical way so far, as we shall see in the case study.

Coyoacán

In the case of México City the impact of urban transformation processes is such that only a few of its historic areas have managed to retain their distinctive character. This is the case of Coyoacán, one of the villages founded in 1521 in the Southeast part of the City (Figure 5.1), where the first government of New Spain and the first municipal government of the city were established (Aceves 1988). Different orders of monks founded churches and monasteries in the area in the sixteenth century, and mansions were built in the seventeenth and eighteenth centuries along the Calle Real, today Francisco Sosa street (Figure 5.2), some of which still stand (Dubernard 1992). Since 1940 Coyoacán has attained an impressive growth: wide avenues, suited for fast traffic, have been opened also in that decade (Novo 1996).

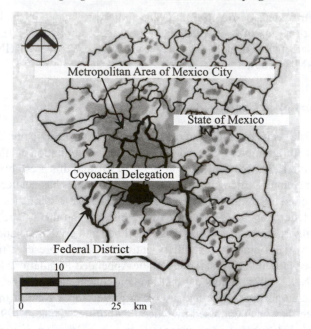

Figure 5.1   The historic zone of Coyoacán in the Federal District[1]

**Figure 5.2   San Juan Bautista church and convent at the main plazas, and
                 Francisco Sosa street**

---

[1]   All maps and photos by the author unless otherwise credited.

In 1934 Coyoacán, together with San Angel and Xochimilco, were recognised by the government as a 'typical and picturesque' zones as a result of their 'characteristic features', and the need to give them special protection (Flores-Marini 1968). In 1972 a new study of the area aimed to protect it and drew new boundaries, increasing the perimeter by including Colonia del Carmen which became part of the district in 1890, and five *barrios* (Rodríguez 1995). The next unpublished study (INAH 1984), did not consider the *colonia*, yet included in the so-called 'perimeter B' the ancient *barrios*. Eventually, official designation took place in 1990 (INAH 1990). Coyoacán's HMZ perimeter includes Francisco Sosa street, the main plazas of the area and its surroundings: *colonia* del Carmen and six *barrios* were left out in the designation, despite 'having conserved the streets layout as a testimony of history' (Rodríguez 1995: 46) (Figure 5.3).

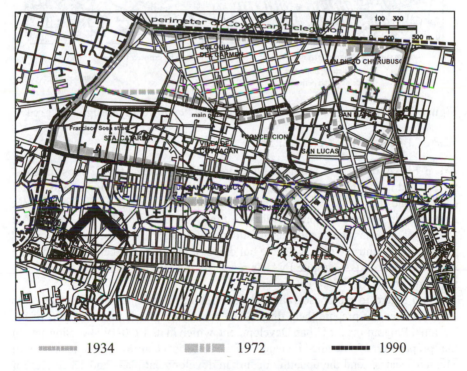

■■■■■■■■ 1934   ■■ ■■■■ 1972   ■■■■■■■■■ 1990

Figure 5.3   Boundaries for the historic area of Coyoacán since 1934

Source: After Rodríguez 1995. Base map: SCINCE, INEGI 1995.

As can be seen in Figure 5.4 and according to the official decree, Coyoacán HMZ has an approximate area of 1.64 km^2, and 50 listed historic monuments, dated between the sixteenth century and the end of the nineteenth century, according to

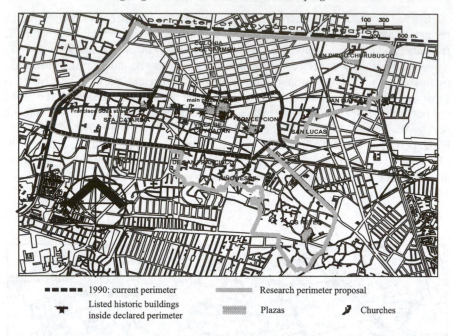

■ ■ ■ ■ ■   1990: current perimeter   ▨▨▨▨▨ Research perimeter proposal

⊤   Listed historic buildings
    inside declared perimeter   ▨▨▨ Plazas   𝄢 Churches

Figure 5.4   The historic area of Coyoacán 1990 – officially designated area

Source: Base map: SCINCE, INEGI 1995.

Art. 3 FLAAHMZ. Five religious buildings and 31 'relevant civil constructions' were listed in the decree (INAH 1990). Designation of Artistic Monuments Zones (AMZ), and listing the 'artistic monuments' (dated in the twentieth century), are responsibilities of the National Institute of Fine Arts and Literature (INBA) (INAH 1972), yet there has been neither an artistic inventory for Coyoacán, nor a designated AMZ in the country to date. Valuable buildings of the twentieth century will remain unprotected by INBA, despite INAH's recent listing that included 146 examples in the study area (INAH 2002).

With regard to the conservation plans, although INAH has the competence to do so, it does not prepare them directly. Conservation programmes are part of the National Programme for Urban Development, which in its 1990-1994 version set out the 'preparation of a detailed inventory of the historical centres located in sixteen of Mexico's states', and the updating of 'urban development plans and schemes…for population centres' (Garza 1999: 164). A conservation plan for a *centro histórico* is considered part of the latter. According to Garza (ibid.), the 100 Cities Programme of 1992 (*P-100-199*) (SEDESOL 1994) was meant to provide local governments with technical assistance in planning their urban growth, and had 'helped updating plans for 16 historical centres' (ibid.: 165) up to 1999. He points out that whereas México City had been 'rudderless for almost a decade' in terms of urban development programmes, in the most recent Federal District administration (appointed by the country's President), a new version of the general urban development plan was created in 1996.[2] The local Urban Development and Housing Secretary (SEDUVI) did elaborate the 16 Delegational Programmes for Urban Development. The Delegational Programme for Urban Development (SEDUVI 1997a) conceptualises the historical *barrios* as *Areas de Conservación Patrimonial* (heritage conservation areas) and establishes design guidelines, mostly directed to control the visual appearance of the buildings. The identification of the *barrios* and their boundaries are neither consistent throughout the document nor with the annexed plans: further, the boundaries are considerably smaller than those identified by my own typo-morphological research. The Programme suggested that Partial Programmes for Urban Development should be elaborated for the *barrios*, which did not happen. Coyoacán's programme for its historic centre establishes the regulations concerning the conservation of the zone. The perimeter of this historic centre is comprised of two so-called *ZEDEC*s, controlled development zones, which differs from the official 1990 designation. Furthermore, *ZEDEC*'s historic centre adds the main plazas area to the Colonia del Carmen one, and by doing so, creates a discrepancy with the presidential decree (Coyoacán: Partial Programme for Urban Development of the Historic Centre and Partial Programme Urban Development for Colonia del Carmen: SEDUVI 1997b, 1997c).

The designation of land use as mainly residential involves protection of the so-called green areas (parks and plazas), in terms of prohibiting change of function, limiting the height of any new buildings, and the number of parking places assigned. The programme also tends to focus on maintaining a certain homogeneity in terms of the physical fabric of the area, and aims to protect the current volume of residential land uses, whereas maintenance and improvement should involve many other elements (e.g. traffic management, parking controls, open spaces). It seems that a better integration of conservation and planning as components of urban design is needed. There is, or at least there *should* be more to conservation than the mere prevention of change.

In summary, the official 1990 perimeter of the historic area to be conserved is smaller than the previous studies, goes broader in the Historic Centre and Colonia del Carmen *ZEDEC*. The boundaries clearly need revision. The urban development Partial Programmes are mainly concerned with the physical aspects of the zone. Finally, because the area is an integral part of metropolitan México City, many of the problems found in Coyoacán can only be addressed in this wider context: for example environmental problems more evident in high rates of air pollution, deficient overall public transport policy, housing scarcity, safety issues, and so forth (Conolly 1999).

---

2   The emphasis on the physical aspects of historic areas persists in the last version of the Programme, approved in December 2003 (GODF, 2003) and current Federal District Legislation (see GODF 2000 and SEDUVI, undated).

Community Involvement, Interests and Perceptions

The chapter now addresses the second main aspect, the involvement of the public in the development and implementation of conservation policies.

Although, as we have seen, public participation should have been part of the 'public consultation', considered the norm for elaborating each plan (GODF 1996: Art. 11, 23.III and 24.II), in Coyoacán's current Partial Programme only two general aims are specified with respect to public involvement. First, a 'subsequent analysis' of the boundaries of the Historic Centre and 'unifying the criteria regarding the land uses' is proposed involving several Civil Associations, presumably residents of the area. Second, an evaluation was also proposed of the projects to be authorised in five plots along Francisco Sosa street by representatives of those associations in a Committee dedicated to that purpose (SEDUVI 1997b: 123, 134). In other words, Coyoacán is typical of the situation which prevails in the country as a whole. There is great divergence between the principles and the practice of public involvement in conservation policies.

Turning to a more detailed analysis of local community groups and stakeholders involved in Coyoacán, we can begin to appreciate their different needs and interests in the conservation and rehabilitation of the historic area. At the same time we can understand how the present physical form of the urban tissue supports or constrains community interests, and how these may interface with the broader goals for the conservation and rehabilitation of the area. The initial basis for developing a typology of stakeholders follows earlier social anthropology research on the construction of local identities in Coyoacán Delegation (Safa 1998). The typology was elaborated as part of my own research and by information given by local people surveyed in the annual religious celebration in April. There are five distinct groups.

Residents

There is a number of distinct residents' groups. The original Village of Coyoacán comprised several *barrios* (Aceves 1988, Rodríguez 1995). *Barrio* is a term inherited from the colonial period. They are localities where the indigenous population lived, away from the central nucleus of the city where the Spaniards built their residences (Safa 1998). In Coyoacán some of the indigenous *barrios* of the sixteenth century survived as *pueblos* or villages until the eighteenth century when Spaniards and *mestizos* were gradually incorporated. *Barrios* were later consolidated as different settlements within the urban network when the notion of the 'modern city' emerged (Siembieda and López 1998). This was the case for Los Reyes Coyoacán, consolidated as a *pueblo rural* or rural village by the end of the nineteenth century.

The ancient *barrios* and *pueblos* of Coyoacán can still be recognised, although urban transformation processes have changed their physical appearance, the social relationships of the communities and their way of living. Los Reyes Coyoacán is amongst the best 'preserved' due to the indigenous population which has been living there, and because the village was founded before the Spaniards arrived. These inhabitants have conserved their local customs and traditions. Rituals and community institutions are the basis for their local identity. Their practices allow them to sustain and renew their sense of belonging to the locality and to the group. Thus decisions concerning the community and the 'renovation of the traditions' are taken within the social community organisation, the *Cabildo* or community meetings. *Cabildo*, a political institution inherited from colonial times (Gibson 1967), is the place were the representatives for the festivities are elected, and where the problems of the community are reconciled. Only people born in the *barrio* with well-established roots in the village, *gente del pueblo* or native people, are allowed to take part and to participate with the right to speak and vote. Community decisions are taken after discussion, debate and negotiation. The opinion of the elderly is always taken into account, although decisions are taken by majority of votes. However, hitherto the *Cabildo* has had no official recognition (Safa 1998: 142). Instead, neighbourhood representatives, an official position established by law in the *Ley de Participación Ciudadana del Distrito Federal* – updated in November 1998 – (GODF, 1998) has functioned as the link between *Cabildo* and local authorities, yet the opportunity to participate in decisions affecting them is very limited. For example, elections for neighbourhood representative which took place in July 1999, registered an abstention rate of 90.71 per cent in the Federal District (Romero 1999).

All the ancient *barrios* and villages of Coyoacán take part in the *Señor de las Misericordias* festivities, one of the most important celebrations of Los Reyes Coyoacán village. This highlights the fact that it is the indigenous community of the *barrios* which gets involved and conserves these traditions, and that each *barrio* community maintains its own celebrations nowadays. Of all the *barrios*, Los Reyes had the strongest, best organised and most powerful community in the past. This has now declined, along with the number of celebrations in each *barrio*, as the indigenous population is being removed. Even so, neighbours defend their village, despite their low-income status (INEGI 1990, 1995), by gathering social and economic resources to conserve the public spaces because of the significance of the religious celebrations which take part in them (Figure 5.5). Three main interests emerge from these community groups. First, they seek to improve the urban services and infrastructure in each *barrio* in response to community decisions. Second, they are engaged in resisting the removal of the indigenous population and the take over by new middle and high income residents of the so-called *condominios* (people who live in new development, see Figure 5.6). Third, they seek to reduce the constant conflicts and tensions with the *condominios* in the use of public areas, especially during religious celebrations.

A second community of residents is to be found in *barrios* where the original population has been almost completely displaced. Here, as Safa asserts, it is only the 'memory, the signs and the signals of the past which allow the construction and reconstruction of local identity despite the transformations of the territory and the recomposition of the social groups that live in it' (Safa 1998: 274). The displacement of the original communities by the invasion of middle and high income class groups who want to live in places with a 'deep rooted history' has converted the historic

Figure 5.5   Voluntary labour in Los Reyes Coyoacán and the plaza during celebrations

Figure 5.6   New developments (*condominios*) built by the private sector in Los Reyes

core of Coyoacán, comprised of three *barrios*, into a symbolic and economically valuable location.

What Safa calls *ambiente Coyoacanense* (Coyoacán ambience) is an 'imaginary representation used to legitimise renovation or urban preservation proposals which articulate several local neighbourhood organised groups' (ibid.: 276, 277). In this case, local identity is a subjective and heterogeneous experience which evolves into a collective symbol when the 'local' is transformed into a 'place of tensions and conflicts' caused by the different and sometimes contradictory interests seeking to appropriate and use of the local built landscape and the land. According to her, the preservation of local identity represents the axis of the indigenous community's demands for Coyoacán's historic core in their struggles between the ancient and the contemporary Coyoacán and the accelerated process of change in land use:

In these historic areas, the past (objectified in monuments, streets and listed buildings protected by law) is the base for the "communities re-invention" (Anderson, 1993) which articulate themselves when a conflict arises and therefore question corruption, centralisation and arbitrary decision-making that do not consider their needs and opinions...Neighbours from Coyoacán defend the preservation of an historic zone, which the majority contributed to transform with their arrival (Safa 1998: 280, 281).

Hence, the principal interests of the residents of the historic core are: opposition to the commercialisation of the area, opposition to the growth of street trading, the reduction of the number of visitors at weekends – and the negative effects they produce – in addition to maintaining and enhancing the historic environment as a means for achieving a better quality of life.

Finally, with respect to the last sub-group of residents, there is the *colonias*. By the end of the nineteenth century new residential areas were created in México City. Siembeida and López (1998) point out that these *colonias* were intended as mono-functional spaces for residential use only, according to models of 'cleanliness, health, order and distinction' which the ancient *barrios* did not have. They were created for the middle and upper classes with an idea of 'exclusivity and segregation' (ibid.: 45) in a completely different way to that of the *barrios*. Colonia Del Carmen Coyoacán, located to the north of the designated historic centre, was founded in 1890. It is the most remarkable settlement of this kind and it has been a place of historic significance. Frida Kahlo, the painter, was born and lived there in the so-called Casa Azul, and Leon Trosky spent his last years a few blocks from there (Dubernard 1990). The interests of the residents in this locality remain that of protecting the exclusivity of the area.

Shop Owners

Two different kinds of shops exist in the historic core of Coyoacán. Those which serve the residents living there, and those targeting tourists. The former have been established for many years – groceries and bakeries, stationers, shoe repair shops and so on – whilst the latter have opened more recently and their presence is constantly increasing, especially surrounding the main plazas: they comprise arts and crafts stores, antique shops, bookstores, clothes shops (also known as *boutiques*), cafés, and so forth. This category also comprises, *taquerías* (taco shops), restaurants and bars including branches of multinational chains. The commercialisation of Coyoacán in terms of the rapid growth of a number of shops is evident. Safa (1998: 196) states that the rejection of this phenomenon has caused the mobilisation of the neighbours and the formation of alliances and/or conflicts between the different groups of residents in the locality. According to her, residents are against the indiscriminate granting of permissions for the opening of more shops, especially those that are not the 'traditional uses', and those that just exploit the identity of Coyoacán for commercial ends.

For the shop owners themselves their main interests are: reducing the number of street vendors and attracting more visitors and potential clients. For that purpose, a safe and attractive environment is needed.

Street Vendors

Known as *ambulantes,* street vendors are part of the informal sector of the national economy which has grown rapidly since the 1980s (Harrison and McVey 1997). Between 1982 and 1990, informal sector employment increased by 80 per cent, and a large part of that increase has been attributed to street trading (Barry 1992). Moctezuma and Anaya (1997) note the familiar reasons for the excessive increase – high rates of unemployment, low and decreasing incomes for the majority of the population and the lack of appropriate employment training programmes. Equally, they suggest that the demand for street trading is a social phenomenon too, due to the cheaper prices in comparison with formal sector retailers.

They point out that the use of public areas for informal trade has escalated at such a rate that if the trend continues the number of formal traders in México City will be overtaken by the informal sector. Already there are clashes between the formal and informal traders. Moctezuma and Anaya (1997) claim that street vendors are a 'factor in the deterioration' of the historic centre of México City, for example, because they obstruct pedestrian flow, and because theft and aggressive behaviour are increasing.

However, Méxican urban areas also generate 'acceptable' forms of street activity, such as newspaper vendors and shoeshine 'boys', *boleros*. In Coyoacán traditional vendors like trolleymen selling snacks, *globeros* (balloon traders), *neveros* (ice cream sellers) and indigenous people selling their crafts, are perceived to be part of the picturesque image of the zone by visitors.

A number of street vendors function in Coyoacán during weekends and Bank Holidays. They are only allowed to set their stalls in the main plazas, Plaza Hidalgo and Jardín Centenario, and in a parking lot adjacent to the latter. They are only supposed to sell traditional arts and crafts – pottery, jewellery, silver, etc. – but they draw large crowds from Coyoacán's central plazas. Because the number of street vendors increases imperceptibly, their rejection by local residents is commensurately slow and unorganised (Safa 1998: 197).

Amongst the main interests of the street vendors are: permission to be able to trade on more days a week, reducing the number of street vendors trading without permission, reducing the conflicts with local residents, and providing public amenities to cater for their use.

Artists

Since the turn of the twentieth century, important artists and intellectuals have lived and still live in Coyoacán. Internationally known painters like Frida Kahlo, Diego Rivera, Chávez Morado and Rufino Tamayo, and writers and poets, film directors and musicians, have made Coyoacán widely identified as a 'cultural zone' (GDF 1999, INAH 1990). The cultural infrastructure in the area is extensive and there is a very active cultural life. The activities in the main plazas in the weekends contribute to this: performers, musicians, street painters selling their work, and so on. This cultural life is widely known to the inhabitants of the city, and it has been used as a key element for promoting the identity the zone and to promote it as a tourist attraction, both by local authorities, and commercially by private investors. Although artists are not an homogeneous group, they play an important role in the distinctiveness of the area, maintaining and enhancing the cultural activity of the zone, and maintaining the character of the zone, amongst others factors.

Visitors

Visitors come to the central area attracted by the cultural variety, restaurants, bars, cafes, shops and street trading. Huge quantities of people pack the main plazas during the weekends. Their presence in Coyoacán is a critical factor contributing to the transformation of the zone. Some of the negative effects they produce are parking problems, increasing alcohol and drugs consumption, and traffic congestion.

Perceptions and Perspectives on the Attitudes of the Five Groups

Turning now to a more detailed view of how these groups perceive their own interests and the strengths, weaknesses, opportunities and threats to the area, a number of contrasting and complementary perspectives emerge.

The lack of strategies to include local communities, their concerns and interests, has resulted in an inequitable and fragmented situation in the conservation and enhancement of the public realm. For instance, whereas visible investment has been directed to the main plazas and their surroundings such as Francisco Sosa street, this has not been the case in the historic barrios. This situation is evident in every plaza – ancient atria – of the historic barrios, with the exception Plazuela de Los Reyes, which is maintained by voluntary community labour. Social problems are evident: drugs dealers and alcohol consumption are taking over the main plazas of the area, and street children and prostitution have become alarming issues in parts of San Diego and San Mateo. The main problems the area is facing, which the local groups and communities have articulated, have been considered neither in the conservation programmes, nor in the management of the area.

Conflicts between the different views, concerns and perspectives for the future of the area from the different local groups, also to contribute to the deterioration of the historic zone. As already noted, these factors are not considered in the conservation programmes. They include: the continuous increasing in street trading; commercialisation of the zone in terms of speculative land markets and proliferation of shops; the displacement of indigenous communities; rent increases; massive invasion of weekend visitors with all the negative side effects they bring with them, and so forth. Moreover, even if these changes are regulated in theory, for example land controls, the regulations are not respected. Shops, restaurants and bars open indiscriminately. They are increasingly appearing in areas which are primarily residential (SEDUVI 1997b, 1997c). Different neighbourhood organisations in the historic core Colonia del Carmen – both formal and informal – are trying to prevent this phenomenon, but in vain.

On the whole the different groups seem to want to retain the cultural infrastructure and activities on offer, the main plazas and the streets around them, the architecture and the historical significance of the area: these are the most valued features for all the local groups. Concerning the negative aspects of the area (i.e. excluding the impact of city wide factors noted earlier), the main issues to be resolved are: the proliferation of the street vendors and the consequent 'weekend invasion of local visitors'; the increasing number of bars and restaurants selling alcohol; the uncontrolled opening of shops targeting local tourism; and the commercialisation of the area. These issues are exacerbated by the lack of commitment, and the lack of powers and capacity by the authorities to regulate the pressures for change more effectively.

As far as priorities are concerned, then, reinforcing the cultural potential is the first challenge confronting the area. Second, there is the challenge of recovering the positive features which Coyoacán once had and which local groups perceive are being lost – in other words its 'typical assets', its social health, attractiveness and 'dignity as an historic area', but most of all its peaceful character. Finally, there is the challenge of maintaining the local character and traditions (including the *barrios*). The main threat which local groups perceived is the apparently inevitable destruction caused by all the pressures on Coyoacán which central and local authorities fail to be aware of and incapable of understanding and tackling.

In this respect, what emerges most strongly is the way local groups have been marginalised from planning and conservation processes by the various public agencies charged with these responsibilities. The lack of opportunities to participate in decision-making affecting them and the consequent failure to articulate public interests remains an enduring threat to the sustainability of Coyoacán.

What is needed is a more detailed analysis of the area, its structure, activity patterns, and urban character and morphology which could lead to developing urban design proposals which would better serve the interests and needs of the different local community groups, in order to protect and enhance Coyoacán HMZ, whilst still maintaining its social and cultural diversity. Guidelines could be developed to indicate key parameters relating to evaluation, conservation and rehabilitation of the historic area. These proposals would then need to be tested to assess their acceptability with the key actors and stakeholders, to deal with the main conflicts identified, and to develop the implementation potential.

Conclusion

This chapter has discussed how federal legislation and the practices for the protection of México's cultural patrimony focus on the physical aspects of the HMZ. It has also elaborated the failure of current conservation practice to articulate the interests of local groups in the development of their neighbourhoods. The consequence of these shortcomings is the declining capacity of the area to sustain its social and physical patrimony.

As regards the physical character of the area, the legislation leaves the 'artistic patrimony' of the twentieth century largely unprotected. As regards public participation the chapter has shown how much progress is still needed to make this a reality. Although there is provision in the federal legislation (DOF 1994, INAH 1972), and despite the growing awareness that community participation is also a means for achieving greater sustainability in the built environment, conservation policies and the main federal institutions responsible for the national heritage have not taken appropriate steps to engage participatory planning and design. Linking community involvement with the programmes for the conservation and rehabilitation of heritage complexes can contribute to an integrated and sustainable form of conservation. However, on the evidence of this case study, urban development plans involving conservation programmes address community participation as a diffuse concept: participatory practice varies from one situation to another.

Finally, in the case of Coyoacán, evidence in this chapter illustrates the contrasting existence of consensus and fundamental conflicts between the different interest groups in the historic area. But it is the competing interests which have lead to inequitable and fragmented outcomes in the conservation and enhancement of the public realm, a situation that, as stated above, neither the current conservation programme nor the main government agencies have taken into account. Future programmes for conservation and rehabilitation must be designed so as to involve local community groups. In this field, as in many others, equity and freedom to participate in decision making affecting local communities are seminal. By balancing the community's aspirations, interests and concerns, whilst maintaining their social and cultural diversity, potentially more equitable and sustainable solutions to the problems faced in historic areas like Coyoacán may be achieved.

Acknowledgements

The research that this chapter is based on has been sponsored by the National Science and Technology Council (CONACYT) and the National Anthropology and History Institute (INAH).

References

Aceves, J. (1988), *Apuntes para la construcción de la historia local de Coyoacán (Notes for the Construction of the Local History of Coyoacán)*, unpublished Master's thesis in History, México, UAM Iztapalapa.

Anderson, B. (1993), *Comunidades imaginadas. Reflexiones sobre el origen y la difusion del Nacionalismo (Imagined Communities: Reflections on the Origin and the Spreading of Nationalism)*, México, FCE.

Barry, T. (1992), *México*, USA, Albuquerque Inter-Hemispheric Education Resource Centre.

Brandon, P.S., Lombardi, P.L. and Bentivengna, V. (1997), *Evaluation of the Built Environment for Sustainability*, London, E. and F.N. Spon.

Connolly, P. (1999), 'México City: Our Common Future?', *Environment and Urbanization*, 11:1, pp. 53–78.

Delafons, J. (1997), 'Sustainable Conservation', *Built Environment*, 23:2, pp. 111–20.

Diaz-Berrio, S. (1990), *Conservación del Patrimonio Cultural (Conservation of the Cultural Patrimony)*, México, INAH.

DOF Diario Oficial de la Federación (Official Gazette of the Federation) (1993) *Ley General de Asentamientos Humanos (General Law on Human Settlements)*, 21 July.

Dubernard, L. (1990), 'Presentación' (foreword), in Sosa, F., *Bosquejo Historico de Coyoacán 1890–1900*, México, author's edition.

Dubernard, L. (1992), *Coyoacán a vuela pluma*, México, Banco del Atlantico.

Flores-Marini, C. (1968), 'Architectural Aspects of Coyoacán Today: Ciudad de México, sus Villas Coyoacán y Churubusco', *Revista Artes de México*, No. 105 año XV, 2a, México, Epoca.

Franco, T. (1997), 'Presentación' (foreword), in Barros, C. (ed.), *El Centro Historico*, México, DDF, INAH.

Gaceta Oficial del Distrito Federal (GODF) (Official Gazette of the Federal District) (1996), *Ley de Desarrollo Urbano del Distrito Federal (Urban Development Law for the Federal District)*, 29 January, Mexico.

Gaceta Oficial del Distrito Federal (GODF) (Official Gazette of the Federal District) (1998), *Ley de Participación Ciudadana del Distrito Federal (Citizen Participation Law for the Federal District)*, 21 December, Mexico.

Gaceta Oficial del Distrito Federal (GODF) (Official Gazette of the Federal District) (2003) *Decreto por el que se Aprueba el Programa General de Desarrollo Urbano del Distrito Federal (Decree for the General Programme of Urban Development for the Federal District is Approved)*, 31 December.

Garcia-Moll, R. (1991), 'Perspectivas de la Conservación de los Centros Históricos a la luz de la polémica actual' (Perspectives on the Conservation of the Historic Centres in the Light of the Current Polemic), *Antropología. Boletín oficial del Instituto Nacional de Antropología e Historia*, 34, pp. 53–57.

Garza, G. (1999), 'Global Economy, Metropolitan Dynamics and Urban Policies in México', *Cities*, 16:3, pp. 149–70.

Gibson, C. (1967), *Los aztecas bajo el dominio español, 1519–1821*, México, Siglo XXI.

Gobierno del Distrito Federal (GODF) (Federal District Government) (1999), *Delegación Coyoacán: turismo*.

Harrison, M. and McVey, C.M. (1997), 'Street Trading in México City', *Third World Planning Review*, 19:3, pp. 313–26.

Instituto Nacional de Antropología e Historia (INAH) (National Institute of Anthropology and History) (1972), *Ley Federal sobre Monumentos y Zonas Arqueológicos, Artísticos e Históricos (Federal Law on Archaeological, Artistic and Historical Monuments' and Zones)*, México, INAH.

Instituto Nacional de Antropología e Historia (INAH) (National Institute of Anthropology and History) (1975), *Reglamento de la Ley Federal Sobre Monumentos y Zonas Arqueológicos, Artísticos e Históricos (Attached Regulations of the Federal Law on Archaeological, Artistic and Historical Monuments and Zones)*, México, INAH.

Instituto Nacional de Antropología e Historia (INAH) (National Institute of Anthropology and History) (1984), *Estudio para la Delimitación de la Zona de Monumentos Históricos de Coyoacán* (Study for the declaration of Coyoacán's Zone of Historic Monuments), México, DMH-INAH.

Instituto Nacional de Antropología e Historia (INAH) (National Institute of Anthropology and History) (1990), 'Decreto de Zona: Delegación Coyoacán, D.F.', in *Diario Oficial de la Federación (Decree of Zone: Coyoacán Delegation, Federal District,* in *Official Gazette of the Federation)*, 19 December, México.

Instituto Nacional de Antropología e Historia (INAH) (National Institute of Anthropology and History) (2001), 'Estudio y Delimitación de Zonas de Monumentos Históricos', *Monumentos Históricos: Catalogación de Monumentos (Study and Delimitation of Historical Monuments' Zones*, in *Historical Monuments: Monuments' Catalogue)*, http:/www.inah.gob.mx/index_.html, visited 2 March 2002.

INAH/SCZ-CNMH Subdirección de Catálogo y Zonas de la Coordinación Nacional de Monumentos Históricos del Instituto Nacional de Antropología e Historia (2004), 'Zonas de Monumentos Históricos Declaradas', in *Manuales de Catalogación de Monumentos Históricos y Manifestación de Impacto Regulatorio de Zonas de Monumentos Históricos (Historical Monuments Zones in Historical Monuments Catalogue Manual and Regulatory Impact of Historical Monuments Zones)*, CD ROM, México.

INEGI (1990), *XI Censo Nacional de Poblacion y Vivienda (XI National Population Census*, México, INEGI.

INEGI (1995), *Conteo Nacional de Población (National Population Census)*, México, INEGI.

Lombardo, S. (1985), 'Antecedentes de las Leyes Sobre Conservación de Monumentos' (Background Laws on Conservation of Monuments, Nineteenth and Twentieth Centuries), in *Primera Reunión para Definir una Política Nacional de Conservación de Monumentos. Las Legislaciones Sobre la Conservación de los Monumentos Históricos (First Meeting for Defining a National Policy for the Conservation of Monuments, Legislation on the Conservation of Historical Monuments)*, Cuaderno de Trabajo 1, Proceedings No. 1, 9–50, México, Dirección de Monumentos Históricos, DMH, INAH.

Moctezuma, P. and Anaya, E. (1997), 'Gestión Social', in Eibenschutz, R. (ed.), *Bases para la Planeación del Desarrollo Urbano de la Ciudad de México Tomo I: Economía y sociedad en la Metrópoli (Basis for the Planning of the Urban Development of México City, Vol 1: Economics and Society in the Metropolis)*, México, UAM, pp. 75–151.

Novo, S. (1996), *Historia y Leyenda de Coyoacán (History and Legend of Coyoacán)*, first published 1971, México, Novaro.

Olive, J. (1997), 'Problemas legales sobre la protección del Patrimonio' (Legal Problems on the Protection of the Patrimony), in Barros. C. (ed.), *El Centro Histórico*, México, INAH, DDF.

Romero, G. (1999), 'Abstencionismo de 90.1% en los comicios vecinales' (Abstention of 90.1 per cent in the Neighbourhood Elections), in *La Jornada*, Mexican Newspaper, 10 July.

Rodríguez, M. (1995), *Restauración de la Capilla de San Lucas Coyoacán, D.F (Restoration of the Chapel of San Lucas)*, unpublished Master's thesis on Restoration of Monuments, México, INAH-ENCRYM.

Rosas-Mantecón, A. (1996), 'La Exploración Antropológica sobre la Conservación, Apreciación y Usos del Patrimonio Cultural Urbano', in Sevilla, A. and Aguilar, M. (eds), *Estudios recientes sobre cultura urbana en México (The Anthropological Exploration of Conservation, Appreciation and Uses of Urban Cultural Heritage, in Recent Studies on Urban Culture in Mexico)*, México, Plaza y Valdés Editores, pp. 65–88.

Rosas-Mantecón, A. (1994), 'Antropología y Revitalización de Centros Históricos', in PMD-INAH (ed.), *Revitalización de Centros Históricos (Anthropology and Revitalization of Historic Centres*, in *Revitalization of Historic Centres)*, México, PMD-INAH, pp. 29–51.

Safa, P. (1998), *Vecinos y Vecindarios en la Ciudad de México: un Estudio sobre la Construcción de las Identidades Vecinales en Coyoacán (Neighbours and Neighbourhoods in México City: A Study on the Construction of Neighbourhood Identities in Coyoacán)*, México, UAM, Porrúa.

Satterthwaite, D. (1999), 'Sustainable Cities or Cities that Contribute to Sustainable Development', in Satterthwaite, D. (ed.), *The Earthscan Reader in Sustainable Cities*, London, Earthscan.

SEDESOL Secretaria de Desarrollo Social (Social Development Secretary) (1994), *Programa de 100 Ciudades: Una Estrategia de Desarrollo Urbano Regional Sustentable y Concertado (100 Cities Programme: A Sustainable and Comprehensive Urban Development Strategy)*, México, Dirección General de Desarrollo Urbano.

SEDUVI Secretaría de Desarrollo Urbano y Vivienda del D.F. (Urban Development And Housing Secretary of the Federal District) (1997a), *Programa Delegacional de Desarrollo Urbano de la Delegación Coyoacán (Urban Development Delgational Programme for Coyoacán Delegation)*, México, SEDUVI.

SEDUVI Secretaría de Desarrollo Urbano y Vivienda del D.F. (Urban Development And Housing Secretary of the Federal District) (1997b), *Programa Parcial de Desarrollo Urbano del Centro Histórico de Coyoacán (Partial Urban Development Programme for the Historic Centre of Coyoacán)*, México, SEDUVI.

SEDUVI Secretaría de Desarrollo Urbano y Vivienda del D.F. (Urban Development And Housing Secretary of the Federal District) (1997c), *Programa Parcial de Desarrollo Urbano de la Colonia del Carmen Coyoacán (Urban Development Partial Programme for Colonia del Carmen Coyoacán)*, México, SEDUVI.

SEDUVI Secretaría de Desarrollo Urbano y Vivienda del D.F. (Urban Development And Housing Secretary of the Federal District) (undated), *Normas de Conservación e Intervención en Inmuebles Patrimoniales y en Zonas Patrimoniales (Norms on Conservation and Intervention in Heritage Buildings and Zones)*, http://www.seduvi.df.gob.mx/patrimonio/index.html, visited 2 October 2004.

Siembeida, W. and López, E. (1998), 'Barrios and the Hispanamerican City', *Journal of Urban Design*, 3:1, pp. 39–52.

Trevor, W. (1999), 'Community and Sustainable Development: Participation in the Future, by Warburton, D.', book review in *Sustainable Development*, v7:2, pp. 112–12.

Wates, N. and Urban Design Group (UDG) (1998), 'Involving Local Communities in Urban Design: Promoting Good Practice', *Urban Design Quarterly*, 67.

World Commission on Environment Development (WCED) (1987), *Our Common Future*, G.H. Brundtland, Oxford, Oxford University Press.

Chapter 6

Value-led Heritage and Sustainable Development: The Case of Bijapur, India

Anwar Punekar

Introduction

For heritage resources such as cultural heritage sites and landscapes which cannot be physically regenerated but only retained, modified, or lost, sustainability means ensuring the continuing contribution of heritage to the present through the thoughtful management of change responsive to the historic environment (Teutonico and Matero 2003). This involves not only preserving the built and natural environment, but also the fundamental elements of the social environment. In fact, there is increasing agreement on the definition of heritage as a social ensemble of many different, complex and interdependent manifestations, reflecting a culture of humanity (Luxen 2004). Thus the challenges of the conservation field stem not only from cultural heritage sites themselves, but from the context in which society embeds them. These contexts – the values people draw from cultural heritage and the uses to which the cultural heritage is put – are the real source of meaning of heritage, and the raison d'être for conservation in all senses (Avrami and Mason 2000). The term 'values' is most often used in one of two senses: first, as morals, principles, or other ideas that serve as guides to action (individual or collective); and second, in reference to the qualities and characteristics seen in things, in particular the positive characteristics (actual and potential) (Mason 2002). This chapter deals with the second definition and there is a large body of research emerging in this direction particularly from Getty Conservation Institute.

At the same time, international debates have also deepened and expanded the notions of heritage and conservation from conserving individual historical monuments in the 1960s to conserving the more encompassing cultural properties themselves (Erder 2004). This evolution includes the drawing up of charters and conventions, which in turn gives impetus to conservation practice. The scope of conservation practice has thus expanded from an initial concern with the preservation or enhancement of important isolated monuments to area conservation strategies and a full integration with local planning practice (Larkham 1996) based on value led planning. Value – be it historical, aesthetic, social or other – is what justifies the protection of cultural heritage resources in the first place and it is the basis of any public support (Clark 2001).

At present, in developing countries, most cultural heritage sites are identified solely in terms of their historical rather than contemporary importance to the communities (Low 1987: 31), an approach which often alienates local communities from their own heritage. However, in order successfully to conserve and manage a heritage building, site or a landscape on a day-to-day basis, there is a need to take into account a much wider bandwidth of values. This bandwidth involves the values of different communities, professionals from other fields, and special interest groups in the conservation field with their own criteria and opinions, which often differ from those of the conservation professionals. This democratisation is a positive development in the conservation field and bears witness to the importance of heritage in today's society (Torre and Mason 2002). In this changed environment, the articulation and understanding of values have acquired greater importance when heritage decisions are being made about what to conserve, how to conserve, where to set priorities, and how to handle conflicting interests.

This chapter addresses a key concern for conservation in Indian historic cities with particular emphasis on Bijapur. It argues that conservation initiatives must be value-led, considering both social as well as physical conditions in culturally and religiously diverse historic urban settings. Value-led conservation initiatives may trigger the impetus for partnerships and collective responsibility both between different local communities and between them and the agencies concerning the historic urban environment. Through its dual focus on engaging diverse communities and enabling partnerships between local communities and agencies, this chapter also makes a significant contribution towards the democratisation of urban conservation in an emerging society.

Conflicting Heritage Values in Diverse Contexts

Historically, cultural heritage and its very existence within a society has been viewed as culturally consensual. But since the 1980s, cultural consensus and norms have been replaced by an atmosphere of openly contentious and fractious cultural politics. If we look back to the 1970s, cultural heritage was defined by critics such as Lowenthal as 'things worth saving [which] need not necessarily be beautiful or historic as long as they are familiar or well loved' (1979: 555). There is, however, compelling evidence that that which previously held true has been replaced by its precise opposite. In other words, heritage at its core is politicised, and thus conservation must not hide behind its traditional philosophical matters of faith (Avrami and Mason 2000). At the heart of inter-disciplinary, critical research on heritage is the notion that cultural heritage is a social construction, which emerges from social processes in a specific time and place (Avrami and Mason 2000) involving different communities, who are often unable to contribute equally or consistently to the construction of heritage (Tunbridge and Ashworth 1996).

There is, therefore, a nexus between the identities of places and tensions between communities that seek to create, or to modify these identities (Tunbridge, Jones and Shaw 1996). Conservation authorities, planners, city management authorities as well as politicians have always recognised these tensions as endemic to urban conservation initiatives. This has been more so in India considering India's vulnerability to religious sensitivities. In an attempt to intervene, the built environment professionals and social and political scientists have always called for a convergence of opposites and an association of differences for mutual benefit in the design of policy, spatial plans and buildings (Hamdi 2004). What must be recognised is the representation of both opposites, not either/or and what we need is an understanding of 'natural scales and limits' in order that polarities can co-exist (Hamdi 2004).

As Sharon Sullivan, the former director of the Australian Heritage Commission, has noted:

> In most cases, the white Australian practitioner can have no way of really assessing the value of a site, except in European terms, unless there is a process of real consultation, and a genuine attempt to accept as equally valuable the views of another culture (cited in Clark 2001: 9–10).

In the Indian context, as we shall see, the government may be claiming Islamic cultural heritage sites as 'national' treasures, ancient masterpieces created many centuries ago by cultures totally different from their own and whose descendents may even be considered to be their cultural opponents. But, it is increasingly important to assess the value of an Islamic site through the eyes of the local Muslim communities, to take into consideration their view as well in the conservation process. Since the sacred space belongs to the devout as much as it does to the custodians of heritage (Baig 2004). The 73rd and 74th amendments to the Indian Constitution mandate a role for the public in the decision making process, which is used marginally without genuine participation (ibid. 2004). In this connection, the 1981 Burra Charter emphasised the process of decision making as involving more than just formal rules placing significance or value at the centre of conservation. 'Conservation of a place should take into consideration all aspects of its cultural significance without unwarranted emphasis on any one at the expense of others' (Burra Charter 1981). This emphasis on discovering significance as part of the planning process has its analogy in the sustainable development of natural sites. The 1992 Rio Conference on Sustainable Development (UN Conference on Environment and Development 1992) noted that development and nature conservation should work together, rather than be separated. In *agenda21* (ibid. 1992) – the plan for action adopted by the conference – the delegates also acknowledged that conservation needs to be seen as both a 'bottom-up' and a 'top-down' process and that successful conservation meant working with, rather than dictating to, communities.

In order to work with communities in culturally diverse contexts, an understanding of how communities are formed is essential. There is a large body of research which has been produced in recent years concerning the concept of 'communities' (Leeds 1994, Harvey 2000). Hamdi has suggested that there are at least five kinds of communities in any given urban setting, they are interlinked and probably we are all the members of at least one of them (Hamdi 2004). These include: communities of interest; communities of culture or religion; communities of practice; communities of place and communities of resistance. These communities differ from one another in their constituencies, value systems, codes of conduct, and in their beliefs and aspirations. They also vary in their terms of engagement with their partners. The challenge for the conservation field is to strengthen its ability to deal constructively with the many, diverse and often conflicting communities and values ascribed to heritage – values that strongly shape conservation decision making (Avrami 2000).

The challenges of assessing diverse and conflicting values identified in the case study of Bijapur's historic core, enables the evolution of methods based on both a conceptual framework and an operational approach. The historic city of Bijapur represents Islamic urban heritage and is 50 per cent inhabited by Muslims co-existing with 50 per cent non-Muslim communities. Bijapur's historic core offers an appropriate physical and social context for research concerning both the city's historic urban form and its contemporary local communities. But first we need to review the Indian context as a whole.

Conservation of Urban Heritage in India

In the legal framework of India, conservation initiatives began as far back as 1774 (Thaper 1989: 165). Nonetheless, only in April 1906, at the instigation of Lord Curzon (1899–1905) was the Archaeological Survey of India (ASI) established (Singh 1997). The Act of 1951 was passed under the auspices of the ASI largely due to a need to provide a central list of well known monuments and sites located in former princely states. No guidelines or criteria exist in the 1951 Act, or in subsequent regulations, as to what counts as a listed monument or site (Thapar 1992). According to this Act, the main heritage site or a building declared as a monument of national importance is to be protected excluding the context within which the site is embedded. As we shall see, this legislative framework aimed at 'conservation as monumentalism' clearly does not lend itself to the contemporary conservation needs of India in the terms argued in this chapter.

In contexts as diverse as the Indian, it is increasingly important to shift the traditional conservation approach – involving experts' archaic vision – to a situation where the 'experts views are a few among many' as Torre and Mason express it (2002). Conservation initiatives need to be more sensitive to community concerns as Indian historic cities represent the cultural heritage of particular communities co-existing with other communities. Conservation initiatives need to evolve processes that build on both diverse community concerns and the physical context of cultural heritage. For, the greater the relevance and sustainability of conservation efforts and the more they serve to foster community building and civic dialogue, the more cultural heritage conservation will be embraced by society as a 'public good' (Avrami et al. 2000).

The social and physical sustainability of conservation initiatives in the Indian context involves enhancing the linkages between cultural heritage sites and local communities on the social front, and on the physical front by enhancing partnerships between departments and agencies concerned with public infrastructure in the historic urban environment. For instance, heritage conservation work often includes collateral investments in public infrastructure to guarantee the sustainability of the investment in the building fabric (Burnham 2004). Commitments to pave the streets and to provide conduits, lighting, street furniture and other public amenities may be critical to the future of the cultural heritage building, site or a landscape that is being preserved. Regulating land use, limiting the height of new buildings and maintaining sympathetic development involving aesthetic as well as spatial linkages within an historic urban setting are often the tasks of town planning and city management authorities. However, in contexts such as this, which involve social as well as physical intervention, partnerships are crucial in order 'to leverage limited resources, as well as – and equally important – to expand the capacity of the conservation community' (Whalen and Bouchenaki 2004: 4).

In India, rapid urbanisation and intra-urban population growth have affected most historic cities to an extent that the advancement in conservation policy and its integration with local planning and management of cultural heritage resources remain inappropriate. This is partly because, while the highly recommended conservation management guidelines such as charters and recommendations from UNESCO and other public international agencies are signed and endorsed by various member states such as India and other countries, they are not incorporated into the conservation planning and management of their historic cities. This is particularly because there are increasing concerns as to the relevance of these contributions in non-Western contexts. Some argue that developing countries have more pressing socio-economic needs to address (Orbasli 1999) and that recommendations and charters are not informed by the local issues concerning the historic urban settings (Bryne 2004). Meanwhile, others argue that there is no institutional framework at the local level that can serve to plan, conserve and manage the historic cities (Punekar 2000). Nonetheless, this gap between conservation policy and practice points to the fact that conservation must be as much a bottom-up as a top-down process.

Stepping down to Indian practice, we find that the local authorities who bear the responsibility for the conservation of built heritage face several conflicting concerns. Firstly, they are expected to protect the authenticity and integrity of their cities' historic urban legacy and to preserve their cultural heritage in the terms of the 1951 Act. Secondly, they have to address development pressures and to allow the historic urban form to accommodate modern societal needs; they have to balance diverse community concerns and, lastly, they have to struggle for funding or find ways of negotiating with other government interests, tourist agencies, lobby groups, private sector and the interests of influential people.

Unable to address this array of competing demands the local authorities – overburdened with providing basic services and overrun by financial deficit as they usually are – often disregard the importance and relevance of protecting and maintaining local cultural heritage, traditions and their social and physical context. Meanwhile the conservation authorities continue protecting cultural heritage sites as individual sites. This disregard for the social and physical context of historic urban environments by the municipal authorities, when placed against the practice of conserving individual heritage sites devoid of their social and physical context, often isolates these sites from the concerns of contemporary local communities. This results in a widening gap between the cultural heritage sites themselves and their social and physical context.

This gap demands increasing attention, considering India's diverse cultures and people. Indeed the uniqueness of India's urban heritage is its demarcation in terms of local and foreign cultures which mark definite phases of historical transition in the Indian cultural landscape up to 1947 (Indian independence). These phases also include Islamic and colonial influences, which are evident in India's composite cultural heritage. Cultural heritage sites, buildings and landscapes representing particular historic phases have varying connotations for contemporary communities because of the values ascribed to them by professional, ethnic or religious groups and local communities or other social groups.

These values in turn have increasing implications for these diverse groups in terms of engagement with the conservation initiatives. For instance, in the process of conserving Mumbai's (Bombay) colonial heritage in the Kala Ghoda Area, Mehrotra (2000) acknowledged the conservation movement as growing out of the environmental movement rather than as a cultural desire to preserve historic icons. He considers that, to an entire generation of citizens, the Victorian core of the city represents repression and exclusion (Mehrotra 2000: 161).

Conservation approaches in this context may be able to treat their 'object' purely as a resource in terms of buildings and environment, devoid of iconographic and symbolic content (ibid. 2000). Such an approach may be possible in relation to Mumbai's colonial heritage, since the colonial rulers who left their influence on the Indian landscape no longer live in India as a demographic constituent. However, conservation approaches with regard to the cultural heritage representing contemporary religious communities co-existing with others pose complex challenges. These complex challenges are the context of Bijapur within which this chapter proposes intervention.

The Case Study of Bijapur's Historic Core

Bijapur is a working city with culturally and religiously diverse communities, Muslims form half the city's population while the other is made up of Hindus (major castes include Brahmins, Lingayats, and Scheduled Castes or Tribes), Christians and Buddhists. Bijapur has a traditional agriculture and horticulture economy. However, in the recent past the education sector has grown attracting students for professional courses from all over India. Past urban heritage together with the education sector have partly enabled Bijapur to connect its past to current and future functions, while the deteriorating historic urban environment has yet to be addressed.

Bijapur's Islamic cultural heritage sites derive from the *Adilshahi* regime (1489–1656 AD) and comprise essentially public buildings, which are both secular and religious. These may be grouped into four categories: forts, bastions and watch towers; water reservoirs and conduit systems; mosques and mausoleums; and palaces, judicial courts and office buildings. The morphology of the historic part of Bijapur offers three distinct quarters: the historic core; modern quarters; and the informal residential and mixed-use settlements.

Despite Bijapur being off the main tourist route, nearly 570,000 domestic tourists and nearly 2,250 international tourists visited Bijapur in 2003, and these numbers are increasing every year. However, the deteriorating historic urban fabric has also led to cultural alienation and segregation among communities largely due to policies that are not under-pinned by a deeper understanding of how Muslim and other communities operate.

Current State of Bijapur's Historic Core

Some monuments and monument precincts are in good repair and surrounded by well maintained landscaping. But the historic core as a whole is in a rundown condition. However, the urban morphology of Bijapur's central historic core, as in other Indian medieval historic cities, is not well served by the Act of 1951 since, although the historic core has significant historic monuments, the urban areas that are integral to the cultural heritage sites and buildings are essentially non-monumental.

Drawing on morphological references to Bijapur from other authors writing on similar contexts worldwide, we can begin to understand how this narrow vision has come about. Only the monumental buildings were conceived and built as cultural symbols in order to last as a legacy of political power. The non-monumental building stock was utilitarian, built to serve its contemporary users and destined to disappear when it became physically or functionally obsolete (Serageldin 2000). Evans also acknowledges that 'unlike Roman towns, Islamic urban centres had no master planning' (1998: 56). As a result, varied residential and civic clusters emerged over time with the monuments and landmarks forming the connecting elements both within and among the clusters. Concerning the clusters, Abu-Lughod (1980: 6–10) discerns some certain common features of Islamic urban form. One, for example, is that property in extensive ownership which gradually evolved into a residential locality was assigned to a group which was empowered to divide it. Naidu (1994: 300) adds that the granting of urban space which was subsequently subdivided into separate ownership enabled a clear distinction between semi-public and public spaces. This type of urban form is the expression of a fundamentally different set of rules: rules generated by a society defining itself on an individual basis rather than in accordance with an imposed centralised rulebook, like that of Rome (Evans 1998: 56).

However, conservation in Indian historic cities in general, and Bijapur in particular, has been both physically and financially sustainable only in respect of the protection of isolated monumental buildings. In addition, the Ancient Monuments and Archaeological Sites and Remains Rules of 1958 have a provision in Rules 31 and 33 declaring certain areas near or adjoining the protected monuments as 'a prohibited or a regulated area' (Thapar 1992). This 'prohibited or regulated area,' which has been defined with the aim of retaining the identity of the historic urban environment and to promote sympathetic development has often proved detrimental to its place identity largely because this provision involves the role of city management and development control authorities noted earlier in this chapter. The problem in Bijapur, and for India as a whole, is the weak institutional capacity. Building control regulations in the 'prohibited and regulated area' are not complied with because of weak building and development control mechanisms and a lack of incentives for the property owners to forego building development rights. In the meantime, in Bijapur, the local communities, developers and entrepreneurs believe the conservation authorities to be inflexible and capable only of imposing an archaic vision of heritage conservation. This situation has led to development which is not in sympathy with the historic core and to dilapidation, encroachment and polarisation of communities.

The parts of the historic core which link different commercial areas are unable to resist development pressures, resulting in illegal mixed-use developments. The old housing stock within the historic core is becoming dilapidated because of the constant subdivision and lack of maintenance. Open spaces surrounding the monument precincts are owned by the government, municipality or absentee landlords, and these areas are often encroached on by squatter settlements.

This rundown physical form is inhabited by communities based on caste, creed and religion partly resulting from friction and local disagreements among different communities concerning use and disuse of cultural heritage precincts.

Bijapur's historic central core can thus be identified with four basic issues:

• development unsympathetic with the historic core;
• dilapidated housing stock;
• squatter settlements; and
• establishment of exclusive polarised communities.

This type of physical and social deterioration can be found in most Indian historic cities. Bijapur is a representative example, which similarly offers the potential for both conservation and conflict. In Bijapur, the social and physical conservation issues identified above, though seen as separate social and physical issues, are in fact largely interlinked – not only because they involve cultural heritage but because they also form the constituents of both a cultural landscape and a working urban environment. It is increasingly important to intervene in historic urban environments inhabited by diverse community groups from the cultural landscape perspective because this approach focuses not only on the humanised environment but, more specifically on Lowenthal's notion of history as dynamic – continuous history, not restricted to the past (1979).

Developing a Values-based Analytical Approach

Urban designers, planners, conservation professionals and social scientists are increasingly aware that the approach of conserving individual buildings devoid of the socio-spatial context, as we have seen, contributes to the deterioration of the physical fabric (Punekar 2000). The challenge, then, is to develop an appropriate methodological and analytical apparatus which will allow us to bridge the gap between narrowly conceived conservation practice, as evident in India but obviously extending much wider than this, and a wider vision of conservation as the process of safeguarding and managing the cultural landscape.

The concept of cultural landscape employed here consists not only of socio-cultural and politically detached scenes lying before our eyes and in our minds as Meinig terms it (1979: 33–34), but also the *inhabited* landscape, the physical world that people participate in directly, modifying it as they are able to according to their needs, aspirations and means. This triple faceted concept of the cultural landscape (natural setting, human modifications and meanings) embodies the whole living landscape associated with a strong ideological perspective, not just the landscape of the past; not just the beautiful and 'unspoilt', not just romantic, bypassed, or religious landscapes. In this concept, the same physical landscape may be simultaneously a shared cultural landscape and a multiple and inconsistent landscape. The urban conservation concept in this chapter is based on a concern with the management of change to this multi-faceted cultural landscape (Figure 6.1).

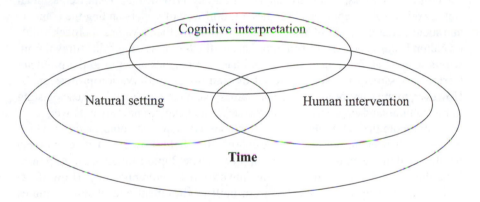

Figure 6.1   **The dialectics of the cultural landscape: Natural landscape, human modification, and interpretation continually evolving over time**

Source: Developed from O'Hare 1997: 30.

A cultural landscape approach enables diverse community groups to be seen as part of that landscape. That is, cultural, historical and political conditions affecting contemporary communities are part of the process of human engagement with the place. The cultural landscape approach can be a means of reuniting fragmented approaches to valuing and constructing the environments we inhabit, a means of overcoming distinctions between historic environment and new development, nature and culture, built heritage and the context. Urban conservation is often faced with the challenge of mediating potential and actual conflicts between such polarities. This is so particularly because present human actions shape and in turn are shaped by not only the natural landscape, but also the previous human modifications of that landscape and because the existing cultural landscape, for instance Bijapur's central historic core, is the locus in which most contemporary needs and desires are to be met.

This may also involve interactions of different communities within themselves or with the historic environment concerning, for instance, the use and neglect of heritage sites. As noted earlier, until recent times the conservation field was relatively isolated, composed of small groups of specialists and experts. These groups determined what constituted cultural heritage and how it should be conserved. However, since the 1980s the concept of heritage has evolved and expanded; new groups have joined the specialists in its identification. These groups of communities, of professionals from other disciplines, and of representatives of special interests arrive in the conservation field with their own criteria and opinions – their own values which often differ from those of conservation professionals. This democratisation is a positive development in the conservation field and chimes with the cultural landscape theories. It is therefore proposed to integrate the cultural landscape approach with that of a values approach.

While the cultural landscape approach largely provides an overall conceptual framework, a values approach becomes a useful way of understanding the contexts and socio-cultural aspects of heritage conservation. Further, a values approach builds on cultural landscape to identify appropriate methods of assessing values drawn from within as well as from other interdisciplinary approaches specific to the problem. Certain assessment methods are used by traditional conservation professionals. However, to measure or assess 'social' values, we must both identify those existing in the cultural landscape and values approaches and explore new areas as well.

Anthropological and ethnographic methods are amongst some of those which have recently been introduced in to the conservation field (Low 2002) which can also be identified in the cultural landscape approach. The Rapid Ethnographic Appraisal Procedures (REAP) methodologies are drawn from agricultural studies (Low 2002) and the inquiry by design method from built environment and planning studies (Bentley 1999, Butina Watson and Bentley 2005), where these methods have been established and in use over a comparatively longer span of time than they have been in the field of conservation. Action planning (Hamdi 2004) and impact assessment (Clark 2001) are also useful tools, performing different but complementary roles with the ultimate intent to transform, ameliorate and humanise the built environment through engaging communities.

The values approach has gained increasing momentum particularly through the efforts of the Getty Conservation Institute and Australian National Heritage. It allows in-depth insight into the values of cultural heritage within its socio-cultural, political, economic and physical context. The values approach employs interdisciplinary qualitative techniques that include constituency analysis; ethnography; mental mapping; inquiry by design; and REAP procedures.

Such an analytical approach to integrate both the social as well as the physical world seems appropriate to Bijapur's central historic core. The social context can be addressed, based on the fact that such historic cities are used by different communities who acquire different interpretations and utilisation of the urban environment. Different communities and different interpretations involve instances of conflicting values. Indeed, most of the damage that happens to sites is not usually a result of deliberate mismanagement but, rather, arises from the need to reconcile different priorities (Clark 2001). There is no simple way of accommodating conflicting values among local communities, but there are approaches which could be adopted to overcome some of these conflicts.

Impact assessment is one approach to dealing with conflicting values. Whatever change needs to be carried out on a heritage site will have an impact on the site's values. Impact assessment enables exploration of what those impacts might be before making any decision. By understanding the values associated with the site, ways of mitigating or reducing impact can be found (Clark 2001).

Exploring the Analytical Potential in Bijapur

All of this may seem a long way from the practical business of repairing an arch or cutting the grass but conservation is about handing on what we value to future generations and that requires us to look not at just what we have but what is happening to it (Clark 2001) and around it. This wider scope involves a shift from the present top-down conservation approaches to those involving 'values and stakeholders' – words that in recent years have become central in the method and implementation of heritage conservation and management (Agnew 2004).

However preliminary findings of the development and piloting of such an approach in Bijapur's historic core, although only briefly reported here, suggest positive results from the application of the analytical process. The method was designed to reveal the values and different cultural identities of the historic core, in from the perspectives of all the stakeholders and communities, as well as the potential for conservation in the wider meaning of the term developed in the chapter.

The Pilot Sites

Three separate heritage sites in Bijapur's central historic core were designated for this pilot. They are all essentially public precincts: *Asar-Mahal Phasari Kaman* complex, *Gagan-Mahal-Narsimha* temple complex and *Anand Mahal*. All three sites provide potential for intervention; but they also demonstrate relatively low-level conflict, in terms of both religious sensitivity and physical encroachment. This allowed the opportunity for positive engagement from the start of the process.

The *Asar Mahal Phasari Kaman* complex represents Muslim religious values and comprises a royal hall of justice and mosque (Figure 6.2). The *Gagan-Mahal-Narsimha* (Figure 6.3) temple complex represents both Hindu and secular values and comprises a hall of assembly and a temple, whilst *Anand Mahal* represents secular values – comprising an administrative building. The first two monument precincts

Asar Mahal

Rear view of Asar Mahal complex

Extended Madrasah in Asar Mahal
complex

Pupils from the Madrasah

Figure 6.2   Asar Mahal Phasari Kaman complex[1]

Gagan Mahal

View of Gagan Mahal-Narsimha
temple complex

Figure 6.3   Gagan Mahal-Narsimha temple complex

---

[1]   All photos by the author.

are surrounded by extensive open spaces, and so the potential for leisure uses to serve diverse communities was incorporated into the regeneration proposals.

The third heritage site offers voluminous built spaces with the potential of contemporary secular use. Therefore an art gallery for Bijapur's art work and paintings was identified as a suitable use since Bijapur lacks a central art gallery.

Impact Assessment Process

This process firstly involved assessment of the values for cultural heritage, socio-economic and cultural resources which are shared by different community groups and stakeholders or which are culturally meaningful to them. In addition, it involved assessing conflicts between community groups concerning the use or neglect of the cultural heritage, and their needs and aspirations. Secondly, the survey offered an insight, and more specifically gauged the effect of the willingness among local communities to participate, and equally the responsiveness of key stakeholders – conservation, tourism, development and city management agencies – to the aims of conservation and development for the historic core. The approach also enabled the potential for partnership and the resistance of those in charge to change or adapt to be assessed.

The interviewees were identified from a range of socio-economic and religious backgrounds – from religious to modern and from far left to far right as well as the Archaeological Survey of India (ASI).

The survey methods adopted were urban design, ethnographic, observational and REAP methodologies (Mason 2002, Throsby 2002, Low 2002, Wolf 1987, Joseph 1997, Donnam 1994). The conservation and revitalising proposals were developed as an inquiry by design tool (Zeisel 1984, Bentley 1999) for the impact assessment exercise along with other methods employed in the empirical field survey (Figure 6.4). The impact assessment exercise has been particularly crucial to tease out implicit community and stakeholder concerns in Bijapur's central historic core.

Preliminary findings from the three cases discussed above reveal that conflicts and differences could be mitigated. But the bigger question is that of who is to implement this process? Should it be the local authorities, the conservation authorities or a combination of both, or a third party?

Generic Findings: Linking Agencies to Built Environment

Turning to the question of institutional capacity revealed by this method, the responsibilities of departments such as Conservation and the City Municipal Authority concerning the historic environment are not well delimited and this situation creates confusion in managing the historic environment. There is no conservation management plan for the historic core which defines development policies and an implementation process, or the role for the historic core in relation to the rest of the city. The articles (Rules 31, 33) from the Act of 1958 declaring certain areas near or adjoining the protected monuments as 'a prohibited or a regulated area', have not been enforced. There are ambiguous implementation criteria in the current legislation introduced to

Stage	Qualitative approaches	Interviewees consulted
1	Constituency analysis – triangulation, SWOT and oral histories	All community groups from diverse religious, socio-economic, political affiliations, and formal and informal cultures across the historic core
2	Ethnographic and observational REAP methodologies	All community groups from diverse religious, socio-economic and political affiliations across the historic city of Bijapur
3	REAP methodologies	Key actors – producers, controllers, mediators
4	REAP methodologies	All respondents from Stages 1, 2 and 3 under one roof in a symposium

Figure 6.4   Summary of process

protect the identity of the historic urban environment. The current legislation is top-down and the local authorities do not, at present, have a conservation section which can deal with routine building permission applications in Bijapur's central historic core. Thus there is no close link between ASI, which steers conservation authorities, and the local town planning and city management authorities, let alone the private sector. The ASI is a central government department while all other departments such as the City Municipal Council, Block Development Authority and the Tourism Departments active in Bijapur are state government departments. Involving various departments in conservation means collaborating with more and different disciplines. Such collaboration raises questions about who is in charge and of which part of the process. What are the relative roles and contributions and responsibilities of this different cast of characters?

Ways Forward

The task of conservation and heritage management of Indian historic cities such as Bijapur cannot be tackled primarily by conservation authorities alone. This is particularly the case because conservation is multidisciplinary and the conclusions of the chapter point to collaboration with others. In contexts as diverse and economically challenged as Bijapur, assessing heritage values and engaging communities is not only morally appropriate but rather a political pre-requisite to facilitate partnerships among different fields and agencies. Partnerships among agencies concerned with the historic built environment are crucial to leverage limited resources. This may involve legislative and statutory empowerment to a central agency at the city scale which could synergise different departments for the improvement, future organisation and functioning of the central historic core.

Conservation planning policies and objectives in the form of a 'conservation management plan' emanating from this central agency should be translated into specific actions. Some might be physical interventions – linking major heritage sites with the surrounding localities, rearranging traffic networks, pedestrianising some key public areas. Others will result in the enactment of specific regulations – use and reuse of heritage sites. Others again, may involve defining implementation guidelines and setting up alternative administrative or management procedures such as establishing a public subsidy initiative, or creating a mixed public-private investment programme.

Finally, a conservation management plan for Bijapur's central historic core should not be considered as a single comprehensive document, defined once and for all. Rather it should be revisited as values and conditions change. It will, however, act as a regulatory framework for different actions required to plan and manage Bijapur's central historic core over the long term.

References

Abu-lughod, J. (1987), 'The Islamic City: Historic Myth, Islamic Essence, and Contemporary Relevance', *International Journal of Middle Eastern Studies*, 19, pp. 155–76.

Agnew, N. (2004), *Partnerships*, a joint issue with UNESCO, Los Angeles, The J. Paul Getty Trust, The Getty Conservation Institute, 19:3.

Avrami, E. and Mason, R. (2000), 'Report on Research', in Avrami, E., Mason, R. and de la Torre, M. (eds), *Values and Heritage Conservation, Research Report*, Los Angeles, The J. Paul Getty Trust, The Getty Conservation Institute, pp. 3–10.

Baig, A. (2004), 'Managing Cultural Significance', in Tandon, R. (ed.), *INTACT Virasat*, National Convention INTACH Vision 2020, INTACH, New Delhi.

Bentley, I. (1999), *Urban Transformations: Power, People and Urban Design*, London, Routledge.

Bryne, D. (2004), 'Chartering Heritage in Asia's Post-modern World Heritage', *Charters and Conventions*, 19:2, Los Angeles, Getty Conservation Institute, pp. 16–19.

Burnham, B. (2004), *Heritage Partnership: Exploring the Unknown*, Los Angeles, The J. Paul Getty Trust, The Getty Conservation Institute Newsletter, 19:3.

Clark, K. (2001), *Preserving What Matters: Value-led Planning for Cultural Heritage*, Los Angeles, The J. Paul Getty Trust, The Getty Conservation Institute Newsletter, 16:3.

Erder, C. (2004), *Principles, Practice, and Process: 'Heritage Charters and Conventions*, Los Angeles, Getty Conservation Institute, 19:2, pp. 16–19.

Evans, M. (ed.) (1998), *Key Moments in Architecture*, Cambridge MA, MIT Press.

Hamdi, N. (2004), *Small Change: About the Art of Practice and the Limits of Planning in Cities*, London, Earthscan.

Harvey, D. (2000), 'Social Movement and the City: A Theoretical Positioning', in Long, O.G. (ed.), *Model Cities, Urban Best Practice*, Singapore, Urban Redevelopment Authority and The Institute of Policy Studies, pp. 104–16.

Joseph, R. (1997), 'Cranberry Bogs to Parks: Ethnography and the Women's History', *CRM Bulletin*, 20, pp. 20–24.

Larkham, P. (1996), *Conservation and the City*, London, Routledge.

Leeds, A. (1994), *Cities, Classes and the Social Order*, Ithaca, NY, Cornell University Press.

Low, S.M. (1987), 'Social Science Methods in Landscape Architecture', *Landscape Planning*, 8, pp. 137–48.

Low, S.M. (2002), 'Anthropological-Ethnographic methods for the Assessment of Cultural Values in Heritage Conservation', in de la Torre, M. (ed.), *Assessing the Values of Cultural Heritage*, Los Angeles, The J. Paul Getty Trust, The Getty Conservation Institute, pp. 31–51.

Lowental, D. (1979), 'Environmental Perception: Preserving the Past', *Progress in Human Geography*, 3, pp. 550–59.

Luxen, J.L. (2004), *Reflections on the Use of Heritage Charters and Convections*, Los Angeles, The J. Paul Getty Trust, The Getty Conservation Institute, pp. 4–10.

Mason, R. (2002), 'Assessing Values in Conservation Planning: Methodological Issues and Choices', in de la Torre, M., (ed) *Assessing the Values of Cultural Heritage*, Los Angeles, The J. Paul Getty Trust, The Getty Conservation Institute, pp. 5–31.

Meinig, D. (1979), *Interpretations of Ordinary Landscapes: Geographic Essays*, New York, Oxford University Press.

Mehrotra, R. (2000), 'Introduction', in *Historic Cities and Sacred Sites*, Washington, DC, The World Bank, pp. xi–xix.

O'Hare, D.J. (1997), *Tourism and Small Coastal Settlements: A Cultural Landscape Approach for Urban Design*, PhD thesis. Oxford Brookes University.

Orbasli, A. (2000), *Tourists in Historic Towns Urban Conservation and Heritage Management*, London, E. and F.N. Spon.

Ratna, N. (1994), 'A Conceptual Framework for the Renewal of Walled Cities in India', *Ekistics*, 368 and 369, Cambridge, Mass.

Punekar, A. S. (2000), *Urban Rehabilitation and Regeneration of Indian Historic Cities-Bijapur, a Case Study*, Unpublished MA Dissertation, Oxford, Joint Centre for Urban Design, Oxford Brookes University.

Serageldin, M. (2000), 'Preserving the Historic Urban Fabric in a Context of Fast-Paced Change', in Avrami, E., Mason, R. and de la Torre, M. (eds), *Values and Heritage Conservation*, Los Angeles, The J. Paul Getty Trust, The Getty Conservation Institute, pp. 51–59.

Singh, R. (1997), 'Sacredscape and Urban Heritage in India: Contestation and Perspective', in Shaw, B.J. and Jones, R. (eds), *Contested Urban Heritage, Voices from the Periphery*, Aldershot, Ashgate Publishing Company, pp. 101–32.

Teutonico, J.M. and Matero, F. (2003), *Managing Change: Sustainable Approaches to the Conservation of the Built Environment*, Los Angeles, The J. Paul Getty Trust, Getty Trust Publications.

Thapar, R. (1992), 'Tradition and Change', in Taylor, B.B. (ed.), *Raj Rewal*, India, Ahmedabad, pp. 21–24.

Thaper, B.K. (1989), 'Agencies for the Preservation of Cultural Heritage in India', in Allichin, B., Allichin, F.R. and Thaper, B.K. (eds), *Conservation of the Indian Heritage*, New Delhi, Cosmo Publications, pp. 164–68.

Throsby, D. (2002), 'Assessing the Values of Cultural Heritage: Cultural Capital and Sustainability Concepts in the Economics of Cultural Heritage', *Essays*, pp. 101–18.

Torre, M. and Mason, R (2002), 'Assessing Values in Conservation Planning: Methodological Issues and Choices', in de la Torre, M. (ed.) *Assessing the Values of Cultural Heritage*, Los Angeles, The J. Paul Getty Trust, The Getty Conservation Institute, pp. 3–5.

Tunbridge, J.E. and Ashworth, G.J. (1996), *Dissonant Heritage*, London, Wiley.

Tunbridge, J.E., Jones, R. and Shaw, B.J. (eds) (1996), 'Contested Heritage: Perth, 1995 Special Issue', *International Journal of Heritage Studies*, 2:1 and 2.

United Nations Conference on Environment and Development (1992), *agenda21*, Rio de Janeiro, Brazil, http://www.un.org/esa/sustdev/agenda21.htm.

Whalen, T.P. and Bouchenaki, M. (2004), *Partnerships: A Joint Issue with UNESCO*, Los Angeles, The J. Paul Getty Trust, The Getty Conservation Institute, editorial note.

Wolf, J.C. (1987), 'Martin Luther King Jr', *CRM Bulletin*, 10:1, pp. 12-13.

Zeisel, J. (1984), *Inquiry by Design: Tools for Environment-Behaviour Research*, Cambridge, Cambridge University Press.

Chapter 7

Urban Planning and Sustainability in South Africa

Koyi Mchunu

Introduction

This chapter examines the contradictory relationship between modern rational planning, the productive and transformation processes that accompany globalisation, and the sustainability discourse. The argument presented is that the 'will to plan' for spatial and social integration is occasioned by post-apartheid urban planning challenges in South Africa. These challenges have necessitated a shift towards Integrated Development Planning as articulated in the Integrated Development Plans (IDPs) since 1996. Although IDP's out of necessity deal with both substantive and procedural issues, post-apartheid urban planning (practice) has fallen prey to standardised concepts and formula, and to new dogma enshrined in legislation, manuals and government regulation (Harrison 2001: 79).

The chapter draws from the examples of two contemporary issues of increasing pertinence to urban spatial planning in South Africa: these are the impact of gated community developments, and the claim for space to practice initiation. These two examples represent new forms of fragmentation along class and ethnic lines respectively, in contradiction to the official policy of IDPs. However, both also relate to the ironic central role of state institutions, particularly in developing countries, in the provision of basic goods and services at a time when their capacity to act is increasingly being undercut by forces beyond their control. The chapter attempts to locate these issues within the broader discussions on environmental sustainability, the economic globalisation process and the persistence of modern planning practice. It also suggests that in both instances, the realities and limits of power tend to reduce both positions to oftentimes less desirable ends (Mabin and Smit 1997). Above all, these contradictions highlight the need for a more robust urban planning theory and practice that is more at ease with these contradictions than is presently the case.

Planning, Sustainability and Fragmentation

The macro-economic neo-liberalism of policy of growth, employment and economic redistribution (GEAR) in South Africa accentuated a shift towards a productive and profiteering motive of a commodifying and flexible accumulation process driven by global capitalism. Within the built environment, planning has served to facilitate this process of market penetration as exemplified by an increasingly marked shift towards consumption in the form of ubiquitous shopping atria and gated communities (Bremner 2002). As a result, the urban footprint is largely dictated by developers (Dewar 2000). Since both modern rational planning methods and global capital favour hierarchical and centralised decision-making processes, this does not augur well for sustainability not only because an array of people are excluded in the decision-making processes but also because it makes a mockery of and raises questions about the government's policy of integrated development planning.

Sustainable development suggests a conflict-free consensus around the urban development processes. Yet in the arena of urban development, the idea of universal acceptance is an exercise in futility because of inherent endemic conflicts of interests. Sustainability supports the promotion of participatory democratic decision-making processes both for procedural and substantive reasons. Decisions made in this manner are supposedly more conducive to translation into sustainable development programmes than a situation where groups of people are marginalised (see Watson 1998, 2002 for example). The universal appeal of sustainability within the context of the environment gives impetus for urban planning to continue to aspire for a universally acceptable planning model. This is particularly appealing to a nascent democracy characterised largely by endeavours at transcending these divisions both spatially and symbolically.

Current attempts at celebrating cultural diversity with the advent of democracy in 1994 are, rather ironically, also serving to reify fragmentation. Urban planners in South Africa are increasingly becoming more sensitised to the issues of difference and diversity as espoused mainly in the works of Sandercock (1998), Thomas and Krishnarayan (1994), Bollens (1998), and others. However, this foregrounding of difference and identity has also been criticised, among other issues, for creating moral pressure for group conformity, obscuring intra-group struggles and the sidelining of distributional issues in favour of misrecognition (Watson 2002: 44), and for contributing towards the very fragmentation upon which a mobile and flexible capital can feed on (Watson and Gibson 1995: 261). So, on the one hand is a marginalising and homogenising rational urban planning process of modern planning whose 'currency is valued because it supports the accumulation processes' (Handal, Chapter 3 in this volume). On the other hand is the reification of identity and difference upon which a mobile and flexible capital can feed on (Watson and Gibson 1995: 261).

Current Context of Urban Planning

Urban planning in South Africa takes place in the context of unprecedented social and political changes. Urban planners are at the forefront of trying to understand these changes and using that understanding to inform theory and practice. The profession is therefore largely still in a state of flux. There is therefore a sense in which urban planners are (still) making the road by walking it (Muller 1998).

Social challenges have to do with high levels of unemployment and poverty, the devastating HIV/AIDS epidemic, and increase in crime and concern for personal and property safety according to the Institute for Security Studies (ISS). Politically, the challenge has to do with the struggle to balance the need for a decentralised system of governance from national to municipal and eventually to the local level of neighbourhood/ward, with more centralised and hierarchical decision-making processes. The latter tends to be more favourable to the needs of government and vested interests. The economic challenges have to do with implications for the increased insertion of South Africa into the global economic arena, which marked a change in the macro-economic policy to the neo-liberalism of GEAR.

Since 1994, the professional challenge has had largely to do with the (hard to fault) grand and romantic endeavour of reconstructing a damaged society (Harrison 2001: 69). Concepts such as the compact cities approach, integrated development planning, sustainable development and participatory planning approaches have become common jargon in post-apartheid urban planning lexicon.

However, the application of these concepts has been fraught with problems partly due to the scale of the challenges at hand, the relative lack in the adequate level of experience and capacity at the 'coal face' of urban planning practice within the public sector, and the sheer contradictions that accompany planning practice. For example, consider the rise in the fragmenting efforts of securing, walling-off and cordoning streets and neighbourhoods from each other and the growing phenomenon of gated-communities, contrasted with the logic behind integrated development plans (IDP), which seek to achieve the exact opposite through major investment in public infrastructure to combat the same fragmentation and spatial separation of the apartheid past (see Landman 2000). The laudable suggestion for attempting to reconcile elements of a productive city, an inclusive city, sustainability and good governance, represent a rational ideal, a rhetoric divorced from the messy world that characterises planning practice. In reality, the elements of inclusivity and good governance are far too contentious and tend to lag far behind the element of a productive city. Meanwhile, the element of sustainability masks these contradictions and conflicts, at least in the urban development process.

According to Graham and Healey (1999: 641), the implications for planning practicioners consist in the following:

> Because the discourse community which clusters around planning practice has such a confused and limited conceptual vocabulary with which to describe what they are adjusting to, planners readily slip back into earlier conceptions, or slide away into the specifications thrust on them by the dominant circuits of power, with their emphases on sectoralised, producer-driven and largely aspatial conceptions of which relationships to consider.

It comes as no surprise therefore that urban planning processes in South Africa metamorphosed from the 'planned oppression' that characterised apartheid state urban planning into post-apartheid 'planned emancipation' (Mabin 1995). This 'will to plan' was somewhat toned down with introduction of the macro-economic neo-liberal policies of the growth, employment and redistribution (GEAR) in 1996. This had two implications for procedural planning. Firstly, there is the necessary but subjective and power-laden process of prioritisation, which inevitably means that other issues become tangential, disregarded, or deferred. The claim for space to practice initiation is a case in point. The issue was sidelined during apartheid urban planning (Mchunu 2005). During post-apartheid planning, the claim was indirectly forced into planners' radar screens as a result of issues that were worth considering but tangential to the spatial claim as will be argued later.

Secondly, there is the persistence of a sterile scientism that is concerned more with the exercise of a narrowly prescribed reason (Harrison 2001: 70), about which much has been written in urban planning literature. Baum (1996) and Hamdi et al. (1997) offer insights into the persistence of the rational planning model which provide valuable discerning views on the issue. Current normative urban planning theories, which compete to supplant modern rational urban planning theory and practice, although useful, are also not robust enough to address the complexities and often-contradictory world that characterise planning practice.

The Globalisation Processes and Urban Planning

Graham and Healey (1999: 632) have argued that 'globalisation seems to demand localisation in the favoured places of the emerging planetary urban system'. Cities therefore aspire to achieve the nebulous ideal of classification as one of these 'emerging planetary urban system(s)' of 'global cities', 'world-class cities', and 'successful cities'. In reality this has translated into the sanitised islands of prosperity in the form of Central Improvement Districts (CIDs) or Business Improvement Districts (BIDs) and Gated Communities (GCs) in the midst of a raging sea of general malaise characterised by rising unemployment, increasing inequality, poverty and declining health for the majority of citizens as alluded to earlier on. Clearly, this cannot be sustainable, at least in the manner in which the World Summit on Sustainable Development WSSD (held in South Africa in 2002) or WCED report (1987) intended. For postmodern neoliberal cities, 'driven by the twin engines of state penetration and corporate commodification' (Dear 1986), sustainability need to be defined in broad terms to encompass more than the physical environment.

Notwithstanding vested interests in the current dominant urban planning approach, the impact of economic globalisation is undermining efforts to develop and nurture robust alternative urban planning approaches in South Africa. This is largely as a result of the forms of production and transformation associated with global capitalism that are underpinned by both the macro-economic neo-liberal policies of GEAR and modern planning theory and practices based on the principle of a supposed universal rationality. This relationship between a globalising capital and modern urban planning coincides with the manifestation of two paradoxical phenomena.

Firstly, there has been a marked increase in the international phenomenon of gated communities (GCs) as a preferred form of lifestyle for the middle and upper classes. This is largely as a response to the perceived lack of personal safety and security for property (Schönteich 2002). Consequently, there has been a shift towards a relatively new form of spatial fragmentation along class lines and, as a result, the reinforcement of previous residential race segregation since the majority of GCs inhabitants' is predominantly from one racial group. This process is facilitated by the planning system and lubricated by market forces that play on these insecurities, real or imagined.

In South Africa, fear and perceived lack of security were cited as the main reasons behind the rising international phenomenon of gated communities (Landman 2000, 2002). This has partly contributed to the uncritical foregrounding of misrecognition and reification of difference. Normative theories that espouse this approach put emphasis on processes and consciousness (Beauregard 1998, cited in Watson 2002: 32), instead of outcomes and consequences. Ironically though, just processes do not necessarily lead to just outcomes (see Watson 2002, for example). The persistence of modern urban planning with its emphasis on hierarchical and centralist decision-making processes undermines procedural justice. In addition, foregrounding difference and identity has also come under criticism for being naïve about the ability for capital to feed on such fragmentation (Watson and Gibson 1995: 261).

Secondly, this relationship between global capital and modern planning represents yet another instance of the adaptability and dynamic nature of international capital. Urban planning is reduced to a commodity to be consumed during the accumulation process. Others have also pointed to the susceptibility for modern rational urban planning to manipulation (see for example Sandercock 1995, 1998, Yiftachel 1995; Flyvbjerg 1998), the so-called 'darker-side' or 'double-edged sword' of modern planning. There is therefore a sense in which the South African planning profession has still to come to terms with its past as Beauregard (1998) suggested whilst simultaneously forging for a new identity or identities in an arguably new context.

The combination between an increasingly globalising capital and an urban planning based on a supposedly universal rationality is more akin to a dialectic power relation. Capital and the government's macro-economic neo-liberal policy of growth, employment and redistribution (GEAR) serves to legitimise the need for a society run along rational lines as Harrison (2001) has argued, whilst the persistence of urban rational planning could be rationalised in terms of these broader processes they continue to serve and facilitate. The idea of planning as rationalisation has also been eloquently demonstrated by Flyvbjerg (1998, 2001).

So far the discussion has focused on the dialectic power relations between urban planning and the globalisation process. The next section brings the discussion full-circle by analysing the role of the sustainable development discourse as it relates to the developing world, and South African urban planning in particular, and the processes of transformation and production associated with economic globalisation.

Sustainable Development

The most recent World Summit on Sustainable Development (WSSD) was held in South Africa in 2002. More recently however, towards the end of February 2005, South Africa hosted a week long International Symposium on Gated Communities (GCs) wherein the very issue of sustainable development was the focus of some of the conference proceedings. The significance of these two events lies not only in South Africa's emerging profile as a major player in the region and continent, and relative influence in global politics. It also lies in the fact that the increasing international phenomenon of GCs raises important questions about sustainability as it relates to social justice and urban form.

This exploration of a sustainable city represents a logical extension of the quest for the ideal city, a quest that has captivated planners for centuries. The definition of an ideal city, the utopian ideal, has evolved with time. In the early twenty-first century, urban planners seek to understand how cities can enthral the senses as well as fulfil basic human needs while controlling and minimising the impact on the environment for the benefit of future generations. Sustainable development is therefore very much context dependent, long term and a work in progress. It is also the subject of much controversy concerning its interpretation and specific standards of application.

Sustainability also resonates well within the South African context because of the sprawling suburbia, mono-functional zoning, low-density development, and separated and fragmented urban landscape. These spatial characteristics exacerbate existing social inequities by concentrating poverty and unemployment, as well as limiting access to opportunities and amenities for the already marginalised and vulnerable groups. According to Landman (2000: 6), sustainability is important because of its integrative and holistic approach:

> In essence urban sustainability calls for a holistic and integrated approach towards city-making, considering not only the parts, but emphasizing their relationship to each other and importantly the sum total of the parts. Thus sustainability is concerned with the city as a whole, and this includes the city of today and tomorrow.

In the South African context, the principles of sustainable development are more encapsulated in the Integrated Development Plans (IDP) that all municipal governments are mandated by the Municipal Systems Act (2000) to prepare in order to access funds from central government for infrastructure, improvement of services and the delivery process. These are budget driven strategic plans upon which all developments within municipal areas are based. The plan is developed in consultation with the community stakeholders, provincial and national governments. It is also a plan that not only concentrates on the provision of fundamental municipal services, but in addition it seeks to eradicate poverty, boost local economic development, eradicate unemployment and promote the process of reconstruction and development. IDPs therefore address both the substantive and procedural aspects of planning.

IDPs propose an integrated planning and implementation framework for urban development, improving services and infrastructure, promoting urban economic development, creating institutions for delivery with emphasis on inter-sectoral collaboration, and the transformation of the public sector.

However, the universal acceptance of sustainability in the environment arena encourages clamour for an urban planning system with universal appeal. Yet in the arena of urban development, this idea of universal acceptance is futile not least because even within the environmental arena there is still no consensus around acceptable standards and differing interpretations (Reese 1988 cited in Marcuse 2005, McGranahan et al. 1996). Unlike in the environment arena, urban development processes involve the allocation of scarce resources and as such tend to be conflict-ridden. Yet sustainability evokes a nuance of procedural charm about it as an intrinsically good practice. In addition, the literal meaning of sustainability is the preservation of the status quo. No one interested in issues of social justice for example would like to see the status quo sustained in any form or shape. The following sections deal with the two issues of GCs and the claim for space to practice initiation as instances of fragmentation that undermine sustainability.

Sustainability and Fragmentation: Gated Communities

The increasing phenomenon of GCs in South Africa lies at the heart of sustainable development initiatives. Notwithstanding the validity of safety and security concerns that are cited as the primary catalyst for these developments and the role of the market in the form of developers who cater to this need, the spatial fragmentation they impose on the landscape is a moot point, more especially as it relates to issues of sustainability.

Figure 7.1   Entrance to a gated development in Johannesburg

Source: Landman 2000.

The GCs' spatial structure contradicts one of the centrepieces of post-apartheid legislation of IDPs. Security and safety concerns may be interpreted as masking a new form of exclusion and segregation along class as opposed to racial lines. Segregation in any form is a throwback to the apartheid-past.

The World Commission on Environment and Development report (1987) states that 'Sustainable development is development that meets the needs of the present without compromising the ability of future generations to meet their own needs'. This definition allows for opportunistic subjective interpretations of the term. Although the definition clearly puts a constraint on the appropriate means to be used in meeting our present needs, i.e. in a sustainable manner, the issue of conflicting standards leaves it open to various interpretations. In a market-driven economy, sustainability becomes easily intertwined with a question of market saturation, in this instance with GCs. An urban footprint that is largely determined by private developers (Dewar 2000) raises questions regarding the sustainability of that trajectory and the need for the current definition of sustainable development to be reformulated as suggested by McGranaham (1996). Marcuse (2005) proposes that sustainable development should be one of the constraints (together with issues of justice) whose absence may limit the usefulness of a good programme.

Sustainability and Fragmentation: Space to Practice Initiation

The claim for space to practice initiation predates post-apartheid urban planning (Mchunu 2005). These spaces were not provided when African townships were originally built with the result that any vacant ground sufficed, a situation which still largely persists. As pressure on urban land increases in order to provide more housing and amenities, the practice is marginalised, forced to survive on whatever patch of land is still within reach.

What finally brought the practice to the planning agendas of local government officials had less to do with the claim for space than with issues around health concerns emanating from botched circumcisions and environmental protection. Consequently, these aspatial elements of the claim overwhelmed the equally important spatial aspects of the practice (Mchunu 2005). It was no surprise therefore that the affected communities received the official spatial proposal with caution not least among the reasons being the highhanded manner in which the whole process of site selection and design of facilities was handled.

In Cape Town, the final design proposal called for a permanent facility to be located within the Delft Nature Reserve. Initiation, as currently practiced, was therefore deemed unsustainable, i.e., as far as access to urban land was concerned and the manner in which initiation was traditionally practiced.

This meant for example that, among other things, the traditional burning of temporary shelter after initiation would no longer be possible nor desirable within the confines of the reserve. This also meant that within the current official agendas for urban space, the claim was not top priority as compared to housing and related infrastructure.

Urban planners play a crucial role in ensuring that local expectations and needs are accommodated and articulated within the larger spatial frameworks of the city, and (should) 'proceed on the basis of a thorough understanding of the socio-spatial and political processes which shape the contexts in which we work' (Watson 2002:28). But ironically, it is during such processes of articulation by urban planners that community-driven planning initiatives tend to loose their emotive and imaginary content, oftentimes the 'emotive voice of the people are reduced to an inaccessible and technical language' (Harrison 2001: 80).

Sustainability in this case was defined in terms of access to the dwindling vacant spaces, and the unacceptable (read unnatural/polluting) building materials used for constructing temporary huts (cardboards, plastics), and the unacceptable burning of temporary shelters. This amounts to the sheer opportunism that Marcuse (2005) has pointed out. I have in mind a different approach, which consists in facilitating access to natural building materials and designating certain spaces as permanent initiation sites.

The practicability of initiation therefore depended on submission to scrutiny under the gaze of environment and health regulations. As McGranahan (1996) pointed out, the environmental concerns of the more disadvantaged urban dwellers are not issues of sustainability, narrowly defined. The practice has demonstrated its resilience over decades of spatial misrecognition and marginalisation by urban planning. In spite of this, it has so far been successful in 'carving its mark' into the deeply contested fabric of the urban landscape. This belated endeavour at spatial intervention under the rubric of the environment risks turning the facilities into a white elephant as some of the affected communities threatened not to use the facility (Mchunu 2005).

Concluding Remarks

Harrison (2001) has pointed out that the objectives of post-apartheid planning are generally good and progressive. Whilst this sentiment is shared, the latter part of the 1990's has witnessed a plethora of academic literature expressing a sense of foreboding (Watson 2002, 1998, Harrison 2001, Mabin 1995, 1998, Oranje 2001 and Muller 1998). The optimism of the early 1990s is being overshadowed by the unforgiving realities of the negotiated and contested arena of planning practice that has reduced planning outcomes to less desirable ends.

Whilst a sense of vigilance may be called for by planners in terms of how tools in our arsenal may be susceptible to manipulation towards unintended consequences, it is rarely acknowledged enough that urban planners are not a monolith as Baum (1996) has eloquently articulated. Whilst there may be vested interests towards the maintenance of the status quo, there is also an imperative for urban planners to seriously reflect on the impact of the processes of economic globalisation, particularly as it is implicated in the resurgence of local politics of identity, in part as a response to the impersonal and homogenising forces it engenders and also as a result of the democratic wave currently in vogue.

Though it is hard to fault the current preoccupation with certain idealised urban forms in South African urban planning, given the context of continuing fragmentation and sprawling nature of the cities these need to be interpreted taking into consideration the plurality and cultural diversity of the local context instead of their supposedly intrinsic good qualities.

Urban planning processes are complex and oftentimes contradictory. For example, the decentralisation of central government responsibility and resources is driven as much by fiscal austerity as it is by a desire for a more accountable and effective service delivery system. Environmental issues are also deeply intertwined with the quintessential consumerism in the form of tourism under the portfolio of the Minister of Environmental Affairs and Tourism. These are some of the contradictions that characterise neo-liberal, post-modern cities. Sustainability is therefore not enough as Marcuse (2005) has pointed out, unless it takes into consideration some of the contradictions that accompany planning practice.

References

Beauregard, R. (1998), 'Subversive Histories: Texts from South Africa', in L. Sandercock (ed.), *Making the Invisible Visible*, Berkeley, University of California Press, pp. 184–97.

Bollens, S. (1998), *Urban-Peace Building in Divided Societies: Belfast and Johannesburg*, Boulder CO, Westview Press.

Bremner, L. (2000), *On Narrow Ground: Urban Policy and Ethnic Conflict in Jerusalem and Belfast*, Albany, State University of New York Press.

Bremner, L. (2002), *Johannesburg: One City, Colliding Worlds, Johannesburg*, STE Publishers.

Dewar, D. (2000), 'The Relevance of the Compact City Approach: The Management of Urban Growth in South African Cities', in Jenks, M. and Burgess, R. (eds), *Compact Cities: Sustainability and Urban Form in Developing Countries*, London, E. and F.N. Spon.

Flyvbjerg, B. (1998), *Rationality and Power: Democracy in Practice*, Chicago IL, University of Chicago Press.

Flyvbjerg, B. (2001), *Making Social Science Matter: Why Social Science Fails and How it Can Succeed Again*, Cambridge, Cambridge University Press.

Friedman, J. (2001), 'Intercity Networks in a Globalizing Era', in Scott, A.J. (ed.), *Global City-regions: Trends, Theory and Policy*, New York, Oxford University Press, pp. 119–38.

Graham, S. and Healey, P. (1999), 'Relational Concepts of Space and Place: Issues for Planning Theory and Practice', *European Planning Studies*, 7:5, pp. 623–43.

Hamdi, N. and Goethert, R. (1997), *Action Planning For Cities: A Guide to Community Practice*, Chichester, John Wiley.

Harrison, P. (2001), 'Romance and Tragedy in (Post) Modern Planning: A Pragmatist Perspective', *International Planning Studies*, 6:1, pp. 69–81.

Integrated Development Plan, Cape Town 2004/2005, www.capetown.org.za/idp/default. asp.

Landman, K. (2000) 'Gated Communities and Urban Sustainability: Taking a Closer Look', paper presented at the *2nd Southern African Conference on Sustainable Development in the Built Environment*, 'Strategies for a Sustainable Built Environment', 23–25 August 2000, Pretoria, South Africa.

Landman, K. (2002), 'Planning in the African Context: Reconsidering Current Approaches to Gated Communities in South Africa', paper presented at the *Planning Africa 2002: Regenerating Africa through Planning Conference*, Durban, 18–20 September 2002.

Mabin, A. and Smith, D. (1997), 'Reconstructing South Africa's Cities? The Making of Urban Planning 1900–2000', *Planning Perspectives*, 12, pp. 193–223.

Mail and *Guardian* online, 3 May 2005.

Marcuse, P. (2005), 'Sustainability is not Enough', *Environment and Urbanization*, 10:2 pp. 103–11.

McGranahan, G., Songsore, J. and Kjellén, M. (1996), 'Sustainability, Poverty and Urban Environmental Transitions', in Pugh, C. (ed.), *Sustainability, the Environment and Urbanisation*, London, Earthscan, pp. 103–34.

Mchunu, K. (2005), 'Claiming Space in Cape Town', unpublished PhD thesis, Oxford Brookes University Department of Planning.

Muller, J. (1998), 'Paradigms in Planning Practice: Conceptual and Contextual Considerations', *International Planning Studies*, 3:3, pp. 287–302.

Rees, W. (1988), 'A Role for Environmental Impact Assessment in Achieving Sustainable Development', *Environmental Impact Assessment Review*, 8, p. 279.

Sandercock, L. (1998), *Towards Cosmopolis: Planning for Multicultural Cities*, Chichester, John Wiley.

Schönteich, M. (2002), 'Crime Levels in South Africa, its Provinces and Cities', http://www.gatedcomsa.co.za/crime.htm.

South African Cities Network (2005).

Thomas, H. and Krishnarayan, V. (eds) (1994), *Race Equality and Planning: Policies and Procedures*, Aldershot, Avebury.

World Commission on Environment Development (WCED) (1987), *Our Common Future*, G.H. Brundtland, Oxford, Oxford University Press.

Watson, S. and Gibson, K. (eds) (1995), 'Postmodern Politics and Planning: A Postscript', in *Postmodern Cities and Spaces*, Oxford, Blackwell, pp. 254–64.

Watson, V. (1998), 'Planning under Political Transition – Lessons from Cape Town's Metropolitan Planning Forum', *International Planning Studies*, 3:3, pp. 335–50.

Watson, V. (2002), 'The Usefulness of Normative Planning Theories in the Context of Sub-Saharan Africa', *Planning Theory*, 1:1, pp. 27–52.

Yiftachel, O. (1995), 'The Dark Side of Modernism: Planning as Control of an Ethnic Minority', in Watson, S. and Gibson, K. (eds), *Postmodern Cities and Spaces*, Oxford, Blackwell, pp. 216–42.

PART II
Designing People-based Environments

Chapter 8

Urban Reform and Development Regulation: The Case of Belém, Brazil

Jose Julio Lima

Introduction

From the beginning of sustainability concerns in the 1980s, equity in the distribution of the benefits of urbanisation was recognised as a principle to guide the enhancement of the quality of human life. Social equity and social justice are interchangeable terms, used to refer to fairness in the distribution of benefits to all social groups (Harvey 1973, Young 1990, Blalock 1991). Within the sustainable development debate, there is the proposition that equity is a natural consequence of economic growth, which, once achieved, can automatically enhance quality of life, regardless of differences between social groups (applied as intergenerational equity by WCED 1987). Opponents of that proposition argue that economic growth is inadequate by itself to deliver improvements through an equal distribution of benefits in developing countries (Trainer 1990, Turner et al. 1994, Burgess et al. 1997). There, deliberate distribution of infrastructure and services to minimise socio-spatial segregation in the city and thus enhance social equity is needed. In discussing urban policies, the importance of social equity seems crucial in Brazil, in order to minimise the effects of acute socio-economic differences by reverting expenditure priorities.

The concept of social equity in the sustainable development debate has been used to support environmental sustainability principles (in Haughton 1999, social justice is related to environmental justice). It is argued that social equity presupposes a proportional distribution of the benefit of improvements to urban layout and infrastructure to disadvantaged groups with a consequential enhancement of environmental quality. There are claims that less advantaged groups do not cause much environmental degradation, since they are responsible for less consumption of CO_2 and in some cases are involved in recycling (Hardoy et al. 1992).

The applicability of the theoretical discussion of social equity within sustainable development in cities has been discussed in developed countries. There, the discussion has concentrated on the form of the city and, in particular, about which degree of compactness can be a means of delivering some of the advantages of sustainable development, including social equity (Breheny 1992, Jenks et al. 1996). In developing countries like in Brazil, the focus of sustainable development concerns has been on environmental aspects and politics for regional development (Becker 1997), without much attention to possible links between urban form and social equity. This chapter analyses urban policies in order to identify possible relationships between the concept of social equity and the contents of plans and inquires about its applicability in the city.

Social Equity in the Sustainable Development Debate and Urban Reform in Brazil

The emergence and consolidation of the sustainable development debate in the world coincided with the end of military dictatorship in Brazil in the 1980s. At the same time as the sustainable development debate grew in importance and issues such as environmental sustainability and social equity were included in development, a re-democratisation process was triggered by the first non-military president in 20 years and direct elections for major positions in central and local governments. After 20 years in which citizens' political rights were limited by central and local governments controlled by military forces, re-democratisation began. As part of this process, calls for urban reform culminated with the inclusion of urban non-governmental organisations proposed in the 1988 Brazilian Federal constitution (Bittar and Coelho 1994, IPPUR/FASE 1994, Ribeiro 1994).

For the first time, a Brazilian constitution contained a chapter on urban policy and urban reform. Under its clauses, every city with more than twenty thousand inhabitants must have a masterplan (or *plano diretor*, singular and *planos diretores*, plural; hereafter used in Portuguese in this chapter) drawn up by local government with the direct participation of citizens. It must contain spatial and social objectives to guide the development of the city. This signals an attempt to redirect urban policy at the level of local institutions through the more democratic participation of private agents. In every city, the *planos diretores* ought to address what was called in the constitution the 'social function of the city and of property' (articles 182 and 183 of the 1988 Brazilian Federal constitution) (Brasil 1989).

In practical terms, 'social function' conveys the meaning of an attempt to establish a balance between economic uses of urban land and a fairer distribution of the benefits of urbanisation through attention to social justice. Mechanisms, mainly for controlling land speculation and provision of infrastructure and to secure housing for the poor, were incorporated in the *planos diretores*. Each municipality was made responsible for defining in specific terms how the *plano diretor* would be applied in parallel with other mechanisms, such as ordinances for occupation patterns and zoning laws (Campos Filho 1989).

The main aspect of *planos diretores* considered here is that they are supposed to embody the social function of the city and of property. Interpretation of such concepts has challenged several municipalities. The task of defining them in housing and urban development policies, such as infrastructure provision and in practical decision-making, is not easy; there are problems with the implementation of urban policies at the local level which stem from the power of interests and the physical constraints which occur in every city. The master plan idea is central to the assumption that cities in developing countries should search for their own solutions; many commentators maintain that there should be no preconceived solutions (Devas and Rakodi 1993).

The Contents and Objectives of Urban Policies in *Planos Diretores*

Urban policies in Brazil take different forms; they appear as planning guidelines in *planos diretores*, transport plans, and urban regulations, mainly land use zoning and land parcelling. This section discusses the contents of *planos diretores* and urban regulations, called non-fiscal instruments, for Belém in the last three decades (Figure 8.1).

Planos diretores are comprehensive city-wide strategic plans and are the main regulatory instruments setting out spatial determinants and social objectives to be achieved through urban public policies, including housing, infrastructure and services provision. Together with land use and parcelling, they are the instruments for urban regulation in Brazilian cities and the responsibility of local government.

Planning level	Instruments
Structure plans	*Planos diretores* (masterplans) and transport plans
Urban regulations	*Lei de uso do solo* (land use laws)
	Lei de parcelamento do solo (land parcelling laws)

Figure 8.1   Principal local level planning documents in Brazil

The time scale for this investigation includes plans and documents from the 1970s, when the origins of urban regulations were formed, to the 1990s, when initiatives incorporating social objectives in urban policy became part of urban reform. The focus of analysis of the objectives of *planos diretores* is on how social objectives have been related to propositions for spatial organisation. *Planos diretores* aim at guiding public and private investment at the local level to create conditions to facilitate socio-economic development through a spatial organisation of the city, by, for example, job-creation, by setting aside areas for industrial development and infrastructure provision, and associate regulations.

Development Plan for Greater Belém, 1975

The first comprehensive plan for the development of the Belém metropolitan region was drawn up between 1973 and 1975. It is called Development Plan for the Greater Belém (or *Plano de Desenvolvimento da Grande Belém,* hereafter PDGB) (Companhia de Desenvolvimento e Administração da Área Metropolitana de Belém et al. 1975). The PDGB can be considered a plan typical of the 1970s in Brazil. Its contents follow what the Federal Service of Housing and Urbanism (*Serviço Federal de Habitação e Urbanismo* or SERFHAU) set out in terms of methodology and means of implementation. This first plan was a plan of general principles; its objectives 'recognise and indicate guidelines for the development of Belém Metropolitan region. In fact the plan did not set up welfare and transport policies. Instead, it set up a spatial structure based on zoning' (CODEM et al. 1975: 55) and urban projects for the improvement of certain areas of the city. The objectives of urban projects are related to encouragement of historical heritage protection and work for improvement of the design of open spaces in the centre of the city.

The PDGB was influenced by central government urban strategies set out in the 1960s to consolidate the power of military dictatorship (Valença 1999). SERFHAU and the National Housing Bank (*Banco Nacional da Habitação* or hereafter the BNH) were created in 1964, the first aiming to give guidance to municipalities for urban planning, and the second to implement a federal housing policy in states and municipalities. Later, in the beginning of the 1970s, nine metropolitan regions were created through legislation (Law no. 14 08/06/73 and Law no. 20 20/03/74) and *planos diretores* aimed to guide the development of urban areas in the nine metropolitan regions – São Paulo, Rio de Janeiro, Belo Horizonte, Recife, Porto Alegre, Salvador, Florianópolis, Curitiba and Belém, the smallest one, with just two municipalities. Since then, influences of changes in theoretical perspective of the relationship between space (urban form) and socio-economic development can be perceived in the contents and implementation of the plans and urban regulations.

The theory behind SERFHAU was that the development of urban areas would be achieved through economic measures, such as job creation and coherent land use distribution, influencing the organisation of the territory of metropolitan regions. *Planos diretores* were responsible for applying an 'urban development strategy' in the country, based on social housing and urban policies set up by SERFHAU and BNH. At that time, urban development strategy was 'functionalist'; land use could be organised, like the planned new towns, to achieve 'coherent' urban development.

The PDGB set up the first zoning scheme to guide the occupation of the Belém metropolitan region. The scheme depended entirely on the implementation of the road network proposed in the same plan; as it contained no consideration of the existing road layout, the zones identified do not correspond to any existing feature of the urban form, such as block layout or open spaces. Residential zones were classified according to the population density that should be housed in each of them. The criteria for the occupation of plots in mixed use zones were based on the size of the buildings to house commercial developments and services. The densities set up for each zone by the PDGB take for granted that there should be a gradation between the high income areas and the poor areas, the first associated with higher densities (to be obtained through high rise housing types) and the second with lower densities.

It is important to note the creation of Exclusive Residential Zones in the city. The PDGB stated that:

In the expansion area of Belém two areas are identified with potential for [exclusive residential] use. One of them is located on the surroundings of Bolonha Lake, aiming to avoid occupation of this area by other uses incompatible with the preservation of that water resource, as is currently happening. Invasion of a portion of the area by a low income population (Guanabara housing area), without the means to implement needed sanitary services, can cause pollution to the water of the lake, due to sewage infiltration. It is more appropriate to make the occupation of this area by higher income families, with the ability to pay for the required sanitary treatment, which would not cause that problem. So there are more advantages for COSANPA (the water provision state company) to allow parcelling for a population of better income, establishing the required sanitary care, than to prohibit its occupation and yet not to have the ability to control its invasion (CODEM et al. 1975: 134, author's translation).

The other area is on the surrounding of Azul Lake, where there is already a private high income dwellers' land parcelling housing scheme.

This passage is important in identifying that the PDBG wished to promote locational advantages through its zoning policy. The construction of high income housing developments was a condition of maintaining the quality of the main water resource of the city. The construction of the housing units with their own sanitary facilities, however, does not guarantee adequate sanitary conditions, because government actions should have followed, implementing public services only for the beneficiaries who occupy that zone, which did not happen.

The implementation of the first *plano diretor* coincided with the introduction by law of the metropolitan region government in Belém, when the military dictatorship reached its most rigid phase in the first years of the 1970s. The effects of SERFHAU and BNH are best described as in opposition. While the first established guidelines for urban development, based on delivery of infrastructure, with the aim of urban consolidation, the second imposed housing policies based on the construction of mass housing in areas with difficult accessibility and no infrastructure. BNH funded the construction of *conjuntos habitacionais* which were against SERFHAU's proposed strategies to organise the space of the cities, in particular the peripheries of municipalities of the metropolitan regions.

Metropolitan Structural Plan, 1980

The second plan set up for the Belém metropolitan region in 1980 was called the Metropolitan Structural Plan (*Plano de Estruturação Metropolitana* or hereafter PEM). The PEM drew up policies to develop the local economy through strategies for distribution of population and jobs, which were to be created throughout the whole Metropolitan region, although, once more, this was to be achieved simply by setting aside land for industrial development. In the methodology of PEM, use of Castells' approach (Castells 1977) to analyse the organisation of an urban system in advanced capitalist societies is explicit. It attempts to 'identify the behaviour [of capital] and its relationships as a result of the needs of the economic system and also to include the excluded portion of the population' (Geotécnica et al. 1980: 42). In the PEM, the spatial dimension depends on identification of a system of values in the social structure, organised in terms of the function of mode of production. The use of Castells' approach to the nature of the urban space served as a guide to set out policies, dividing urban space into the elements which, according to Marxism, constitute the urban system. Each element, according to this theory is formed by activities and spaces responsible for production (of products in the material sense) including industrial activities; consumption is organised including housing; exchange, including retail and services, and also the relationships between production and consumption through road and transport networks. Management was the term used to refer to urban regulations set out by metropolitan, state and local institutions.

The spatial strategies of the PEM consisted of setting out guidelines for the distribution of population and jobs within the territory of the metropolitan region. The metropolitan spatial structure set up in the PEM was to be achieved by macro zoning, consisting of:

- dense residential areas to be located in the city's main core, where there was sufficient infrastructure, and non-dense residential areas in low-income areas of the city's main core and the periphery;
- centres for service and commerce are sub centres set up to decentralise activities from the city centre;
- industrial uses are to be located on the coast and in designated industrial districts;
- environmental protection should be achieved through setting up parks of different sizes and located on areas with remaining natural flora and fauna.

The spatial structure set up by the PEM to implement its development policy came from a more sophisticated methodology than that used in PDGB. A mathematical model based on a model by Lowry developed for North American cities in the 1960s (for a description of the original model see Batty 1976) produced a complex system of 'urban models' of land occupation, with a set of indices for building and land parcelling, based on a land use zoning scheme. Lowry's original model had to undergo some adaptations for use in a city of a developing country. The original model is based on use of the calculation of attraction forces within each zone to determine location of population and services, taking into consideration accessibility to work and shopping. It assumed that the majority of families choose their living place near their jobs. In developing countries, other factors such as land prices have to be considered. Due to income constraints, land prices are more decisive on choice of living place for the majority of the population. Accordingly, living place options for low-income populations are as follows:

- areas with low market values, determined either by location further from the centre or being without infrastructure or in areas with unfavourable features such as water-logging and/or on hillsides;
- areas subject to illegal invasions, vacant sites, or unfinished housing schemes;
- illegally parcelled areas (or *loteamentos clandestinos* in Portuguese) which do not meet legal official requirements, and so may not be permanent.

The model defined parameters by which to distribute populations of each income class and jobs in different zones in Belém Metropolitan Region. Coherent distribution of land uses was to be achieved through a transport network linked to an existing road network linking the zones. The model's results were transformed into urban indices to control occupation in each zone and thus to implement the objectives of the plan through land use proposed distribution and parameters for land parcelling and building typologies. Accordingly, each zone of the city was supposed to be occupied by a given number of dwellings which permitted a certain prescribed density of housing. Other land uses, such as for retail and services, were permitted according to their importance in generating the required number of jobs.

Criteria for distributing population and employment within the territory were the projected densities of land use zones. Guidelines also indicated the size and characteristics of built up areas within them and a transport network based on a road hierarchy network and urban land use zones at a micro scale, later to be implemented through urban zoning and occupation patterns, identified according to housing densities. This formed a detailed land use scheme to implement the PEM's metropolitan structural principles.

Zoning consisted of marking residential zones set up for use for urban and urban expansion areas already occupied. The main aspects of the land use scheme were:

- Limits for construction were set up according to land use. Mixed land use zones to house high density developments were located in city sub-centres.
- Environmental protection was included as part of zoning.
- The main novel characteristic of the urban zoning scheme of the PEM was the creation of zones of mixed use in the areas identified by the plan for sub-centres.
- A road network covered all Belém's periphery and established a system of main roads and local roads linking pockets of existing social housing developments.

The occupation density of the zones was set according to the model of land use, and established high densities for areas located along the main axes and around sub centres formed by mixed use. And a certain 'hesitation' to organise the periphery is apparent in the land use zoning scheme, according to which the expansion of the urban periphery would follow existing axes. The main axis on the periphery was to organise the zones' boundaries. It is also important to highlight two features for the periphery: the creation of a green belt and areas for environmental preservation, located on the edge of the metropolitan region.

The PEM zoning follows the same principles as the PDGB. There is a clear separation between residential zones and sub centres (one of the main principles of spatial organisation of the plan). The differentiation of zones depended on the models of occupation for the plots in each zone. On the periphery, the main axis, as in the PDGB, gave a structural impetus to the creation of sub centres; at the same time the maintenance of institutional uses was included in the plan.

The mathematically measurable outputs of the PEM continued the trend of the zoning law of 1979. Like it, PEM prescribed densities and indices for building regulations which became decisive for the real estate market. Restrictions on the construction of high rise buildings rather than on land uses became, for a time, the only aspect of the PEM considered by planners and developers. Floor area ratios became the main element for achieving the density parameters set out in the zone location.

The contents of the PEM reveal that there was concern for social equity to be achieved through the urban structure. It is found in the methodology employed and in the mechanisms of distribution of transport infrastructure, which aimed to provide the periphery with the same standards as the centre of the city. The means of implementing the plan, however, show a function-based approach for development control which seems contradictory to the social aspects of the plan. During the implementation of the plan, problems caused by lack of political alignment between state and prefecture emphasised the bureaucratic aspects of the plan and compromised its efficacy.

Belém Urban Masterplan, 1993

By 1996, five of the nine metropolitan regions had new *planos diretores*. These were the cities of Belém, Fortaleza, Recife, Belo Horizonte and Salvador, where the emphasis of newly elected authorities in 1993 has been on their implementation and on other legal instruments such as progressive property taxation on unoccupied and thus speculative land use and direct participation in local government decision-making. The challenge was to rethink how existing institutional bureaucracy could be altered to include new social objectives in traditional instruments of land use control and management. Claims by NGOs, scholars and departments of government indicate the need to integrate central government urban development policies with local government management actions. The legal framework and administrative schemes in the 1988 constitution depend on land use and parcelling regulations and the effect of the property taxation system on the ability of local authority management to use income constructively for effective performance.

Belém Urban Masterplan (or *Plano Diretor Urbano de Belém*, hereafter PDU) is the third and the most recent plan for Belém. It was promulgated as a municipal law (Municipal Law no. 7,603 13/01/93) in January 1993. The PDU designed policies to promote the social function of the city, and of property, as urban planning should do under the 1988 constitution. The plan established its definition of social function of the city and of property in article number 140 as follows:

> Article 140 – Urban property fulfils its social function when it guarantees [to dwellers] that it will meet their fundamental social requirements by the city's structure, searching for equity in access to goods and public services, as expressed in the *Plano Diretor*, [with the condition that] government actions to the benefit of the city are carried out [in the property] and it does not become a means to yield speculative real estate gains from public investment.
>
> Paragraph 1. The activities with urban impact are those inherent in the social functions of the city and collective well being, including
> * housing

- production of goods and services
- provision of services
- circulation of people, vehicles and goods
- preservation of historic, cultural, environmental and landscape heritage
- safety
- preservation of resources needed for good urban living conditions, such as mangrove swamps, forests, trees, rivers and streams, and the coast.

Paragraph 2. Urban owners shall give back, according to the terms of this law, real estate gains yielded by public investment (Prefeitura de Belém 1993: 21, author's translation).

The PDU is the culmination of trends of thought about spatial structure in previous plans, and sets out alternative social instruments to fulfil social needs under the new constitution. For improved equity in the city, the plan identified strategies to tackle real estate speculation through alterations to property rights in areas with acceptable infrastructure and to re-direct investment priorities to poor areas. The PDU indicates physical and institutional developments needed to achieve a better balance in the city in terms of social function and development. It was the first time that physical determinants for the design of *barrios* were connected with social functions in terms of housing and environmental quality (Prefeitura Municipal de Belém 1993).

A solution for socio-economic and urban spatial problems advocated by the PEM and the PDU was deconcentration of retail activities and services from the city centre to the periphery. Job-creation policies are also recommended with zoning and transport coordinated to create new centres for services beyond the limits of the city's main core. Urban policies, also set out in the plans, should be incorporated into the management of the city. The assumptions about urban development in the plans take for granted that a state and market coalition will continue the same pattern of development that has created urban problems: city core concentration of commercial development and services and shortage of housing units (IPEA 1997). The need for land use decentralisation became, after the PEM, widely accepted, and also recommended in later transport plans and regulations.

At the beginning of the 1990s, when the PDU was set up, the city inevitably needed policies for upgrading sites and services. Function-oriented ideas for decentralisation of land use from the city centre were not the main aspect of the plan. Under the new constitution, development regulations were required to take into account the social function of the city, and provide a better balance between the areas with infrastructure and public and private investments. This divided planners and others called by the municipality to design the PDU; there were 'traditional' planners who did not take part in arranging the popular participation demanded by the constitution, and those who considered this the most important aspect of the plan and neglected functional aspects of zoning.

The land use zoning and transport organisation schemes of the PDU are entirely committed to making the city fulfil its social function through reducing real estate speculation, and a housing policy to guide local government actions in housing provision and control of land uses and designating built-up areas. At the beginning of the 1990s when the plan was drawn up, Belém was characterised by high rise buildings in the city centre and an accelerated expansion of its periphery. The land use and density scheme set out for the city, in the PDU, does not alter the existing trends. Its innovative aspect is the priority given to consolidating illegal occupation on the periphery by upgrading services. Funding was to be raised by selling building rights for providing infrastructure and social housing in socially deprived areas. The mechanisms for money raising are fiscally-based and aim to 'add' social concerns to traditional land use zoning.

In 1998, land use and land parcelling laws set out in 1988 under the PEM's land use zoning scheme were still in force, although undergoing alterations to incorporate principles outlined in the *plano diretor* of 1993. The regulations of 1988 were not invalid under the PDU; on the contrary, 1988 zoning was considered the basis for the spatial structure it set up. Building and land use regulations had to be adapted to help enforcement of 'additional' zonings based on social objectives of the PDU's housing policy. These additional zonings classified zones in accordance with use and proposed densities for each district of the city and for supporting mechanisms for the city and property, to enable them to fulfil their social function. For that purpose, the plan created financial mechanisms to fund upgrading projects and set guidelines for drawing up neighbourhood plans. The financial mechanisms consist first of 'selling' building rights (known as *solo criado*, which means created land) in areas where there is enough infrastructure to accommodate an increase in density. The areas to have this increase in building rights are located in the city centre and along the main axis on the periphery. Second, money to be raised from this mechanism should be spent on the urbanisation of Zones of Special Social Need (*Zonas Especiais de Interesse Social* or hereafter ZEIS). ZEIS, poor districts located in the water-logged areas of the city centre and in illegal occupations on the periphery, were transformed into special zones. That is, the scheme has a mix of financial and spatial policies.

The PDU asserts that the total buildable area permitted for developers is determined by the existing infrastructure capacity in the zone where the development is proposed. The plan holds that the infrastructure imposes limits on the total buildable area as do the capacity of the public transport network and the road network. The two networks, in their turn, provide the conditions for Floor Area Ratios (FAR) in different areas of the city. Total buildable area is established by the sum of the floor area permitted by a 'basic FAR' (incorporated in land use zoning), plus 'created land' (i.e. 'extra' area to be 'sold', under an additional zoning regulation, in areas of the city with higher standards of transport and road conditions). Purchase of 'created land' is regulated by conditions in the zoning law. The PDU also established that in order to avoid giving privileges to landowners and the real estate sector, urban legislation should establish in each zone a potential buildable area, higher than the actual limit of extra floor area to be sold. The PDU established ZEIS to where local government infrastructure improvements and housing should be first directed. They are poor areas without acceptable infrastructure.

The principle was to establish criteria for increasing the quality of the urban environment by meeting socially-orientated demands for infrastructure and services

(Prefeitura Municipal de Belém, 1993). This was done during the drawing up of the *plano diretor*, and was the result of public participation in the *plano diretor*. For the time being, the expected upgrading actions contained in the ZEIS as set up in the *plano diretor* are not to proceed. Neighbourhood plans are to be drawn up by the district authority, and should be implemented in different portions of the city. Thus, on the one hand, expectations of upgrading actions resulting from local government expenditure from an 'urban fund', financed by selling created soil in areas with infrastructure (part of a compensation mechanism), have appeared among local communities. On the other, the plans for the ZEIS, or neighbourhood plans, are seen by local authority managers to contain a potential for enforcement of ordinances as well as upgrading actions.

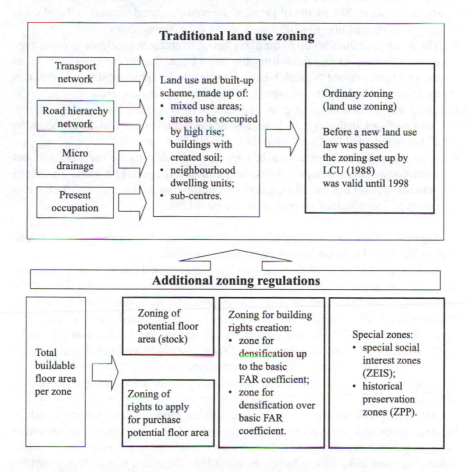

Figure 8.2   Traditional land use zoning and additional schemes in PDU

Source: Prefeitura Municipal de Belém, 1993.

Conclusion: Intended Effects of Development Control and Social Equity

The distribution of social groups in the city and the ability of this distribution to create a just urban structure depend partly on the direct interference of the state through housing programmes and partly on the indirect regulation, through the study and definitions of parameters for settlement densification and configuration. Investigation of the plan contents permitted identification of how the ideas about their intended distributional effects, explicitly the concept of bringing about social equity, could be implemented.

The diverse spatial strategies have in common the following aims:

- Concentrated decentralised development for urban peripheral expansion, based on a metropolitan scale of development which was assumed to be suitable for the urban scale. The model of peripheral development advocated in the plans is argued to be the only possible model, given the circumstances.
- The zoning schemes set up in the plans aimed to create sub-centres to encourage decentralisation of activities from the city centre. The occupation patterns in the city were defined through higher densities, to be achieved through high rise buildings for higher income areas, and low densities in poor areas.
- Land distribution according to land use, density zoning and road hierarchy, 'imposed' on existing layouts in order to achieve sub-centres and decentralisation of non-residential land uses from the city centre.
- A functional hierarchy of roads to be imposed on the existing road network, without much consideration of the existing configuration of the grid. This hierarchical road network was set out with the objective of improving the bus network in the city centre and to integrate the pockets of the periphery.

Figure 8.3 shows a summary of policy content according to the plans described in the chapter and their objectives and spatial strategies.

Investigation of *plano diretor* contents has demonstrated that the manipulation of urban form according to spatial strategies is the envisaged means of implementing the objectives of social justice in the plans. The emphasis on spatial issues in the plans was higher before 1988, revealing that social issues were implicit and scarcely considered by government. PDGB, the first plan analysed, had no explicit reference to social equity in the distribution of infrastructure. Yet social objectives were implicit. Until 1988, *planos diretores* were nothing but bureaucratic tools for guiding implementation of urban planning, based on physical assumptions, to assist economic improvement of urban areas.

All three plans set out for Belém had similar approaches to the relationships between space and socio-economic development. Their assumptions about socio-economic development are based on their view of economic relations in urban space. The main difference between the plans is in the extent to which they assume that their proposed spatial strategies will translate into the means of solving urban problems and promote economic development. The PDGB, at the beginning of the 1970s, the PEM at the end of 1970s and the PDU in the 1990s show that the city

Contents	Policy objectives	(Spatial) means of implementation
• Policies for socio-economic development through job-creation and infrastructure provision. ○ Measures for spatial organisation through control of land use distribution and provision of public transport.	• To promote location of jobs in the periphery. • To encourage compatibility of land uses with socio economic development. • Formal occupation with compatible land uses and densities in accordance with infrastructure levels. • Compliance with prescribed health, education, employment and environmental standards. • Just urban structures in the sense that land use distribution facilitates access of all residents to infrastructure and services. • To promote equal access to services in new developments.	• Land uses distribution according to zoning and road hierarchy 'imposed' on existing layouts in order to achieve concentrated decentralisation through: ○ Creation of sub-centres and decentralisation of land uses from the city centre. ○ Expansion of the urban periphery with infrastructure provision and expansion of housing.

Figure 8.3 Summary of *planos diretores*' contents, objectives and means of implementation

form was considered a consequence of the economic forces that shape society at any given time. The strategy of the PDU to divert spending priorities to ZEIS was seen as an important policy departure which would, for the first time in Belém, establish links between development control and popular housing initiatives and infrastructure provision. Although the initiative was timely, investigation of the plans, in particular of land use schemes, shows that at the end of the 1980s, management mechanisms, such as those demanded by the PDU, were difficult to put into practice. This is shown in the evidence that *planos diretores* believed that structural alterations in the urban form *per se* would be responsible for improvements in social equity, although their zoning schemes for territorial organisation were contradictory, based on spontaneous trends in the occupation of the city. The *plano diretor* of 1980 had a structure based on less concentration of retail and services in the centre and more on the outskirts of the city. The 1993 proposals, however, only followed the natural tendency to increase mixed land uses in areas where there was already infrastructure, usually city centre locations with pavement, sanitation and regular refuse collection. Thus making the fiscal mechanisms of created soil difficult to deliver improvements and contribute to social equity.

References

Batty, M. (1976), *Urban Modelling: Algorithms, Calibrations, Predictions*, Cambridge, Cambridge University Press.

Becker, B. (1997), 'Novos Rumos da Política Regional: por um Desenvolvimento Sustentável da Fronteira Amazônica', in Becker, B. and Miranda, M. (eds), *A Geografia Política do Desenvolvimento Sustentável*, Rio de Janeiro, Editora UFRJ.

Bittar, J. and Coelho, F. (1994), 'Gestão Democrática, Inversão de Prioridades e os Caminhos da Administração Pública Municipa', in Ribeiro, L. and Santos Jr., O. (eds), *Globlização, Fragmentação e Reforma Urbana: o Futuro das Cidades Brasileiras na Crise*, Rio de Janeiro, Civilização Brasileira, pp. 327–350.

Blalock Jr, H. (1991), *Understanding Social Inequality*, London, Sage.

Brasil (1989), *Constituição da República Federativa do Brasil Promulgada em 5 de Outubro de 1988, Organização do texto, notas remissivas e índices por Oliveira*, Juarez, São Paulo, Saraiva.

Breheny, M. (ed.) (1992), *Sustainable Development and Urban Form*, London, Pion.

Burgess, R., Carmona, M. and Kolstee, T. (eds) (1997), *The Challenge of Sustainable Cities Development: Neo-liberalism and Urban Strategies in the Developing World*, London, Zed.

Campos Filho, C. (1990), *Cidades Brasileiras, Seu Ccontrole ou o Caos*, São Paulo, Nobel.

Castells, M. (1977), *The Urban Question*, London, Edward Arnold.

Companhia de Desenvolvimento e Administração da Área Metropolitana de Belém (CODEM), Banco Nacional da Habitação (BNH) and Desenvolvimento e Sistemas Consultants (DS) (1975), *Plano de Desenvolvimento da Grande Belém PDGB*, Belém, CODEM/BNH/DS.

Devas, N. and Rakodi, C. (eds) (1993), *Managing Fast Growing Cities*, New York, Longman.

Geotécnica, CODEM and SEPLAN (1980), *Planos Diretores para Areas Urbanas de Belém*, Belém, Geotécnica.

Hardoy, J., Mitlin, D. and Satterthwaite, D. (1992), *Environmental Problems in Third World Cities*, London, Earthscan.

Harvey, D. (1973), *Social Justice and the City*, Oxford, Blackwell.

Haughton, G. (1999), 'Environmental Justice and the Sustainable City', *Journal of Planning Education and Research*, 18:3, pp. 233–43.

IPPUR/FASE (1994), *Questão Urbana, Desigualdades Sociais e Políticas Públicas: Avaliação do Programa Nacional de Reforma Urbana*, Research Report, Rio de Janeiro, Rio de Janeiro University.

Jenks, M., Burton, E. and Williams, K. (1996), *The Compact City*, London, E. and F.N. Spon.

Prefeitura Municipal de Belém (1993), *Plano Diretor 1991–2010*, Belém, Diário Oficial do Município.

Ribeiro, L. (1994), 'Reforma Urbana na Cidade da Crise: Balanço Teórico e Dsafios', in Ribeiro, L. and Santos Jr, O. (eds), *Globlização, Fragmentação e Reforma Urbana: o Futuro das Cidades Brasileiras na Crise*, Rio de Janeiro, Civilização Brasileira, pp. 261–90.

Trainer, T. (1990), 'A Rejection of the Brundtland Report', *IFDA Dossier*, May–June, pp. 71–84.

Turner, R., Pearce, D. and Baterman, I. (1994), *Environmental Economics*, Hemel Hempstead, UK, Harvester Wheatsheaf.

Valença, M. (1999), 'The Closure of the Brazilian Housing Bank and Beyond', *Urban Studies*, 36:10, pp. 1747–68.

Young, I. (1990), *Justice and the Politics of Difference*, Princeton NJ, Princeton University Press.

World Commission on Environment Development (WCED) (1987), *Our Common Future*, G.H. Brundtland, Oxford, Oxford University Press.

Chapter 9

The Impact of Land Subdivision Processes on Residential Layouts in Makkah City, Saudi Arabia

Mohammed Abdullah Edrees

Introduction

Residential environments are the complex product of user preferences, developers' interests, cultural traditions and statutory regulation. At the same time they should reflect the influence of community values and respond to the residents' needs and aspirations whilst evolving in respect of prevailing environmental circumstances.

This chapter examines how disjuncture occurs, and with what effects, when new residential environments (Figure 9.1) fail to accommodate and sustain the values and needs of the community. It examines these conflicts in the context of modern residential layouts in Makkah city, Saudi Arabia which, by adopting the grid pattern, have neglected basic characteristics and standards to be found in older more traditional settlement forms of the city (Figure 9.1). Specifically, the chapter considers the residential *barha*, (public space between houses) which constitutes a major component of traditional residential layouts, but which is lacking in contemporary development.

The *barha* (Figures 9.2) is the lung of the residential area and an important open space and cultural feature in the design of these areas. It permits residents to carry out different outdoor activities such as the gathering of older people, children's play, and a space used for religious and other celebrations for the residents. These functions contribute to the enhancement of social interaction among the residents, and help to conserve cultural traditions. Equally, the *barha* plays other roles: it helps to improve microclimatic conditions and it provides security to the residential area.

Urban Expansion in Makkah City

The expansion of the city and the demand for new residential development arises from several factors. The growth of an urban based economy, migration to the city, and the large number of expatriates working in the country have all stimulated the growth of the city and the emergence of the modern residential layouts.

More local factors are also at play. There have been several expansions of the Holy Mosque during the last centuries which have played a distinctive role in the urban development of the city and this has affected the residential development pattern.

Figure 9.1   Modern (left) and traditional (right) residential layouts

Figure 9.2   Modern (left) and traditional (right) *barha*

The last two very large expansions during the Saudi era have increased the Mosque area twofold, which has required the demolition of several of the traditional areas and increased the demand for new housing. However, even without the expansion of the Mosque, it is also important to recognise that recent decades have witnessed a remarkable increase in residential mobility out of the traditional areas to the modern areas in Makkah city. Establishing the factors which have caused residents to move, and the factors which influenced the selection of the new residential areas, is significant here since these reasons will help to identify more clearly residents' aspirations and the way these may be fulfilled by better design of the residential layouts.

In this context, residents' perceptions suggest that the three most important reasons which have caused this outward movement from traditional to modern areas are: the demolition caused by the Mosque expansion; lack of car parking; and the perceived poor quality of the traditional residential environments. At the same time, proximity of work place, accessibility and good location, and proximity of relatives and friends are the three most important factors which positively influence the selection of the modern areas. However, as we shall see, perceived poor quality of the traditional residential locations by no means implies that residents are satisfied with the new residential layouts.

Comparing Traditional and Modern Residential Layouts

A number of findings emerge from the comparison between traditional and modern residential layouts.

Recognition of *Shariah* (Islamic law) principles and guidance in the new residential layouts is lacking. Shariah law provides an essential body of legislation to enhance the social life of people, including the built environment: it encourages people to live peacefully and to share responsibilities to enhance their social and urban life (Akbar 1992, Allam et al. 1993, Ibrahim 1994, Eben Saleh 1998). Despite the fact that Shariah is a major part of planning control in Saudi Arabia, in recent practice it has often been completely ignored. Thus in most of the modern residential layouts surveyed in this study, neither the layouts nor the *barha* (discussed below), appear to have respected these principles in the land subdivision process. This has resulted in negative impacts on the built environment of Makkah.

The characteristics, experience and qualities of residential areas in the traditional Arab Muslim city and the residential *barha* have also been ignored. Although Arab Muslim cities are largely the outcome of spontaneous growth, the contextual needs and environmental conditions which satisfied residents' aspirations were taken into consideration. At the strategic level, cities developed pragmatically, whilst, at the local level, detailed design was guided by Shariah law regarding privacy, seclusion and so on. In modern residential layouts and the *barha* the advantages of this experience do not appear to have taken into account in order to underpin their efficiency and functionality. The opportunity of linking the best of the traditional concepts with modern needs of the community has been lost

Comparing the traditional areas with recent modern areas in Makkah, it can be concluded that the planners and master builders of the traditional areas spent considerable effort, with limited resources, to create and develop comfortable and satisfying residential environments. In particular, building enclosure, adaptation to climatic extremes, adaptation to topographical requirements to create attractive and varied layouts, the *barha* effectively integrated into the urban design process: these features are all evident. However, the situation with the modern layouts is different. Here what is evident are formalised 'western style' grid layouts which give precedence to satisfying the landowners and speculators, often using imported layout patterns and styles (Abdulaal 1999). There is little evidence that effective site analysis has been conducted prior to privately owned land subdivision. The designs are largely drawing board exercises and site visits by either the consultants or the municipality engineers approving the proposed subdivision schemes, are rare. The design process is dominated by the need to satisfy the formal requirements of the municipality in land subdivision in terms of density, road layout and configuration of plots, and to satisfy the landowners by providing as many plots as possible. Thus topographical geological features are ignored. Open space provision is neglected as this is not important for the landowners.

The problems, of course, arise at the implementation stage when the whole site has already been sold. When the new owners want to build their houses, they discover that they need to grade and level their plots, undertake expensive cut and fill or construct retaining walls to develop their houses; this may cost them more than the land value. In some cases, upgrading costs are about three times the original land value.

Whilst, as we have seen, residents cite the perceived poor quality of the traditional residential environments as one of the reasons for moving out, even so, there are many positive aspects to the living environment of the traditional areas. These locations are enhanced by: coherent layouts which address the topographic impacts; encouraging pedestrian movement which in turn encourages social interaction among the residents; reducing the extra construction costs. Conversely, my research confirms the negative impacts of the modern residential areas: incoherent layouts which ignore the topography; vehicle-oriented development which discourages social interaction among the residents; increased construction costs; the discouragement of pedestrian movements inside the areas.

Assessment of residents' level of satisfaction with the residential layouts confirm these findings. They indicate a significant difference between perceptions of the traditional and the modern areas. The coherent traditional layout, developed considering the social, economic and environmental circumstances and the evolving Shariah guidance, resulted in the large majority of the traditional area residents being satisfied with the residential layout. However, the situation in most of the modern residential areas is different. The incoherent modern layouts which lack the more intimate form of traditional residential areas, fail to incorporate the residential *barha*, and ignore the social, economic and environmental circumstances and Shariah guidance, result in a large majority of the residents being dissatisfied with these new residential layouts.

As regards the future, the 1998 comprehensive development plan anticipates a large expansion of residential development in the city within the next 50 years. This requires specific consideration of residents' opinions and preferences to avoid the existing problems and inefficient residential layouts. As the evidence from my own study suggests, a number of key factors should be taken into account to develop design guidance based on the shortcomings in the patterns of recent new developments. These include: consideration of how best to design layouts which can accommodate social interaction among the residents; recognition of climatic conditions; security. Still important, but a lesser priority amongst residents are: costs of development (i.e.

topography and land preparation costs); accessibility; maintaining privacy; vehicular movement; pedestrian movement; and the availability and location of facilities and services.

Overall, what emerges most strongly in this evaluation of residents' preferences is that the functions and the importance of residential *barha* need to be acknowledged in the design process. Consideration of the residential *barha*, as the major component of residential layouts, will ensure that new layouts will be more positively perceived by the residents, because a significant number of the perceived problems currently emerging in new layouts can be overcome. It is on the residential *barha*, therefore, which the chapter now focuses.

The Residential *Barha*

The residential *barha* is perceived as an extension of the house and it is developed to be used mainly by the residents for outdoor family activities (Figure 9.3) such as: different types of children's play; social interchange for mothers and children; elderly people gathering; residents' special occasions; religious and other celebrations; and some commercial activities.

Figure 9.3   Outdoor activities of residents (left), and gathering of elderly residents (right)

The residential *barha* has a direct effect on the visual form of the residential area, and at the same time, it has a strong impact in enhancing the social features, some of the economic and commercial aspects of the neighbourhood, in conserving cultural traditions, and in creating environmental quality. It plays an important role in the microclimate of residential areas as well. Thus in traditional areas the quality of the residential *barha* plays a distinctive role in the residents' relationship with their neighbourhood. A good quality residential *barha* – i.e. one that is located close to residential uses, includes different spaces, user facilities and activities, and is attractively designed and landscaped – encourages the residents to carry out these activities, while a poor quality residential *barha* discourages them (see Figure 9.2).

Given the significance of the *barha* to residents' perceptions of the quality and functionality of residential areas, it is important to establish more precisely what role it plays and how this role can be adapted and incorporated into new residential neighbourhoods.

A number of factors are relevant here which include: the availability, social and cultural importance, and use of the residential *barha* in the residential area; the design quality and facilities of the *barha* itself; and its impact on the living environment. Residents' preferences, aspirations and opinions, together with comparison between the active use of the *barha* in traditional areas compared with its more restricted uses in modern residential areas, can also inform an understanding of the relationship between the residents and the residential *barha* and how this might be better established in new developments.

The large majority of the residents of seven surveyed areas value the recreational, social, cultural, economic and environmental importance of the residential *barha* as an integral component of the residential layout and strongly support its provision in future residential development. The three most important aspects are that it: enhances social interaction among residents; provides secure areas for social needs whilst respecting cultural determinants for privacy; and provides children's playgrounds.

In most of the modern developments however, the basic design and location factors, as well as essential user facilities, have been ignored and so the residential *barha* in its traditional form is no longer viable. This has created residential *barhas* of poor quality and has restricted their use (Figures 9.2, left and 9.4).

Where they exist they are scattered and unevenly distributed, and they often remain vacant for long periods with limited, if any, active use. This has resulted in the disappearance of most of the traditional outdoor activities, and the degradation of the functions and the importance of the residential *barha* for the residential area as a whole. This is confirmed by the substantial number of the residents of modern residential areas who appear never to use the residential *barha*. Family and female use is almost completely absent. Of the small number of the residents using the residential *barha*, this is mainly children (boys) playing football.

The other traditional activities found in the residential *barha* noted above, are scarcely evident in the modern residential areas. The maintenance and management are problematic, as neither the residents nor the authorities seem to undertake these responsibilities. As a result of all these factors, the residential *barha* becomes an eyesore.

User surveys indicate the main concerns which residents have, and the strong relationship between the poor quality of residential *barha* and reasons restricting the use. The unsuitable location is a first major reason which restricts the use of the residential *barha* in the modern areas, since most of them are away from the houses and in locations which are perceived to be insecure. They are all surrounded by roads,

Figure 9.4   Residential *barha* in poor quality modern developments

since vehicular movement is given priority in the modern residential layouts, but this further isolates the residential *barha*. Consequently, lack of safety and security is a second major reason for lack of use, since most of the available residential *barhas* ignore the need for safety and security; this prevents families from sending their children to play. Lack of seclusion and privacy in most of the residential *barhas* is a third major reason which restricts their use. These features, especially in the Saudi context, are essential in the open spaces and in the mixed-use areas because separation between men and women is a key cultural determinant. But, most of the residential *barhas* are very open in their design, overlooked by the surrounding buildings and lack privacy and seclusion.

In addition to those reasons, there is a wide range of features which also restricts the use of the residential *barha* in these new developments, although these are of less importance. These are: neglect of microclimate; poor topography and landscaping; lack of facilities and services to allow flexibility for different activities and uses; and the lack of private places.

Overall, the complete lack of the residential *barha* in most of the modern areas, or the poor quality where provision is made, are major factors in the dissatisfaction which the majority of the residents have with the environment of the modern residential areas.

As my research shows, the socio-economic characteristics of the residents also have a significant influence on the satisfaction levels with the residential *barha*, particularly in association with the type of housing design which is now developing. Thus villa residents have the opportunity to use their private outdoor spaces and the roof areas; at the same time, the size of villa developments allows residents to carry out varied indoor activities without necessarily needing to use the public space of the residential *barha*. By contrast, apartment residents, and especially large families with low incomes, find it difficult to carry out any indoor social and recreational activities due to the limited space and the size of the family. But, at the same time, it is difficult for them to use the residential *barha* for the reasons discussed above.

To summarise: the residential *barha* is one of the integral components of residential layout in Saudi society, but it has been substantially ignored in most of the modern residential developments. Thus the evidence set out in this chapter has important implications for design guidance for the residential *barha* specifically, and the quality of the layout of the new residential areas as a whole. These proposals are now reviewed in the context of both existing residential layouts and for the design of future land subdivisions in order to enhance their performance and efficiency in meeting the preferences and aspirations of their residents. The recommendations have wider relevance to the land subdivision and development process in Saudi Arabia as a whole as well as other Muslim countries where these design features obtain.

Design Guidance for the Residential *Barha*

Recommendations relating to the residential *barha* are very important, because the solution to many of the problems of residential areas can be achieved by considering how the quality of the residential *barha* can be improved. As we have seen, residential *barhas* are a vital component of the traditional residential area. They are the spaces where the residents carry out a variety of daily outdoor activities. Thus it is crucial that they are retained as a key design feature of residential areas, but updated and designed according to modern requirements.

Residents' opinions and preferences, as we have seen, prioritise suitable location, safety and security, and privacy as the three essential factors to be considered in the design and location of the residential *barha*. Significant factors, but of less importance to local residents, are microclimate, topography, planting materials, availability of secluded places, availability of facilities and services, and adequate size of provision are all relevant.

The wider literature on open space provision and the residential *barha* also provide further evidence on how more appropriate guidance might be constructed (Fogg 1986, Heseltine 1987, Al-Olet 1990, El-Akbabi 1991, Aldous 1992, Lutley 1992, Bahmmam 1995, Gehl 1996, Arendt 1996, Wheway and Millward 1997, El-Diasty 1998, Marcus and Francis 1998, Siksna 2000).

Taking general guidelines first of all, the main requirement is that planning policies and the land subdivision process should include residential *barha* as an essential component of the residential layout, particularly in the areas where apartments are the major house type.

The residential *barha* and its design must be carefully integrated within the urban fabric in future land subdivision, ensuring suitable, safe and secure forms of provision (major concerns of residents), which achieve positive microclimatic effects, which are accessible and within walking distance from the dwellings whilst maintaining privacy and seclusion. Guidelines should also encourage a range of uses in the residential *barha*. These factors will improve the quality of the residential developments thereby improving social interaction among the residents, enhancing the microclimate, preserving cultural traditions, and providing better security.

Specifically, the residential *barha* should be protected from vehicular movement and access since the majority of and, in some areas, all the residential *barhas* have become car-parking spaces.

Developing these general points in more detail, there are ten essential factors affecting the quality and use residential *barha*. These can be used as an analytical tool to evaluate in more detail the qualities of the existing residential *barha*, and to form part of a design brief and an appraisal methodology to develop good quality residential *barha* in new residential areas. These factors are:

- *Location and accessibility*: suitable and easily accessible locations, closely integrated within walking distance of residential areas to encourage the use of the residential *barha*.
- *Safety and security*: children and elderly people are the major users and thus safe and secure access, design standards and features are essential.
- *Privacy*: maintaining appropriate privacy and seclusion are major considerations especially in Saudi society. This can be achieved by design and landscaping and access routes.
- *Microclimate*: microclimatic considerations should be adopted as a basic criterion for the residential *barha* design since the configuration and location of open spaces directly affect local climatic conditions and should thus be integrated into the layout design.
- *Topography*: avoid unsuitable areas such as steep gradients, which are generally more expensive to develop than level sites, less attractive for users and less suitable for the variety of activities in the residential *barha*.
- *Planting and landscaping*: suitable planting and landscaping can enhance quality, use, privacy and microclimatic conditions such as protection from sun and wind. Planting materials should be carefully selected to obtain these advantages.
- *Facilities and services*: flexible and varied provision of facilities and services should be adopted to encourage the residents to use areas and spaces – e.g. play facilities, some small scale commercial uses; space for elderly people; secluded spaces; suitable equipment and street furniture.
- *Availability of private spaces*: especially those which are to be used by women and children.
- *Size*: varied size of residential *barha* according to density, size of residential area and the number of houses it will serve, the demographic and socio-economic structure of the area, the variety of activities practiced.
- *Maintenance*: responsibility for management and maintenance must be established in order to retain quality, either the local authority or a residents' group.

Enhancing Residential Layouts

Whilst better design guidance will lead to improvements in the quality of the residential *barha* in new developments, this needs to be linked to improved design and planning policies for the layout of the new residential areas as a whole.

First of all an appropriate strategic planning programme for future land subdivision in Makkah, based on Shariah (Islamic law) and the characteristics of Arab Muslim cities and societies is needed. On this basis development guidelines should be developed, as part of the planning process, which are sufficiently flexible to meet Makkah's specific circumstances. These might be in the form of supplementary planning guidance.

Next, improvements to the land subdivision process are demanded. In particular, comprehensive site appraisal should precede the design and detailed planning process: as we have seen this does not take place at present. Such appraisal should include topographic analysis showing the areas suitable for development and the areas where development should not take place, including watershed protection. Microclimatic factors such as sunpath, air movement and prevailing wind direction, to indicate suitable orientation, should be assessed as well. These variables, should be considered in conjunction with the study of the socio-economic characteristics and the needs of the proposed residents. Appraisal should be conducted before the plan preparation phase so that these factors form part of a planning design and development brief. A sustainability statement ensuring adequate management of the developed scheme should also be assessed at this stage.

As regards the already developed modern residential areas, where the layout and the provision of the residential *barkha* are generally unsatisfactory, an improvement strategy is needed. This should incorporate the upgrading, and, where feasible, the redesign, of the layouts to a more appropriate design standard.

Special attention is needed for land allocation for social and other facilities both in proposed new development as well as in most of the existing new developments where, as we have seen, current provision is poor. Planning policies and strategies should be developed indicating the required level, types and indicative areas for services and facilities in each residential area. A suggested proportion of about one-third of the residential area should be dedicated to non-residential uses. Guidelines should indicate the range of facilities based on adequate but flexible standards and in suitable locations, within walking distance from the dwellings, so that they can serve the required population. The standards should allow for growth and change.

Accessibility is a major factor, as we have seen this is a primary motive for people to move to new residential areas. This needs to be considered in the design stage by providing better access to and from residential areas and, more particularly, within the residential areas. A reduction in vehicular movement inside the residential areas and the encouragement of pedestrian movement by providing safe, secure and shaded pedestrian networks (alleyways) within the residential areas, is essential. These requirements suggest that a detailed study of transport and pedestrian movement should be included at the layout stage.

Another important design feature for new residential areas is to ensure that privacy and seclusion are maintained in residential layouts by avoiding overlooking and by providing semi-private spaces such as cul-de-sacs, as found in the traditional layouts.

Improvements, such as these, to the layout of residential areas and the provision of social facilities should produce more efficient and environmentally sensitive layouts. Reduction in street areas would have other benefits such as reducing the cumulative heat gains from high temperature and glare levels found in many new residential areas. It will also enhance the environmental quality by reducing vehicular movement inside the residential areas.

As regards the older residential areas some upgrading and redevelopment is both necessary and desirable in order to reduce the cumulative pressure for more new developments. At the same time, conservation policies are necessary in order to maintain the layout and characteristics of the remaining traditional residential areas whilst permitting the necessary upgrading to meet present day environment needs.

A particular concern here is the pressure to accommodate vehicular movement in the traditional residential areas, and the associated objectives of providing appropriate car parking standards, public transport access and policies which balance these provisions with appropriate and comprehensive pedestrian movement systems.

Enhancing the quality and the conservation of traditional residential areas in Makkah should be set in the context of a strategic plan which adopts a variety of short, medium, and long-term objectives.

Conclusions

The chapter has revealed how, under the pressure for rapid urban expansion, the lack of adequate planning, design and land subdivision processes in Saudi Arabia in general, and in Makkah in particular, are major factors affecting the low efficiency of new residential layouts and the availability, and quality of residential *barha*. The unqualified adoption of alien design characteristics severely undermines crucial traditional, indigenous design principles of residential areas. This reinforces the neglect of the experience of traditional Arab-Muslim city design and the contextual and environmental conditions which have satisfied residents in the past but which contribute to dissatisfaction with new developments. Whilst accepting that adaptation and updating are necessary, at the same time, basic cultural and social norms embodied in the design process, as well as physical features which are well adapted to climatic and environmental needs, can still be safeguarded. What is required is: careful assessment and evaluation; detailed awareness of residents' preferences and aspirations; and appropriate planning and design guidance instruments which ensure that essential residential qualities can be retained and enhanced.

References

Abdulaal, W. (1999), 'Urban Land Development Process', in Al-Hathloul, S. and Edadan, N. (eds), *Urban Development in Saudi Arabia: Challenges and Opportunities*, Riyadh, Saudi Arabia, Dar Alsahan, pp. 139–56.

Aldous, T. (1992), *Urban Villages: A Concept for Creating Mixed-use Urban Developments on a Sustainable Scale*, report published by the Urban Villages Group to stimulate discussion and action by all concerned with the quality of the built environment, Arjo Wiggins, Appleton.

Al-Olet, A. (1990), *Cultural Issues as an Approach to Forming and Managing the Future Neighbourhood*, unpublished PhD thesis, Glasgow, University of Strathclyde, Centre for Planning.

Akbar, J. (1992), *Land Development in Islam*, Jeddah, Saudi Arabia, Dar Al-Qeblah for Islamic Culture.

Allam, K., Abdullah, M., and Al-Dinary, M. (1993), *The History of Cities Planning*, 1st edn, Cairo, Egypt, Al-Aangalo.

Arendt, R.G. (1996), *Conservation Design for Subdivisions: A Practical Guide to Creating Open Space Networks*, Washington, DC, Island Press.

Bahammam, O.S. (1995), *The Social Needs of the Users in Public Open Spaces, the Involvement of Social-cultural Aspects in Landscape Design of the Outdoor Urban Environment in Ar-Riyadh, Saudi Arabia*, unpublished PhD thesis, Edinburgh, Department of Architecture and Landscape Architecture, University of Edinburgh.

Eben Saleh, M. (1998), 'The Impact of Islamic Customary Law on Urban Form Development in Southwestern Saudi Arabia', *Habitat International*, 22:4, pp. 143–47.

El-Akbabi, M. (1991), 'Beauty and Function: Values of the Plants in the Urban Spaces, Cairo', *Alam Albena*, 124, November, Society for Revival of Planning and Architecture Heritage, pp. 19–21.

El-Diasty, R. (1998), 'Open Space Planning in Desert Environment', in Freestone, R. (ed.), *Twentieth Century Urban Planning Experience*, Sydney, Australia, University of South Wales, pp. 154–59.

Fogg, G. (1986), *A Site Design Process*, Alexandria, USA, National Recreation and Park Association.

Gehl, J. (1996), *Life Between Buildings, Using Public Space*, 3rd edn, Copenhagen, Arkitektens Forlog.

Heseltine, P. and Holborn, J. (1987), *Playground: The Planning, Design and Construction of Play Environment*, London, Mitchell Publishing Company Ltd.

Ibrahim, A. (1994), *Islamic View to Urban Development*, Cairo, Egypt, Architectural and Planning Studies Centre.

Lutley, W. (1992), *Making Space, Protecting and Creating Open Space for Local Communities*, Milton Keynes, Powage Press.

Marcus, C. and Francis, C. (1998), *People Places: Design Guidelines for Urban Open Spaces*, 2nd edn, Canada, John Wiley.

Siksna, A. (2000), 'Ten Principles for the Design of Successful Urban Space', paper presented at the *27th International Making Cities Liveable Conference*, Vienna, Austria, July, 2000.

Wheway, R. and Millward, A. (1997), *Child's Play: Facilitating Play on Housing Estates*, Report for the Chartered Institute of Housing and the Joseph Rowntree Foundation, York, Chartered Institute of Housing.

Chapter 10

Sustainable Urban Form: Environment and Climate Responsive Design

Silvia de Schiller, Ian Bentley and Georgia Butina Watson

Introduction

The process of globalisation has a clear influence on urban development in cities in the developing world. One of these effects is the modification of urban tissue, leading to a series of environmental impacts related to energy and urban climate. These affect the way that urban space is used, the value of urban investments and the sustainability of cities.

In this chapter four complementary phenomena are discussed relating to environmental impacts at the global, urban, micro-urban and building scales. At all of the scales, buildings and urban spaces have a significant impact on the environment and, at the same time, the external environment has an important influence on buildings, their occupants and the users of the adjacent outdoor spaces. Special attention is paid to thermal impacts and variables that affect human comfort, without ignoring other environmental consequences.

Thermal effects are emphasised, as changes in external air temperature will influence energy demand. Therefore, there is a potential vicious circle whereby the changes provoke reactions that may increase environmental impacts. It should be remembered that the changes in air movement, solar radiation and humidity found within cities also determine the thermal comfort of the users of urban spaces.

Following a general discussion of these phenomena, the evidence of environmental impacts at different scales in the city of Buenos Aires is presented.

At the *global scale*, growing concern about greenhouse gases and global warming is beginning to create pressures for action with special reference to the increasing use of non-renewable energy and the impact of fossil fuels. In the emerging countries of the developing world, the important role of the energy demand of buildings is still insufficiently recognised as a contributory factor. At the same time, the link between climate change and energy demand in buildings is also little understood, even in political, professional and academic circles.

At the *urban scale*, the city creates important modifications of the urban environment, when compared with the surrounding rural zone. The urban heat island, with local increases in the air temperature, is one of these impacts, which affects internal conditions in buildings and their energy demand. This phenomenon is also linked with the increasing concentration of pollution in city centres of the developing world.

At the *micro-urban scale*, changes in development trends have produced variations in the urban tissue, such as the tower block and the free-standing isolated building typology, which increasingly replace the continuous façades of the traditional urban street. These changes, which have been introduced to partly improve ventilation and natural lighting in building interiors, have promoted a more open form of urban development. This change also produces modifications in the environmental conditions of urban spaces, particularly the wind regime, the shading of outdoor spaces and access to winter sun, all of which influence outdoor comfort and the quality of public spaces.

At the *building scale*, changes in construction technology and architectural trends have increased the incidence of overheating of indoor spaces; due to increased intensity of building use, better thermal insulation and larger glazed areas of façades and roofs. This tendency, linked to the dependency on artificial heating and cooling, not only creates discomfort within buildings, but also produces impacts at the urban and global scale through the increasing use of non-renewable energy.

Therefore, the search for sustainable urban form should concentrate on the reduction of unfavourable impacts at all scales (Smith 2001).

However, there may be conflicting results as reduced impacts at one scale may increase unfavourable impacts at other scales. A more detailed consideration of possible impacts in the following sections explains this potential paradox.

Global Warming and the Contribution of the Built Environment

Increasing concentrations of greenhouse gases in the upper atmosphere are creating conditions for climate change and global warming that pose many potential threats for human activity. A decade ago, the Inter-governmental Panel on Climate Change in their United Nations Report (IPCC 1990: xxv) stated, 'We predict that, under *business-as-usual*, emissions of greenhouse gases, a rate of increase of global mean temperature of about 0.3°C per decade ...', although Houghton (1997) predicts a slightly lower figure of 0.25°C per decade.

This rate of change will produce a temperature increase of about 1.5°C by the year 2050, with a sea level rise of 35cm. In addition to temperature changes, other climatic conditions are likely to be modified, with changes such as increased droughts in some areas, heavier rains in others, and increased frequency of cyclones and storms. When considering the impact on the built environment, a 1.5°C temperature rise is equivalent to a 4° latitude shift towards the equator. This increase will occur within the life span of buildings and urban developments planned, designed and constructed today.

The later IPCC Report indicates that, in spite of significant uncertainties, the consequences of climate change on the global environment are sufficiently serious to adopt immediate response strategies (IPCC 1995). Current temperature trends measured at the world scale are consistent with this concern. Temperatures rise steadily, sea ice is receding, glaciers are in retreat and climatic extremes are frequent with more catastrophic events than in previous decades.

The 1997 Meteorological Office Report has observed that modification of temperature patterns can be attributed to anthropogenic activities, especially those which emit greenhouse gases (DETR 1997).

Climate change affects water resources, food supply and coastal areas threatened by sea-level rise with direct impacts on human populations, particularly in low latitude developing countries. These changes are primarily the results of increasing concentrations of man made greenhouse gases from energy use (46 per cent) emission of CFC's and similar chemicals (24 per cent), forestry (18 per cent), agriculture (9 per cent) and other sources (3 per cent).

The IPCC Report indicates that the two most important factors that determine levels of greenhouse gas emissions are the energy demand and the mix of energy resources used to satisfy that demand (IPCC 1990).

According to the alternative scenarios presented, primary energy demand may grow by a factor of two to four in the next century. Large future increases in energy demands are expected in the developing world, which presently uses about 25 per cent of total world energy resources but will double this figure by the year 2100.

Reducing this dramatic increase may delay the development process of the world's poorest regions, which are unprepared to face critical environmental impacts due to severe lack of capital and scarcity of skilled human resources.

Total global energy demand can be divided between buildings, transport, industry and other sectors. The proportional distribution between sectors varies between countries, though typically energy demand in buildings accounts for about 30 per cent of all primary energy, used mainly for controlling the environmental conditions within buildings.

As energy demand for heating, cooling and lighting buildings is closely influenced by external climatic conditions, global warming may reduce energy demand for heating, but will significantly increase requirement for artificial cooling.

Despite the important energy demand in the building sector, the IPCC Report (UNEP 1990) devotes less than half a page to this problem. However it does point out that savings of 25 per cent can be achieved in housing retrofits, up to 50 per cent in commercial developments, and up to 75 per cent in new buildings.

Urban morphology, building design and form of urban space can all make valuable contributions to reduce and save energy resources (Short 1998, Yeang 1999).

The built environment contributes to global warming, while at the same time, buildings and urban areas suffer from global warming and climate change which increases the energy demand for cooling, producing further impacts in a vicious circle (Samuels and Prasad 1994); which complements other circular relationships at the urban and building scale.

Urban Heat Island and Energy Use

A different scale of environmental impact is the local increase of urban air temperature known as the heat island (Chandler 1965, Santamouris 2001b).

Although this is a local warming effect, not directly related to global warming, there is a clear relationship between the two phenomena as a result of the concentrated use of energy in urban areas, which produces both heat and greenhouse gases.

Greenhouse gases produced by energy consumption in buildings today will continue to affect global average temperatures over a very long period, lasting many decades, while the same energy use has a more immediate affect on urban air temperatures.

At the urban scale, significant measures to improve energy efficiency and reduce energy use will have an almost immediate beneficial effect, though the feasibility of achieving this reduction is doubtful.

The heat island effect can be related to four main factors, identified by Lacey (1977), Oke (1982) and Bitan (1991), characteristic of large urban areas:

- Energy use in transport, especially the use of the internal combustion engine. The concentrated use of transport produces heat from exhaust gases, motors and radiators. Though electric trains also produce heat, both in the motors and in the related thermal power plants, road vehicles, especially the private car, produce a far higher heat output per passenger kilometre.
- Energy use in buildings. Part of this energy is the waste heat from boiler flues, air-conditioning cooling towers, etc. Another important source is the heat loss due to transmission through the building skin and ventilation.
- Increased heat absorption and retention on urban surfaces, both buildings and paved external areas. These urban surfaces are typically darker than those of the surrounding rural areas, with higher solar absorption. At the same time, these surfaces have a higher heat capacity or admittance, retaining the heat for longer. Finally the typical urban street section acts as a heat trap, increasing the surface area, reducing the average reflectance, reducing the radiant heat losses from building surfaces and reducing wind speeds. All of these factors contribute to higher temperatures in urban areas.
- Pollution in urban areas and increased cloud cover also trap air and heat within the urban boundary layer, the lower layer of the atmosphere close to the surface where the effect of building surfaces is greatest. The resulting increase in inversion layer frequency and cloud cover also reduces the out-going radiation, reducing cooling at night.

Studies have been made on characteristics of urban areas with high temperature differentials and changes that may reduce the intensity of the heat island effect (Santamouris 2001b). These include the highly beneficial effects of parks and green areas, the reduction of built density and increase of the general reflection (albedo) of urban surfaces.

However, less information is available on other possibilities of reducing the heat island effect by energy conservation in buildings and changes of predominant building typologies. This aspect is related to other environmental changes that have occurred in many urban areas, including Buenos Aires, over the past three decades.

Clearly, the urban heat island promoted by high energy use in buildings also affects their energy demand.

This is especially true of air-conditioned commercial buildings in central areas, where the exhaust heat from air-conditioning cooling towers adds latent and sensible heat to the atmosphere, thus increasing the cooling load of same buildings. These buildings also tend to have important internal heat loads, due to high occupant density, artificial lighting and energy intensive office equipment (Evans 2003).

Large cities are already suffering from this vicious circle, with increasing urban temperatures in central areas. This effect is most critical in temperate subtropical, tropical and equatorial climates, where higher external temperatures increase the demand for artificial air-conditioning. Low energy buildings can provide a significant contribution to reduce the urban heat island. The reduction or elimination of air-conditioning through appropriate climate-responsive design would be an important technically feasible step, even in the warm summers of sub-tropical climates (de Schiller 2000).

However, concerted efforts will be required to tackle the effect of building and urban form on energy demand, as few isolated low energy buildings will have little effect on the overall urban environment (Katzschner 1997).

Urban Morphology and Microclimate

The cities of Latin America have developed within the traditional orthogonal Hispano-American grid pattern, initially established over four hundred years ago, within the framework established by the Spanish Authorities in the Laws of the Indies. These set out the recommendations for the location of new settlements and the land subdivision within them.

The regular city grid of about 100 m^2 was formed with the same basic pattern found in nearly all the cities of Spanish Latin America, showing that global planning trends are not an entirely new phenomenon.

Globalisation of technology and design are modifying the conventional tissue of perimeter blocks, with continuous façades constructed on the front boundary of plots. Up until the 1960s, the planning codes applied in Buenos Aires favoured the use of continuous street façades. Although a series of modifications led to a chaotic skyline as maximum building height limits were successively raised, the continuous frontage, especially on the ground floor, remains a characteristic feature of the urban area.

However, present economic pressures for densification, architectural trends, clients' requirements and planning codes favour the development of free standing high-rise towers to provide more ground-level 'urban space'.

This modification of the urban tissue (de Schiller 2001) also changes the microclimatic conditions in the spaces between buildings.

In this process, the introduction of the tower block responds simultaneously to three separate requirements: symbolic, economic and environmental:

- As symbols, they have a long history, from cathedral spires to skyscrapers, where height symbolised superiority. Today, towers continue to exercise a powerful symbolic attraction for both residential and commercial buildings, especially in highly visible central areas.
- As an economic alternative for urban development, high-rise building costs have become more accessible while the cost of limited land in city centres creates a pressure for denser development, justifying the investment in high buildings.
- As an environmental form of urban development, the free-standing tower supposedly allows denser and higher buildings without blocking access to light and air for adjacent buildings. Light and sun can be received from the space left over at the side of towers, instead of over roofs.

Environmental arguments are especially relevant as the concept of the free standing tower was adopted in Buenos Aires, without the adoption of the complementary design aids developed in other latitudes to ensure achievement of environmental standards (MoHLG 1964, 1958). Another important factor to take into account is the impact of climatic differences on the advantages of tower blocks. The environmental benefits of high-rise buildings that were mentioned before are principally related to daylight, ventilation and solar access to improve conditions in the indoor spaces.

In the colder climates of northern Europe, comfort in outdoor spaces is less important. However, conditions in Buenos Aires are significantly different as overheating is a major problem and daylight levels are higher, while outdoor spaces are more comfortable during a greater proportion of the year, encouraging extended use.

Although free standing high-rise buildings promote open urban tissue, with better air movement as well as higher levels of daylight (Yeang 1999), they also have undesirable environmental side effects.

The open urban tissue may offer an appealing visual image, where individual buildings are clearly identifiable; but for the pedestrian, the interruption of the continuous street façades, the increased wind speeds and the lack of clarity in the spatial enclosure can be seen as environmental and economic disadvantages.

Serious wind effects around high rise buildings in the 1960s generated studies of the problems of wind acceleration around tall buildings and possible measures to reduce or avoid this problem.

The problem is particularly notable in cases when high buildings are located in areas of lower construction.

Energy Demand and Overheating in Buildings

As well as global warming, heat island effects and microclimate modification, design changes related to building use, architectural image and technological development also modify indoor conditions with increased overheating and larger temperature swings and increased demand for air conditioning.

Identified by different authors (Samuels and Prasad 1994, Santamouris 2001), the following major issues are found to be increasingly contributing to this trend:

- building use is becoming more intensive, especially in the fast growing administrative and commercial sector, with lower space standards, greater use of information technology and higher lighting standards, raising internal heat loads;
- thermal insulation standards have improved and costs of lightweight thermal insulation have decreased, reducing heat loads in winter, but increasing summer overheating if ventilation and shading strategies are not implemented;
- larger areas of façade and roof glazing, another architectural trend, cause greater heating demand on cold cloudy days and higher cooling requirements on warm sunny days.

Intensive space use may raise the energy density in buildings measured in $kWhr/m^2$ per annum, but it may not increase energy use per capita. Higher occupation density may also reduce need for new buildings, avoiding resulting environmental impacts. The changes mentioned not only provoke potential discomfort due to overheating but also favour the incorporation of air-conditioning in situations where it was not previously used, or increase the energy demand in building types where air-conditioning is already installed, producing additional environmental impacts.

The introduction of air-conditioning has allowed effective control of indoor thermal conditions in warm climates. Planners and architects are therefore able to disregard problems of discomfort arising from inappropriate design, though at high economic and environmental cost.

In the developed world, the environmental consequences of excessive reliance on artificial conditioning is starting to be understood, though in most developing countries, air conditioning is still regarded as a status symbol necessary to emulate the developed world.

Existing air conditioning is a major cause of CFC emissions, as well as provoking other impacts on occupant's health and indoor air quality, especially in developing countries where poor maintenance of installations is frequent.

Environmental Quality in Buenos Aires

The process of globalisation is generated in the major cities of the developed world, but these influences are received in the developing world with very different cultural, climatic, and economic conditions. These impacts are evaluated in a series of studies carried out in Buenos Aires, Argentina, a large capital city with a total population of 10 million situated in a subtropical climate.

There are significant climatic differences between northern Europe, latitude 45–55°N, and Buenos Aires, latitude 34°S. These differences reflect on the potential and actual use of outdoor space, the bioclimatic design strategies for natural heating and cooling of buildings and the energy demand of heating, lighting and air-conditioning installations.

For example, the high level midday sun reaches a maximum angular height of 79° in Buenos Aires while in London this angle does not exceed 62°, some 17° lower in the sky. In winter the difference is similar (34° to 17°), but the impact on shadow length is much greater.

If the same standard of sunlight is required, buildings in London should be half the height of those in Buenos Aires. In practice, the difference is even less favourable as the length of a winter day at latitude 50° is only eight hours, while in Buenos Aires it is over nine hours, where winter day light levels are also considerably higher.

Global warming in Buenos Aires will produce an average increase in the mean temperature of 1.5°C in the next 50 years. This will reduce winter heating demand by about 15 per cent.

However, cooling degree-days are likely to increase by a higher proportion and net annual building energy demand will rise significantly as a result of global warming.

This may be moderated by climate responsive urban and building design. But even today, it is possible to measure higher temperature differences within the city of Buenos Aires, due to urban development, architectural form and building design.

Different impacts of the global transformation trends as a result of the modification of urban tissue are evaluated in the following surveys:

- *urban heat island experiment*, undertaken for this research, measured increasing urban air temperatures and the relation with higher densities;
- *energy demand of buildings* with different forms was evaluated, taking into account design variables such as building form, compactness and orientation;
- *urban microclimate* in spaces around buildings were studied, using direct observation, computer simulations and model tests in a solar simulator and wind tunnel;
- *user behaviour* in urban spaces was observed and pedestrian flows were measured, in relation to differences in the urban tissue.

The surveys are related to the modification of the urban tissue in the city, contrasting areas of traditional urban blocks with areas where towers have been inserted in the consolidated development and comprehensive development areas of free standing towers.

Urban Heat Island Experiment

Objective

A study of the Buenos Aires urban heat island was undertaken to detect the influence of density, urban form and building typologies on the climate of the city (Leveratto et al. 2000). City wide measurements were made in two different seasons of the year.

Method

The survey was made with seven vehicles moving through the urban area, recording the air temperature every 10 seconds, the location of the vehicle within the city and the characteristics of urban tissue.

Technique

The simultaneous vehicular circuits covered the inner urban area, in a 12 km radius, leaving and returning to the same point in the city centre.

Measurements

Automatic temperature measurements were made using miniature data loggers attached to the outside of the vehicles.

Results

During the surveys carried out in the evening, increases of up to 3°C were measured. The areas of highest temperatures coincide with the highest building densities. The results are consistent with infrared temperature data from satellite images of the metropolitan area.

Discussion

The heat island study in Buenos Aires shows a drop in temperature which appears to coincide with the Catalinas Norte area, an area of free standing towers. The drop may be related to other factors as Catalinas Norte is not only a high-rise tower zone but also the border between the dense city centre and the much lower density area of the Madero Docks, with large areas of water. However, the highest temperatures coincide with the high-density areas with enclosed streets and relatively high continuous frontages.

These areas have the following characteristics:

- enclosed spaces with generally lower air movement, though the continuous street pattern can channel the prevailing wind;
- larger surfaces of heavy building mass, retaining the heat;
- important surfaces with significant heat losses form the heated building interiors;
- slow moving traffic.

This can be contrasted with the characteristics of the area of free-standing high-rise towers in Catalinas Norte where open urban tissue produces significantly higher wind speeds at pedestrian level, night radiation losses are higher, glazed façades reduce the effect of thermal inertia and evening traffic is free flowing.

Figure 10.1   Dense residential area of Belgrano within the Federal Capital conurbation, about 7 km from the centre of the city, coincides with the finger of higher temperatures to the NW of the city in Figure 10.2[1]

The results show the moderating effect of the River Plate on night air temperatures as the water, with a higher thermal capacity, will cool down slower than the land mass. It is also possible to detect the cooling effect of the 3rd of February Park.

The results confirm that high building density and compact built form are important variables that contribute to the heat island effect. The city dense built form is shown in Figure 10.1. Figure 10.2 shows the heat island of Buenos Aires, mapped where each contour represents a change of 0.5°C, with a temperature of over 13.5°C in denser central areas and less than 11.0°C on the shores of the River Plate to the NE.

Energy Demand and Building Form

Objective

The energy demand of different building forms was estimated to detect the impact of alternative urban developments and building forms, and to quantify the consequent environmental impacts.

---

[1]   All illustrations by de Schiller.

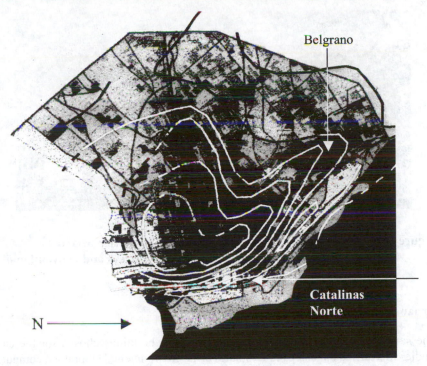

Figure 10.2 **The urban heat island of Buenos Aires, Federal Capital, June 10th, 1999, at 21:00 hrs, showing a 3°C temperature rise in the denser sectors of the city**

Method

The evaluation method was based on a series of computer simulations which show an estimate of annual energy demand for commercial buildings located in Buenos Aires, according to building form, local climate data, etc. The approach used is based on the LT concept developed by Baker in the Martin Centre, Cambridge (Leveratto et al., 2000).

Results

Towers have higher energy demands than conventional urban development with continuous street façades, even when the characteristic differences in façade treatment and glazing areas are discounted. This is largely due to the larger surface area exposed to direct solar radiation in summer. Although variables of design and building materials are important, appropriate architectural form and urban grouping also contribute to reduce energy use and the resulting environmental impacts (Baker and Steemers 2000).

Figure 10.3   Irregular central area skyline of Buenos Aires: Mixed development of tower blocks up to 25 storeys and conventional development up to 12–15 storeys

Urban Microclimate at the Local Scale

The survey of conditions in the spaces around the buildings chosen for the case studies was carried out using model studies in the environmental laboratory, computer simulations and direct observation in the urban tissue, shown in Figure 10.3.

Solar Impact

Areas of sun and shadows in the urban space were studied using scale models in the heliodon, as shown in Figure 10.4. Graphic analysis and computer simulations were also undertaken for different seasons of the year, complemented with direct observation and measurements of the obstructions made by adjacent buildings made on site.

Wind Impact

The wind regime around high buildings was studied in the low speed wind tunnel, using smoke to visualise the flows and anemometers to measure wind speeds at pedestrian level. CFD results from flow patterns computer simulations were also obtained, with measurements and subjective assessments of conditions on site using direct observation.

Comfort

Comfort levels were estimated for each of the urban spaces according to the conditions of sun and wind, with hourly temperature, relative humidity and solar radiation data, measured in a specially constructed meteorological station.

Assessment

With this data, hourly comfort levels were obtained for representative days in different seasons for urban sectors under study and unmodified conventional urban tissue. The contrast between the open tissue of the tower blocks area and the conventional development of the traditional city blocks on the opposite side of the Alem Avenue can be clearly seen in Figure 10.4.

Figure 10.4   Model of Catalinas Norte office complex used for laboratory studies of sunlight, shade and wind: Shadows at 10 am in winter

Results

The preliminary results show that conditions are consistently less comfortable in the spaces around tower buildings. This is principally due to increased wind speeds in winter and the larger areas exposed to strong sun in summer.

Use of Urban Space

Verification

Urban spaces were surveyed to detect possible modification of pedestrian behaviour and its relation to microclimate conditions and comfort levels in each sector.

Method

The survey measured the intensity of pedestrian flows in different locations at the same time of day in urban areas with alternative conditions of urban tissue.

Results

The measurements made in alternative locations and conditions in different sectors of the Central area make it difficult to make comparisons. However, there is a clear decrease in pedestrian movement in pavements around comprehensive development areas with towers. It is also possible to detect variations between pavements on different sides of the street, as a result of differences in sun and shade. This shows that pedestrian behaviour is influenced by microclimatic conditions.

Urban Tissue, Building Form and Environmental Impact

The preceding analysis of environmental impact and its relation to urban form and architectural design variables establish a relationship that has different effects at different scales. There is also a significant indication that changes in urban and energy efficiency policies can produce important changes in the resulting impact.

Energy saving in the built environment can produce greater proportional reductions than other sectors, when considered at the global scale. The IPCC study (UNEP 1990) mentions possible energy savings and reductions of greenhouse gas emission of 25 per cent for residential retrofitting, 50 per cent in retrofitting of commercial buildings and 75 per cent in new buildings. Comparable figures are 15 per cent for transport, 15 per cent for new vehicles, 13–40 per cent for the industrial sector and 15–20 per cent for conventional energy production.

However, the time frame for achieving these reductions is much longer for the built environment. It is therefore vital that modifications of the urban tissue are implemented in present day developments to reduce environmental impacts and avoid unfavourable consequences that may last over centuries.

The comparative examples of options that can be taken in the built environment show the wide variation of periods corresponding to different energy efficiency measures. The period for economic changes of appliance parts is about three to five years for items such as high efficiency lights and ventilator motors, while mechanical systems such as heating and air-conditioning installations, lifts and pumps are likely to be replaced at intervals of about 15 to 30 years. Major changes to the building fabric such as up grading insulation in walls and roofs may take place at intervals of 20 to 50 years. Finally, changes in city infrastructure and urban tissue take place over extended time periods of up to 300 years. It is therefore vital that opportunities should not be missed at the scale where buildings and micro-urban sectors are interacting.

Conclusions

Changes in physical variables at this scale also have a clear impact on users of urban spaces considering that outdoor comfort is related to and modifies pedestrian behaviour, as shown by the surveys undertaken for this study. If pedestrians avoid uncomfortable areas and naturally prefer more comfortable spaces, then this may also modify the image and performance of the area. In this respect, environmental conditions in outdoor spaces in cities are likely to affect the urban quality, as well as the economic value and commercial success of whole urban sectors.

Cities in both the developed and developing worlds produce important environmental impacts. While the increase of aerial pollution and acid rain are two of the better-known results of energy use in urban areas, global warming, heat islands and microclimate are also producing impacts that affect the environmental and economic conditions in cities. If the modification of urban tissues are at present increasing energy demand and reducing comfort in outdoor spaces, the appropriate design of urban developments can therefore make an important contribution to energy efficiency in the built environment, while improving urban conditions and promoting sustainable cities.

Acknowledgements

This study was carried out as part of the research project 'Sustainable urban form' undertaken in the framework of the ALFA-IBIS Programme 'Globalisation, Urban Form and Governance', of the European Union, coordinated by TU Delft, with the participation of the Joint Centre for Urban Design, Oxford Brookes University, and the Faculty of Architecture, Design and Urbanism, University of Buenos Aires.

The authors acknowledge the advice of Professor John Martin Evans, Director of the Research Centre Habitat and Energy, University of Buenos Aires, related to global warming and the urban heat island experiment.

References

Baker, N. and Steemers, K. (2000), *Energy and Environment in Architecture, A Technical Design Guide*, London, E. and F.N. Spon.

Bitan, A. (ed.) (1991), *Urban Climate, Planning and Building*, Lausanne, Elsevier Sequoia.

Chandler, T.J. (1965), *The Climate of London*, London, Hutchinson.

De Schiller, S. (2000), 'Sustainable Urban Form: Environment and Climate Responsive Design', in Proceedings 1, Part III: *Environment, Sustainable Urban Form and Social Issues*, Delft, DUP.

De Schiller, S. (2001), 'Building Form, Transformation of Urban Tissue and the Evaluation of Sustainability', in Pereira, F.O.R., Rüther, R., Souza, R.V.G., Afonso, S. and de Cunha Neto, J.A.B. (eds), *Proceedings of PLEA 2001, Renewable Energy for Sustainable Development of the Built Environment*, Florianopolis, Conference Organizing Committee PLEA.

DETR (Department of the Environment, Transport and the Regions) (1997), *Planning for Sustainable Development: Towards Better Practice*, London, HMSO.

Evans, J.M. (2003), 'Solar Radiation, Design Variables and Environmental Impact: Measurements, Simulation Integrated in Project Development', in Bustamante, W. and Collados, E. (eds), *Rethinking Development*, Proceedings PLEA 2003, Santiago, Pontificia Universidad Catolica de Chile.

Houghton, J. (1997), *Global Warming: The Complete Briefing*, 2nd edn, Cambridge, Cambridge University Press.

Intergovernmental Panel on Climate Change (1990), *Climate Change, The IPCC Response Strategies*, World Meteorological Organization/United Nations Environmental Program.

Intergovernmental Panel on Climate Change (1995), *Climate Change, The Second Assessment Report*, World Meteorological Organization/United Nations Environmental Program.

Katzschner, L. (1997), 'Urban Climate Studies as Tools for Urban Planning and Architecture', in Nery, J., Freire, T. and Lamberts, R. (eds), *Anais IV Encontro Nacional do Conforto no Ambiente Construido*, Bahia, Universidade Federal do Bahia.

Lacey, R.E. (1977), *Climate and Building in Britain*, BRE Report, Department of the Environment, London, HMSO.

Leveratto, M.J., de Schiller, S. and Evans, J.M. (2000), 'Buenos Aires Urban Heat Island: Intensity and Environmental Impact', in Steemers, K. and Yannas, S. (eds), *Architecture, City, Environment*, London, James and James.

MoHLG (Ministry of Housing and Local Government) (1958), *Flats and Houses, Design and Economy*, London, HMSO.

MoHLG (Ministry of Housing and Local Government) (1964), *Design for Daylight and Sunlight*, *Planning Bulletin*, 5, London, HMSO.

Oke, T. (1982), *Boundary Layer Climates*, London, Academic Press.

Samuels, R. and Prasad, D. (eds) (1994), *Global Warming and the Environment*, London, E. and F.N. Spon.

Santamouris, M. (2001), *Energy and Climate in the Urban Built Environment*, London, James and James.

Santamouris, M. (2001a), 'The Energy Impact of the Urban Environment', in Santamouris, M. *Energy and Climate in the Urban Built Environment*, London, James and James.

Santamouris, M. (2001b), 'The Heat Island Effect', in Santamouris, M., *Energy and Climate in the Urban Built Environment*, London, James and James.

Short, A. (1998), 'The Evolution of a Naturally Conditioned Building', in Scott, A. (ed.), *Dimensions of Sustainability*, London, E. and F.N. Spon.

Smith, P. (2001), *Architecture in a Climate of Change, A Guide to Sustainable Design*, Oxford, Architectural Press.

Yeang, K. (1999), *The Green Sky-scraper: The Basis for Designing Sustainable Intensive Buildings*, Munich, Prestel Verlag.

Chapter 11

Collaborative Public Open Space Design in Self-help Housing: Minas-Polvorilla, México City

Luis Gabriel Juárez-Galeana

Introduction

The depletion of natural resources, waste generation and deterioration of human quality of life have become global concerns for sustainable development (Rees 1999). Sustainability, however, is not only about the natural environment. The social dimensions have been recognised as being of equal importance, encompassed by the commonly agreed definition for sustainability, 'meeting the needs of the present without compromising the ability of future generations to meet their own needs' (WCED 1987: 8). Thus, the notion of people and their capacity to survive as individuals and cultures has been incorporated into the current sustainable development discourse. It not only seeks to conserve the environment while permitting a degree of development, it is also an inquiry into how community collaborative participation can lead to creative initiatives for social innovation and environmental preservation.

It is in cities where the greatest environmental and social concerns are concentrated. Thus, considerations about the built environment and how it interacts with people living and working in it are of primary importance. It is also widely recognised that the world's poorest populations are rapidly increasing year by year. Moreover, urban growth and the consequent urban sprawl associated with these populations is largely characterised by self-help settlements. Sheltering these populations, amongst other problems, is thus a worldwide concern, particularly in countries in the 'south'.

In Mexico these issues are of paramount relevance since 40 per cent of its population is considered to be in extreme poverty. For them, self-help settlements are their only option to access land and dwellings. Within this scenario, groups involved in developing housing processes face even greater constraints since they are rarely considered within the institutional housing supply process. They must look for their own means of providing dwellings while facing the additional problem of how to build their settlement.

In self-help settlements, careful open space design in relation to local concerns and residents' real needs is commonly neglected. At best, both are addressed using standardised regulations that only prescribe a required amount of space. The result is alienated housing estates with unstructured public places which, in time, become dysfunctional because of antisocial behaviour, lack of maintenance, waste and pollution. Unless design of the urban realm is closely related to the way people perceive the quality of their built environment, the expressed aims of sustainability will be unachievable.

Using a case study from Mexico City, this chapter discusses how the collaborative approach of local residents and design advisors can surpass the 'provision-only' approach and produce an outcome which creates a more sustainable environment by improving the public space and incorporating other cultural and social variables relevant to design. The case study shows how groups involved in a self-help process can engage in the design of their habitat and, by doing so, move towards a more sustainable urban pattern.

Sustainability and City Growth

Sustainable development and global environmental change have become a major interest in relation to urban settlements since it is here that the highest proportion of the world's production, consumption and waste generation takes place. Compatibility of built form with sustainable urban development in cities is thus crucial from many perspectives (Haughton and Hunter 1994, Satterthwaite 1998).

Cities of the south receive special attention since they experience some of the major emerging environmental impacts, local and global; this is mainly due to their size and nature of urban expansion. Amongst these, population increase and expansion of the built environment are directly associated with environmental degradation (Houghton and Hunter 1994).

Growth *per se* is blamed as the cause by some authors, since it generates higher investment, consumption of resources and energy with consequent impacts on waste production (Rees 1999). Others, however, have a more balanced view that the problem lies not so much in the size of cities but in relation to their organisation and structure. Satterthwaite, for example, asserts that the 'city's rapid growth or an increasingly urbanised population within a nation need not be incompatible with sustainable development goals' (1999: 8).

Concerns about urban sustainability in cities of the south deserve special attention because growth is mainly composed of low-income, self-help settlements. Whilst this is not just a contemporary feature of urban growth, as Hamdi and Goethert (1997) note the magnitude of this process is a fairly recent phenomenon: essentially since the middle of the twentieth century.

Explanations of the origins and causes of these types of urban expansions are varied (see Gilbert 1996 and 1998) and debates about whether self-help schemes are sustainable or not are very much related to issues of compactness and high density versus low-density living (see Haughton and Hunter 1994: 82–88). While the debate continues, such settlements are being produced and will continue to shape today's urban pattern with consequentially critical implications for sustainability in social, economic and environmental terms.

There is some preoccupation regarding public space design as a component of sustainability in relation to the expansion of the urban fabric and the form it takes. Haughton and Hunter (1994: 118) state that:

> ... the heart of the concern of most advocates for improving the natural urban environment in cities is not only the question of how much urban space is provided, but also where it is located and how it is designed and used.

New initiatives should be encouraged which go beyond the 'space provision only' model. Instead, a different approach is needed: how to better address the concerns of sustainability in relation to open space design and the social dimension of self-help settlements.

Self-help Settlements in México City

Since the early 1940s, México City has undergone rapid urbanisation. This is the result of a range of social and economical processes, principally industrialisation and the consequent rural migration to the city (Benitez 1997). One of the impacts, however, of increased labour supply in the city brought about by migration has been the depression of wages and employment opportunities, which, in turn, are reflected in the persistent decay in living standards (Gilbert 1996, 1998).

The main indicator of this outcome is the predominant settlement morphology and the type of housing to which this population has access. While a few received the benefits of institutionalised housing programmes, the majority could only access the informal settlement option, the so-called self-help processes. Today millions of people in México City live in these settlements and they have become an important element of housing provision (Figure 11.1).

Year	Population (millions)	Population in self-help settlements (millions)	%
1952	2,372	330	14
1966	3,287	1,500	46
1970	7,314	3,438	47
1976	11,312	5,656	50
1990	15,783	9,470	60

Note: INEGI (1997) data show a population of 8.5 million in Mexico City and 12.2 for the State of México, which includes most of the metropolitan area. From these data, the percentage currently living in self-help schemes still remains above 50 per cent at least.

Figure 11.1 Trends of self-help settlements in México City up to 1990

Source: Gilbert 1996: 74–75, 1998: 80.

Self-help housing can be described as a process rather than a single intervention, starting with a rudimentary shack made of flimsy materials which is gradually consolidated to a permanent construction. The changes are basically determined by the needs of the family and the security of land tenure (Mitlin 1997, Ward and Macoloo 1992, Siembieda and López 1997). Self-help settlements are usually located at the city's periphery where land prices are affordable for low-income sectors.

The urban morphology also reflects the housing process. In parallel with the improvement to dwellings, the settlements gradually consolidate with the introduction of electricity, water, drainage, road and urban facilities. In terms of design, self-help schemes rarely comply with any architectural trends or current aesthetic concerns. Nevertheless, designs developed by residents usually match their needs rather better than when carried out by professionals – houses allow growth when family size increases or as economic circumstances change. The capacity to use dwellings for informal sector activity such as a local shop or workshop at the side is crucial. Most importantly, all these changes are affordable (Gilbert 1998).

Characterised by their spontaneous origin, high densities, pollution, social conflicts, petty economies, lack of or marginally served by infrastructure, and so forth, self-help settlements have been regarded as places where environmental degradation presents some of its worst manifestations (Aina 1990, Rojas 1997, Sánchez 1997). By contrast, the processes which produce these settlements also offer the potential for solutions. Rees (1998) affirms that it is in cities where the greatest opportunities exist to make the necessary changes to achieve sustainability. Satterthwaite (1999: 8) supports this contention, claiming that 'urbanised populations bring important potential advantages for meeting human needs and reducing resource use and wastes'.

Accordingly it could be argued that seizing the participatory nature of the self-help processes, a better environment is more likely to be achieved if the human resources available in these settlements are fully exploited. That is to say: residents working in collaboration with professionals and technicians can effectively address problems such as the urban form of the settlements, and by doing so environmental improvements are more likely to occur.

It can also be argued that interventions of this kind contain features that help to produce a more sustainable city – for example the supply of shops and services by local entrepreneurs, the use of some on site materials and labour for construction, the extent of recycling, re-use and repair of various goods for consumption, sources of employment within the settlement and so forth.

Collaborative Urban Design Projects as Promoters of Sustainability

Rees (1999) asserts that planners have a predominant role in establishing not only the policies for achieving sustainability, but also for implementation and the physical actions – design and construction – that will support them. Consequently it can be argued that urban designers share that role, focusing on the latter aspect.

Nonetheless, embarking upon the various challenges is a daunting task. Campbell (1999) points out that a range of conflicts is likely to arise when professionals aim to achieve the goals of sustainability – namely conflicts between environmental protection, economic development and social equity. Whilst professional initiatives or solutions might get close to a sustainable outcome, they are unlikely to resolve the conflicts and interactions posed by different interests existing in the city.

Given these complexities, solutions cannot be restricted to the scope and vision of professionals only – planners, designers or related professionals. It cannot be assumed that their interventions alone will provide answers independently from wider cultural and social structures. Moreover, current models of urban planning and design rarely address the social needs portrayed above in an effective way. Rather, more affluent sectors of society have benefited to the detriment of the poorest ones (Hamdi and Goethert 1997).

Conversely, the inclusion of an extended set of players with diverse ideas, perceptions and knowledge of their problems can better resolve the likely conflicts. Plans and designs should be crafted to exploit the spontaneity of community level development, where concerns and eventual solutions are perceived tangibly (Bentley 1999). Moreover, one of the main principles to achieve sustainability claims that people on the ground need to be incorporated into the decision-making and implementation processes at all levels (Haughton and Hunter 1994, OECD 1996).

One of these levels is the urban design realm, specifically in the self-help housing context since, as we have seen, this accounts for most of the urban sprawl. Thus comprehensive urban design practice can be a positive influence in transforming the current use of environmental resources, by acting upon patterns of urban development and promoting changes which entail reduced energy consumption and increased sustainable human activities.

However, it is not only energy and resources which are important matters when speaking about human environments. Fusco Girard (1997: 89) elaborates the concept of *social sustainability* where 'the welfare of the individual in the community is linked to the welfare of the system itself'. Social sustainability depends on active communication, co-operative and self-organisational processes. An urban space that recognises and incorporates plurality of values, cultures and interests is said to be a self-sustainable one by generating a system in which each part takes – to different extents – the other components into account. In the author's words:

> A city that is able to promote a sustainable development is a city whose community is able to choose the goals and instruments of its own development, through communication, participation and constant comparison with the public explanation of good reasons (Fusco Girard 1997: 90).

Bentley (1999) also establishes a connection between the urban form, and social issues at various levels. He claims:

> The physical form of the urban environment, then, is not some sort of designer add-on to 'real' social issues. It is a central aspect of the social world itself, contributing to the

construction of that world through every dimension of the economic through the biotic and the aesthetic (Bentley 1999: 4).

Supporting the involvement of users at the grass-root level, it has been recognised that people in many parts of the world are already handling their own problems through a cumulative learning process within the community. Individual and collective skills are cultivated in order to achieve positive changes in the environment and their lives (Feldman and Westphal 1998).

In summary, these ideas support the argument that pursuing a sustainable built form in terms of social welfare and quality of life; as well as energy use and waste reduction, needs to be sought by involving all the relevant players in the production and consumption of urban space. Moreover, this process needs to put special emphasis on the residents since they are the ones who experience the ills or benefits of their immediate environment.

As regards participation in urban development issues within the Mexican context, practice over the last two decades or so has proved itself capable of addressing a wide range of problems. Communities and civil organisations have jointly worked towards addressing concerns of housing supply and sites and services schemes, by creating partnerships with governmental agencies and occasionally with private initiatives, hence building up some valuable knowledge and experience (Alexander 1985, Basurto 1996, Casa y Ciudad 1997, CEDUAM et al. 1996, CYTED-D 1991, Connolly 1993, Davis 1992).

Yet the issue of designing public spaces from a participatory point of view has not been addressed with the same amount of research and insight. The issue of collaborative design needs to be further examined with a focus that is relevant to the Mexican context. In addition, one feature which needs to be taken into account in the context of Mexican society, is the role of women within these processes. This group usually has more in-depth knowledge of the settlements' situation, since the majority of them work at home and support the organisational and managerial tasks within the settlement. In spite of this, their potential has been systematically minimised due to the social milieu within which the women operate, where initiatives are largely initiated and developed by them, but led and later attributed to the male representatives (Varley 1995).

The case study will show how the residents – especially the women – assisted by professionals, generated a comprehensive design solution for the community's concerns. At the same time sustainability issues related to urban form were addressed by means of this joint work.

Participatory Design Methodology

A methodology for collaborative design was developed based on the theoretical issues and urban development processes outlined above. Additional insights were obtained from interviews with professionals, city authorities, NGO's and self-help community leaders related to the self-help housing context as part of the research. The methodology was developed bearing in mind the following. It had to: be adaptable to the Mexican culture/social milieu; be oriented to public space design in a housing context; involve low cost in implementation and avoid sophisticated technology; have the capacity to capture various groups' perceptions; be time effective and lend itself to evaluation and recording.

Workshops were used as the basic unit of the methodology and structured in four phases (Figure 11.2).

Phase	Purpose
1 Presentation/summary	Explanation of objectives and outcomes expected. Summary of previous workshop.
2 Main activity	Team work developing a specific task using brainstorming, graphic visualisations, drawing and modelling techniques.
3 Group discussion	Discussion of the topics and issues developed in the workshop in relation to: other related concerns and workshops as well as forthcoming activities.
4 Workshop assessment	Evaluation of research team's performance and how to improve the forthcoming workshops.

Figure 11.2   Workshop structure

Five workshops were held (Figure 11.3) which commenced with a general approach to the perceived problems of the settlement up to in-depth investigation of the preferred layout of the estate and the public space requirements and configuration.

The resulting project was then discussed in terms of the implementation strategies likely to follow. Lastly the overall methodology and participatory experience was evaluated by the community and the research team.

Minas-Polvorilla Site Case Study

Community Background

The community occupying the case study site originated over 15 years ago when two groups of dwellers were evicted from different low-income districts within México City around 1988–89. Both decided to combine efforts in order to become a social organisation of housing seekers. Thus the *Popular Front Francisco Villa* (FPFV) was born. It was named after *Francisco Villa*, a Mexican revolution social fighter and war hero. The increase of members coming from the addition of smaller organisations pushed the group to seek an alternative place to better accommodate the FPFV. After a while they settled on a plot in southern México City. Currently it is a radical, powerful and combative left wing organisation that has several offshoots of housing

Workshop	Purpose
1. Identifying problems, advantages, threats and desires	Identify community perception of place in relation to the problems and needs within the settlement.
2. Developing a General Action Plan	Enable the participants to understand and produce a 3D scheme showing a shared vision of the settlement, addressing the issues from workshop 1.
3. Including the children	Collect opinions/perceptions of children on how public space could meet their needs. Enable them to produce a 3D model with their views.
4. Designing the local places	Enable people to develop detailed designs based on the proposals of the General Action Plan and incorporate children's workshop outcomes.
5 Formulating implementation and monitoring outline	Generate awareness of steps to follow towards the implementation of the schemes.

Figure 11.3   The five workshops

cooperatives or housing seeker groups – each with a distinctive name – which resulted from additional organisations joining the main group.

Site location and characteristics

Minas Polvorilla, also known as Frente Popular Francisco Villa Independiente-Acapatzingo (FPFVI-A), is located in the southeast sector of México City, within the Iztapalapa Delegation administrative zone. This part of the city was constituted by communal land, protected areas and also a settlement risk area. In the last forty years it has been occupied by squatter settlements and later urbanised and granted legal status (Figure 11.4).

Originally, mining and extraction activity for construction materials took place on the site. Once exhausted, it was used as waste disposal land mainly for construction refuse from México City's 1985 earthquake. Some parts of the site were supervised during the filling and compacting operations but others were not. Thus it is very unstable land in terms of its bearing capacity, allowing only for low, two storey construction maximum. Only a small area supports multi-storey buildings.

The site is surrounded by other former squatter settlements, multi-storey low income buildings and local shops (Figures 11.5 and 11.6).

Two main roads are adjacent on the east and south boundaries, however access from the main city roads is somewhat difficult due to distance and the conditions of the roads themselves. Water, drainage and electricity are provided. The site is gated with two controlled access points on the east and west sides.

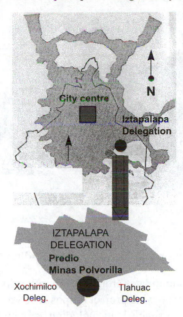

Figure 11.4   Location of Minas Polvorilla within México City[1]

Figure 11.5   Local shops and multi-storey buildings surrounding the site

---

[1]   All illustrations and photos by the author.

Figure 11.6   Former squatter settlements surrounding the site

Currently the site accommodates around 650 families living in shacks distributed in scattered fashion. A new housing project proposes 608 dwellings (490 single units and 188 flats) on 7.95 ha of available land, including basic infrastructure supply (water, drainage, electricity, roads), urban facilities, open spaces and a car park.

The central basketball courts are used as the meeting square and main public place (Figures 11.7 and 11.8).

Figure 11.7   Main square and public space within Minas-Polvorilla

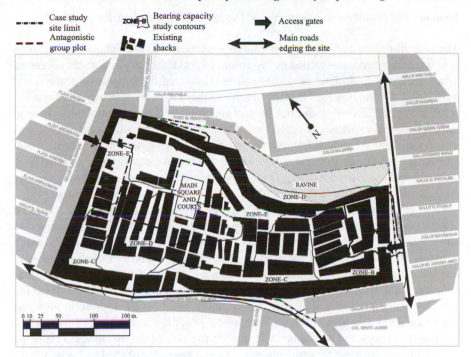

▪▪▬▪▬	Case study site limit	ZONE-B	Bearing capacity study contours	➤	Access gates
▬ ▬ ▬	Antagonistic group plot		Existing shacks	◄►	Main roads edging the site

Figure 11.8   Current layout and spatial organisation of Minas-Polvorilla

Workshop Mobilisation

Negotiations for the the selection of the study area of Minas-Polvorilla and the participatory workshops were conducted with México City Housing Institute (INVI), a city government institution. Contact with the FPFV leadership was made in order to explain the initiative. An initial collaboration between the FPFV, INVI and the research team was proposed. Despite various problems of reaching agreement between the different interests groups, the workshops proceeded. Architecture students were invited to be part of the research team. Their role was to facilitate the activities during the workshops. A training programme was carried out as part of their academic course. This covered general theoretical aspects of design and participation as well as the objectives and necessary skills to facilitate workshop delivery.

A core group of participants from the community was gathered with one representative from each of the 21 brigades constituting the group; the average attendance was around forty people at each workshop. Residents were involved in several tasks aiming to establish the community's problems and needs. Besides designing the layout and specific public spaces, they discussed how to implement the project. A children's workshop was also carried out, and results were shown and incorporated with the adult's work.

Outcomes of Collaborative Open Space Design in Minas Polvorilla

The overall results and learning experience were positive. They show that self-help housing design processes carried out by groups of residents can promote the necessary urban attributes to achieve sustainable cities. However, the support of professional advice and training is needed in order to achieve these aims successfully. Community-professional collaboration did not neglect planning and design principles. Instead the professional expertise, in respect of technical issues and urban regulations, was incorporated into the cultural framework – in effect producing two sets of 'experts' (local knowledge and outside technical expertise). Moreover, participatory tools and techniques were not applied indiscriminately. On the contrary these were adapted throughout the participatory experience to suit the cultural and social milieu of the settlement.

The resulting collaborative project (Figures 11.9 and 11.10) not only shows an enhancement in the design of the public space, but also contributes to sustainability aims. Internally a legible pattern in the layout was achieved by the street-public space network and the location of the main facilities. Thus, every part of the settlement has access to local shopping areas and open space is provided. The designated local shopping and service areas support the sustainable paradigm since they provide for most daily purchases, thus avoiding the inefficiency of transportation time and use of cars. On a smaller scale, the design of a progressive dwelling allows for the inclusion of shops and workshops within or at the side of the dwellings. This helps to provide employment for residents and acts as a generator of the local economy in the settlement.

An equal distribution and adequate provision of open space/green areas is provided throughout the settlement. The scale of these open space areas reflects a more human dimension expressed in a closer relationship to the dwellings. This creates a safer environment by providing easy-to-watch locations. Moreover these spaces can potentially contribute to the green continuum amongst buildings, a necessary aspect to allow local biodiversity and to balance the microclimate.

The location of the community's central facilities can potentially foster various degrees of interactions amongst neighbours, contributing to social cohesion. All these aspects are considered key indicators to achieve and measure sustainability (see Atkinson 1999).

The linkage of, and the potential for the simultaneous use of public spaces with buildings was explored in the detailed designs since participants became aware of the relationships amongst them. An example of this is the central facilities project where a school, communal room, the main square plus other administrative buildings were combined to create an integrative urban space.

Other outcomes were also evident as a result of the collaborative project. A cornerstone argument of the sustainable development discourse is the need to change current attitudes towards the way society operates and its representation in design practice. Throughout the joint work for both groups – students and residents – the learning experience challenged their views on participation, public space design and settlement improvement.

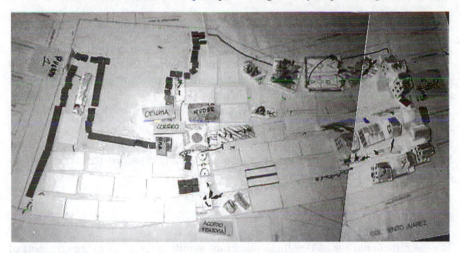

Figure 11.9   Original action plan co-designed by residents and research team

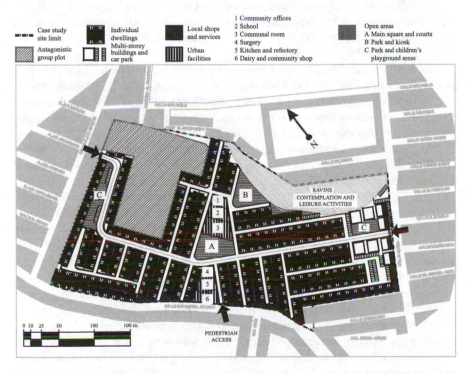

Figure 11.10 Revised action plan by the research team presented to the residents for discussion

The students' group at first regarded this insight as a challenge to their perception of their professional capacity. Thus the collaborative experience helped not only to develop a better project in terms of sustainability and urban form, but also, new generations of designers are already questioning the values underpinning current professional practice, where participation is not considered part of the urban design and decision making process for city planning.

For the residents it constituted a whole new insight into the possibilities of collaborative work. Concerns about public space and the settlement were addressed at various levels within a positive atmosphere for discussion and exchange of ideas. Moreover, during the evaluation community members regarded the experience as positive and beneficial for them.

Conclusions

The overall conclusion is that these outcomes significantly address the concerns of sustainability regarding social and environmental issues. The self-help settlement model is thus seen in a different light, one which shows how it can be part of a sustainable city.

The collaborative workshops incorporated the residents' knowledge of their 'place': the different meanings, life experience and perceptions of the participants came across during the design process. This gave a wider social and cultural dimension to the solutions portrayed by public space design.

The environmental needs were addressed by providing sustainable local activities and facilities that best suit the daily needs of the community. In addition, on-site employment opportunities and economic development were envisaged through discussion of the maintenance and management needs of the settlement as well as by allowing for mixed uses within the dwellings.

The participatory experience showed a successful and creative way of including two of the disadvantaged groups that sustainability aims to address, namely women and children. Incorporating their knowledge and views, the experience promoted a different awareness into the real needs of the community, usually overlooked by professionals. Women provided significant insights to the development of the settlement design. This group has a remarkable understanding of their settlement and social context. This enabled them to visualise a positive transformation of their environment, while providing the strength and necessary liaisons to structure the community towards common objectives (Figure 11.11).

Innovative approaches with children were also implemented, resulting in new insights for the development of public spaces portraying the children's needs (Figure 11.12). Moreover, the involvement of the children stimulated other participatory experiences. Adults became encouraged by watching their children's work. Consequently other sessions addressing vandalism, drug-addiction, study improvement and hygiene were requested.

In summary, the result of the participatory project showed that, working together, residents and design professionals can define an urban form and associated activities

Figure 11.11 Women as main promoters of the collaborative experience

Figure 11.12 Children building 3D models of public spaces

aiming for a more sustainable city. Importantly, it also helps to promote the new attitudes which are imperative if sustainable cities are to be developed.

References

Aina, T.A. (1990), 'The Politics of Sustainable Third World Development', in Cadman, D. and Payne, G. (eds), *The Living City: Towards a Sustainable Future*, London, Routledge, pp. 192–205.

Alexander, C. (1985), *The Production of Houses*, New York, Oxford University Press.

Atkisson, A. (1999), 'Developing Indicators of Sustainable Community: Lessons from Sustainable Seattle', in Satterthwaite, D. (ed.), *The Earthscan Reader in Sustainable Cities*, London, Earthscan, pp. 352–63.

Basurto, A. (1996), 'Making the World More Fit to Live in', *México: NGO's Demand that Habitat be Managed in Social Terms*, http://gate.gtz.de/isat/, visited January 1998.

Benitez, R. (1997), 'Población y Desarrollo en la Gran Ciudad de México', in Alvarez, L. (ed.), *Participacion y Democracia en la Ciudad de México*, México, Centro de Investigaciones Interdisciplinarias en Ciencias y Humanidades.

Bentley, I. (1999), *Urban Transformations: Power, People and Urban Design*, London, Routledge.

Campbell, S. (1999), 'Planning: Green Cities, Growing Cities, Just Cities?', in Satterthwaite, D. (ed.), *The Earthscan Reader in Sustainable Cities*, London, Earthscan, pp. 251–73.

Casa y Ciudad (1997), *Diseño Participativo*, México, Casa y Ciudad A.C.

CEDUAM, CENVI, FOSOVI, GEA and PDP (1994), *Medio ambiente y autogestión urbana. Procesos participativos en problemas ambientales -taller de experiencias*, México, World Resources Institute.

Connolly, P. (1993), 'The "Go-between": CENVI, a Habitat NGO in México City', *Environment and Urbanisation*, 5:1, pp. 68–90.

CYTED-D (1991), *Vivienda Latinoamericana. Tecnología y participación social en la construcción del habitat popular*, México, CYTED-D.

Davis, D. (1990), 'Social Movements in México's Crisis', *Journal of International Affairs*, 43:343, p. 67.

Feldman, R. and Westphal, L. (1998), 'Participation for Empowerment: The Greening of a Public Housing Development', *Places*, 12:2, pp. 34–37.

Fusco Girard, L. (1997), 'Self Sustainable Urban Development', in Brandon, P., Lombardi, P. and Bentivengna, V. (eds), *Evaluation of the Built Environment for Sustainability*, London, E. and F.N. Spon, pp. 82–104.

Gilbert, A. (1996), *The Mega-City in Latin America*, New York, United Nations University Press.

Gilbert, A. (1998), *The Latin American City*, London, Latin American Bureau, revised edition, first published in 1994.

Hamdi, N. and Goethert, R. (1997), *Action Planning for Cities: A Guide to Community Practice*, Chichester, John Wiley and Sons.

Haughton, G. and Hunter, C. (1994), *Sustainable Cities*, London, Jessica Kingsley Publishers and Regional Studies Association.

INEGI (1997), 'Encuesta Nacional de la Dinámica Demografica 1997, Metodologia y Tabulados, 1999', INEGI website, http://www.inegi.gob.mx/poblacion/ingles, visited February, 2000.

Mitlin, D. (1997), 'Building with Credit: House Finance for Low-income Households', *Third World Planning Review*, 19:1, pp. 21–50.

OECD (1996), *Innovative Policies for Sustainable Development: The Ecological City*, Paris, OECD.

Payne, G. (1984), 'Introduction', in Payne, G. (ed.), *Low-Income Housing in the Developing World: The Role of Site and Services and Settlement Upgrading*, Chichester, John Wiley and Sons, pp. 1–14.

Porter, R. and Lloyd-Evans, S. (1998), *The City in the Developing World*, London, Longman.

Rees, W. (1999), 'Achieving Sustainability: Reform or Transformation', in Satterthwaite, D. (ed.), *The Earthscan Reader in Sustainable Cities*, London, Earthscan, pp. 22–52.

Roelofs, J. (1999), 'Building and Designing with Nature: Urban Design', in Satterthwaite, D. (ed.), *The Earthscan Reader in Sustainable Cities*, London, Earthscan.

Rojas, R. (1997), 'Salud y Medio Ambiente', in Castillo, M. and Reyes, S. (eds), *Problemas Emergentes de la Zona Metropolitana de la Ciudad de México*, México, Universidad Nacional Autónoma de México – Programa Universitario de Estudios sobre la Ciudad, pp. 83–88.

Sanchez, M. (1997), 'Asentamientos de alto riesgo físico en el D.F', *Ciudades*, 33, January–March, pp. 27–35.

Satterthwaite, D. (1999), 'The Key Issues and the Works Included', in Satterthwaite, D. (ed.), *The Earthscan Reader in Sustainable Cities*, London, Earthscan, pp. 3–21.

Siembieda, W. and Lopez, E. (1997), 'Expanding Housing Choices for the Sector Popular: Strategies for México', *Housing Policy Debate*, 8, Fannie Mae Foundation.

Varley, A. (1995), 'Neither Victims nor Heroines: Women, Land and Housing in Mexican Cities', *Third World Planning Review*, 17:2, pp. 169–82.

Ward, P. and Macoloo, G. (1992), 'Articulation Theory and Self-help Housing Practice in the 1990s', *International Journal of Urban and Regional Research*, 16:1, pp. 61–80.

World Commission on Environment Development (WCED) (1987), *Our Common Future*, G.H. Brundtland, Oxford, Oxford University Press.

Chapter 12

Community Involvement in Planning and Managing Sustainable Open Space in Mexico

Ana Maria Maldonaldo-Fuse

Introduction

The context and aims of sustainability cover practices in numerous fields and disciplines of human activity since being placed firmly on the international agenda by the World Commission on Environment and Development (WCED 1987, Drakakis-Smith 1997, Franks 1996).

This chapter contends that in the search for more 'sustainable' urban development, green open spaces can contribute significantly to the achievement of this goal. Evidence indicates that the current processes of planning and management of green spaces have not achieved much progress in this respect (Lopez Moreno 1998, SAPM 1999) but that this picture could be improved by developing design and management tools in which the community is involved.

Mexico has not been an exception to the vast set of challenges to sustainability. Issues of pollution, loss of bio-diversity and deforestation of natural areas, erosion, loss of soils and water resources (all of these related to the existence and quality of the green areas) are critical issues to be addressed (Carabias 1990, Mazari et al. 1995, INEGI 1997, SAPM 1999).

The country is one of the 12 in the world considered as 'mega-diverse', i.e. with the highest levels of bio-diversity (INEGI 1997). As in the rest of Latin America, the relationship between resource diversity and population density is generally favourable. However, the demographic explosion has generated strong pressures on the natural resources, particularly because of the irregular and skewed population distribution (overall population growth rates of 2 per cent p.a. are higher in cities, with 2.8 per cent in urban areas compared with 1.6 per cent in semi-rural and 0.6 per cent rural areas) (INEGI 1997, INE 1998).

Historically, Mexicans have had a strong disposition to use urban and suburban green open spaces intensively; this use has been intimately related to culturally important activities, including leisure, religious assembly, and scientific investigation, among other types of activities. In the present era, green public open spaces provide important opportunities for leisure, contact with nature, environmental education, and social interaction among other needs. These functions are particularly important for the low-income sectors of the population (Carabias 1990).

However, the demographic dynamic mentioned above, combined with social and economic change and the lack of effective tools and strategies to manage urban development trends, has resulted in the very low provision of green areas – less than 3 sq. m/inhabitant in some areas (DDF 1983). This threatens the deterioration of existing open spaces and depletion of valuable resources (INE 1998). Demand for green open areas is growing at a much more accelerated rate than the supply (DDF 1983), and hence, the green open space systems are becoming gradually more uniform but also more fragmented. Green open space is increasingly threatened by development and thus a more fragile commodity (Cabeza 1995).

The most detrimental factors are:

• pressures for development – competition for space and resources;
• lack of community interest in using open space as well as the lack of practical tools to defend their existence – there is little scope for the community to promote a sense of belonging;
• poor planning and management guidance or the lack of instruments altogether for green open spaces, resulting in unsustainability – underuse, neglect, potential danger, expensive maintenance (DDF 1983, Cabeza 1995).

The Context for Sustainable Green Open Space in Mexico

In Mexico, by the time of the 1992 Rio Conference, a number of specific environment programmes (under names such as 'Eco-development') had already been implemented to cope with specific problems (Sachs 1992). However, as a consequence of the Rio conference, a more concerted programme of research and action was initiated and greater efforts were made to consolidate environmental politics.

Nevertheless the term 'sustainability', is still used rather vaguely both in discourse and practice, even by government agencies concerned with social and economic development and environmental management. In addition, a particular critique is the lack of linkage between the regional levels of planning and specific action at the local level, together with insufficient instruments for implementation.

In relation to the provision of green public open space, a matter of particular local concern, the situation has not improved. The legislation is fragmented and does not deal specifically with green open space. No guidance has been produced to assist local planning initiatives or the provision of open space in new developments in terms of urban sustainability other than in terms of accessibility, regulatory norms and strategic plans. Even the current norms are largely optional and resources to improve the quality of existing open spaces are scarce unless there is critical and active community engagement.

According to law, the obligation for planning and managing local green areas falls on the local (municipal) authority, within the framework of federal development and environmental legislation. However, human and technical resources are scarce. In any case responsibility is often divided: for example the Department of Ecology will be responsible for larger areas and the Department of Parks and Gardens for the rest of green open space. On the other hand, the federal agencies have more experience regarding the management of green areas (particularly the Protected Areas) with a focus on more sustainable schemes, such as CONABIO (National Board for Bio-diversity Conservation); but these schemes and agencies are not related in any way to the municipality level provision of green open spaces.

Community Involvement: Discourse and Practice

In Mexico, schemes to incorporate community involvement exist both in the legislation and in practice as well – evident in the increasingly wide range of NGOs working in the environmental field in Mexico. Yet their work has been limited and hindered by numerous factors, including the lack of appropriate governance structures. The poor economic situation of the country and the perception of environmental matters as not crucial to the quality of life of the population are factors that discourage the participation.

However, there are alternative modes of action. Civil society engagement with environmental issues through NGOs and family participation through schools show high potential for development if they are well conducted.

Nevertheless, in relation to the specific task of planning and management of green open space, these resources have been used very rarely, mainly when emergencies or critical events within the life of a local community have pressed for action in particular circumstances.

The challenge seems to be, in the first place, to develop an appropriate frame of reference and methodology by which the provision of green open spaces can better incorporate community interests and partnership which might ultimately lead to more sustainable provision and maintenance.

We might conceptualise the challenge in terms of a series of questions which now follows.

What is Understood by the Use of the Term 'Sustainability' in the Context of Planning and Managing Green Open Spaces in Mexico?

It is important to identify in what ways the spatial, social and cultural conditions shape the needs for the provision and use of open space. Establishing clearly what these elements are will help to improve understanding which can guide provision and also provide information to support better monitoring and evaluation.

What is a Sustainable System of Green Open Space?

In order to make progress towards more sustainable open space provision, a profile of the generic characteristics could be drawn up, using the information from the first question. This would also embrace indicators such as the main concerns about provision, people's expectations and critical environmental and social issues reflected in the distribution and use of green open space.

In What Way Could Sustainability be Measured with Respect to the Provision of Green Open Space?

As already noted, a critical gap in Mexico at the present time is the lack of effective control and monitoring tools to assess provision and the achievements of actions and practices already implemented. In other words, an evaluation framework is needed to measure different aspects of sustainability – for example physical structure, design and social value – which is practical, clear and can be used for future policy guidance and provision.

How can Community Involvement be Engaged as a Potentially Critical Resource in the Provision of Sustainable Open Space?

Identifying the role of main actors involved in the planning and management of green open spaces is a fundamental condition in developing strategies as well as implementation and monitoring tools. In this respect, local communities have a crucial role to play in terms of participating in the planning, provision and maintenance of open space in relation to their socio-cultural needs and priorities.

Application of the Matrix

The practical application of these questions has been developed, partly based on the work of Evans (1996), Punter (1990), and Bentley (1990), to generate an evaluation matrix of primary indicators comprising the most relevant aspects of sustainability in relation to the provision of green open space. This matrix links general aspects to measurable qualities and elements (Figure 12.1).

This matrix has been tested in case study locations in Tepotzotlán, Edo. de Mexico, a mid-sized urban settlement. Preliminary results illustrate the value of the matrix in assessing the overall sustainability of green open space in terms of provision, design, use and management, public perceptions of its value, information levels and critical issues currently arising. In other words, this is the beginning of a much more systematic appraisal which can form the basis of sustainable green open space planning and management.

Primary indicators of sustainability	Measurable qualities
A Accessibility to a variety of social, health and age groups	1 Is the OS* easily accessible e.g. by public transport or foot?
B Permeability	2 Is the location permeable in relation to the urban context?
C Choice of areas/activities	3 Is the range of facilities environments sufficient to satisfy different user groups?
D Legibility	4 Can users easily 'read' the space/context?
E Fulfilment of primary/daily needs	5 Are people satisfied with the way the OS fulfils their needs?
F Degree of care/maintenance	6 Is the level of care/maintenance satisfactory?
G Meaning	7 Does the space hold important meaning for people – e.g. culturally, historically?
H Agency	8 What agencies are responsible for provision/maintenance?
I Existent or potential community involvement	9 Is there currently any successful practice of community involvement?
	10 Is the community willing to get involved in provision/maintenance/activities?
	11 Are there any successful local practices for environmental education?
J Safety	12 Is the OS safe?
K Beauty	13 Do local people find the OS attractive?
Environmental sustainability	
L Connectivity	14 Is the area connected with other areas?
M Adequacy of flora, soil and fauna	15 Is the flora/fauna in good condition?
	16 Does the range of flora/fauna include species from the original ecosystem?
	17 Do the species used cause environmental problems by requiring high maintenance or hindering other plant/fauna development?
	18 Are there problems such as compaction, flooding, salination, erosion of the soil?
N Self-sustainability	19 What is the degree of self-sustainability of the flora/fauna?
O Freedom from pollution	20 What levels of pollution are present?
P Efficient resource management	21 Are there any programmes for maximising the use of the natural resources?

* OS = open space

Figure 12.1 Evaluation matrix of primary indicators and measurable qualities

Provision of Green Open Space: System and Characteristics

Green open space in Tepotzotlán lacks systematic provision. Thus, it is the Civic Plaza-Public Garden-Atrium open space grouping which is fundamental to the public perception and image of the city centre in Tepotzotlán, as in practically any settlement in Mexico. Even so, in Tepotzotlán, as elsewhere, this is not technically a 'green area', although residents perceive it as such and emphasise its overwhelming importance in the context of the city as a whole. This open space is, effectively, the only one which is regularly maintained and kept in good condition.

Very close to this nucleus, but inside the Museum building, is a second principal feature of green open space, the orchards of the former Jesuit college. However, significantly in terms of permeability and legibility (Indicators B and D), even though this is the largest green area within central Tepotzotlán, it was not even mentioned by the interviewees – neither the public nor staff of the municipality.

Further investigation of permeability and meaning (Indicators D and F) shows that the Royal Watercourse (Acequia Real) potentially forms a main linear structure of open space linked to the river banks which operate as streets and pathways with areas of planting. This is one of the most important features dating from the pre-Hispanic and colonial era. It is still preserved, constituted by the remaining sections of the hydraulic system which brought water from the Concepcion basin. The Acequia Real and numerous sections of smaller channels were used for irrigated agriculture. Now they remain as a series of residual green linear spaces (parallel to pathways or local streets) within the urban structure which provide green space and even carry water at times.

The orchards and the Acequia Real are the only two connected elements of a sustainable green open space system. The remaining green open spaces in Tepotzotlán are unplanned and unsystematic. There are numerous plots of agricultural or unoccupied land intermixed with residential areas, as well as some residual open spaces; but these are largely neglected and are not perceived as part of a sustainable open space system.

As regards the other provision, there are some private areas of open use which are not usually included in government data and classification although they certainly fulfil leisure and environmental needs such as sports and recreations facilities.

There are also other examples where, even though accessibility (in terms of cost and distance/travel time) is difficult, the value of these areas is very important to city residents such that they should be included in the open space template as green areas associated with natural or historically important sites or monuments.

Planning, Design, Use and Management of Open Space and the Role of Main Actors and Community Involvement

There are no long-term programmes for the planning and design of green open space. It is only in extreme cases of community pressure that the issue is addressed. For the most part, community involvement has been hindered by the low income of the citizens, a lack of trust in the local municipalities and a belief that they are not interested in the issue of open space and sustainability. Conversely, from the perspective of the municipalities, their critical priorities are housing and infrastructure. Green open space attracts few resources and little interest. The current projects have failed to interest the community in changing their unsustainable patterns of consumption or to involve them in a systematic way, in strategy formulation. Where public participation has taken place, this is mostly when critical decisions are being made, not on a long-term basis.

Moreover the responsibility for open space provision and management is uncoordinated. The municipality is responsible for some areas but suffers from a serious lack of resources and expertise to take the lead. Sites owned or managed by the federal government agency responsible for historic conservation, INAH (National Institute of Anthropology and History) or the Museum are not managed from the perspective of open space, but mainly in terms of the architectural structures. Finally, private open space provision and maintenance relies on the decisions of management boards and private funding is, in general, well resourced and handled.

Critical Aspects of Sustainability in the Current System of Green Open Space Provision

The most immediate problem is the lack of resources – financial and human – to ensure the adequate management and improvement of open space, but also the fact that entrenched practices are not sustainable (Indicators F and H). For example, the application of concepts such as efficient resource management and recycling processes are only used in one of the open spaces – the privately provided area (Indicator P). However, the evaluation showed that even a moderate degree of care can be a very influential factor in the process of using open space (Indicator F), whereas the neglected spaces are perceived as unsafe (Indicator J). Conversely, the best maintained spaces are in private ownership but are perceived, not surprisingly, as being inaccessible (Indicator A). The open space with the highest degree of care is in fact a private area, and is perceived by respondents as 'alien' to the city with comments that the ecological character can only be afforded by the better off.

The open space system is centred in one key resource (the Central Garden and Plaza); this is satisfactorily maintained whereas the rest are neglected. The degree of connectivity (Indicators B, D and L) is extremely low, and the system is not balanced in terms of the different features, activities and characteristics which distinct areas could provide (Indicator E).

Residual spaces, which potentially might make the highest contribution to biodiversity in an open space system (Indicator N) are not managed at all. They lack any interest from potential users, being perceived as unsafe and unusable (Indicator J).

As a whole, because the green open spaces are scattered and fragmented, they are much more fragile in terms of negative external impacts and damage (Indicator L). The lack of a holistic strategy reduces their potential robustness.

Community involvement has not made a significant contribution to the development of green open space provision, and there is a lack of environmental education initiatives, which could support and enhance public interest and involvement (Indicator I).

In terms of adequate use of soil and vegetation (Indicator M) a consistently identified factor is the presence of mainly exotic species, some of which hinder or inhibit the adequate growth of the others. Soil, in general, is subject to a high degree of compaction and medium levels of erosion, which is reflected in the generally poor state of the flora. Since many of the plant species require high maintenance, they appear neglected.

The aspect of meaning (Indicator G) turned out to be one of the most important. Specific sites have a particular attraction. Hence, even when the others aspects were performing poorly – such as even safety and permeability – the spaces are used intensively.

Perceptions of Sustainability and Green Open Spaces

According to the responses in the pilot survey, the concept of sustainability is most often perceived in terms of the conservation of green areas and their natural habitat: this emphasises the contention at the start of this chapter that the link between sustainability and open space is critical in the minds of city dwellers. Green open space is perceived as closely related with wellbeing and health, although there were few clear ideas as to how these attributes might be enhanced by environmental improvements. Interestingly, concepts of safeguarding environmental futures, living in harmony with nature, the rational use of the resources and particularly the implications of sustainable lifestyles, were not mentioned by respondents.

Conclusions

The general evaluation framework/matrix has proved to be a valuable tool in seeking to understand how stakeholders perceive the provision, role and management of green open space in their city. Even so, it is evident that more analysis and further refinements to the methodology are needed.

- More attention needs to be paid to the method of evaluation in terms of understanding the open space system as a whole – both perception and use. This lack of a holistic character was as much a critical problem as the individually poor performance of many of the other elements.
- It is clear that there is a disjuncture between how people at the local level perceive and use open space in reality, compared to the top down approaches of public agencies. The evaluation matrix needs to bridge the two different perspectives.
- Issues of accessibility are probably more important than the pilot survey revealed – particularly in terms of the costs of accessing private space.
- The 'performance' of green open space against the evaluation indicators varies enormously between different agencies. These conditions produce a very wide

range of information which is difficult to process and compare. A more selective approach, focusing on priority indicators or open spaces which are critical to the overall system, is needed.

- Community involvement remains the most difficult indicator to develop and gauge. More effectively measurable qualities are needed in order to more thoroughly investigate how green open space is perceived and used and the techniques and schemes that could enhance community involvement.

References

Aldous, T. (1992), *Urban Villages: A Concept for Creating Mixed-use Urban Developments*, London, Urban Villages Group.

Bentley, I. (1990), 'Ecological Issues in Urban Design', *Architects Journal*, 24 October, pp. 69–71.

Carabias, J. (1990), 'Criterios Ecologicos para el Bienestar de las Ciudades', *La Modernización de las Ciudades en Méxic*, Seminar Papers, Mexico, UNAM, pp. 35–38.

DDF (Departamento del Distrito Federal), Cocoder (1983), *Manual de Planeacion, Diseño y Manejo de la Areas Verdes del Distrito Federal*, Mexico, Distrito Federal, DDF.

Drakakis-Smith, D. (1997), 'Third World Cities: Sustainable Urban Development, Basic Needs and Human Rights', *Urban Studies*, 34:5–6, pp. 797–823.

Evans, D. (1996), *Urban Design Qualities in the Planning and Development of Small New Settlements*, PhD thesis, Oxford, Joint Centre for Urban Design, Oxford Brookes University.

Franks, T.R. (1996), 'Managing Sustainable Development: Definitions, Paradigms and Dimensions', *Sustainable Development*, 4, pp. 53–60.

INEGI (1997), *Estadisticas del Medio Ambiente, Mexico 1997. Informe sobre la situacion en materia de equilibrio ecologico y proteccion al ambiente, 1995, 1996*, Mexico, INEGI, SEMARNAP.

Instituto Nacional de Ecologia (INE), SEMARNAP, Sistema Nacional de Informacion Ambiental website (1998), http://www.ine.gob.mx/ord-ecol/introdu.html (Ordenamiento Ecológico).

Lopez Moreno, I. and Diaz-Betancourt, M. (1998), 'Urbanizacion y biodiversidad', *Ciudades*, 38, April–June, Mexico, Puebla, RNIU.

Mazari, M. and Ezcurra, E. (1995), 'Es sustentable el desarrollo urbano en la cuenca de Mexico?', *Universidad de Mexico*, pp. 52–56.

Punter, J. (1990), 'The Ten Commandments of Architecture and Urban Design', *The Planner*, 5 October, pp. 10–14.

Rodriguez Velazquez, D. (1998), 'Vulnerabilidad y Riesgos en el D.F', *Ciudades*, 38, April–June, Mexico, Puebla, RNIU.

Sachs, I. (1992), *Ecodesarrollo: Desarrollo sin Destruccion*, Mexico, Colegio de Mexico, Series Programa sobre Desarrollo y Medio Ambiente.

SAPM (1999), *Procedure Papers for the 1st National Congress of Landscape Architect*, Mexico, DF.

World Commission on Environment Development (WCED) (1987), *Our Common Future*, G.H. Brundtland, Oxford, Oxford University Press.

Index

Page numbers in *italics* refer to figures and tables.